RETURN TO THE OLD PATHS
A HISTORY OF THE RESTORATION MOVEMENT

by
V. Glenn McCoy

RETURN TO THE OLD PATHS
A HISTORY OF THE RESTORATION MOVEMENT

by
V. Glenn McCoy

Copyright © 2020 World Video Bible School®
ISBN: 9780996700375

Originally published in 1998
by McCoy Publications

WVBS is thankful to the V. Glenn McCoy family
for the right to republish this book for the Lord's Church.

Printed in the United States of America
All Rights Reserved.

Published by
World Video Bible School®
25 Lantana Lane
Maxwell, Texas 78656
www.WVBS.org

TABLE OF CONTENTS

Part I: The Necessity of Restoration

Introduction: 2
Chapter 1: Seed Produces After its Kind 3
Chapter 2: The Great Apostasy 11
Chapter 3: Forerunners of the Reformation 17
Chapter 4: The Protestant Reformation.................................. 21
Chapter 5: Resulting Movements 35
Chapter 6: Early Beginnings of Restoration in Great Britain 43

Part II: Restoration Leaders in America

Chapter 7: Early Beginnings of Restoration in America 53
Chapter 8: Barton W. Stone 67
Chapter 9: Thomas Campbell 107
Chapter 10: Alexander Campbell 121
Chapter 11: Raccoon John Smith 171
Chapter 12: Walter Scott 195
Chapter 13: The Growth of the Church 215
Chapter 14: American Christian Missionary Society 219
Chapter 15: Instrumental Music in Worship 229

Part III: Other Influential Leaders

Chapter 16: Jacob Creath, Sr. 267
Chapter 17: John T. Johnson 271
Chapter 18: Aylette Rains 279
Chapter 19: Thomas M. Allen 283
Chapter 20: Philip S. Fall 287
Chapter 21: Jacob Creath, Jr. 291
Chapter 22: John Allen Gano 301
Chapter 23: Tolbert Fanning 305
Chapter 24: Benjamin Franklin 311

Chapter 25: W.K. Pendleton 321
Chapter 26: Moses E. Lard 325
Chapter 27: J.W. McGarvey 333
Chapter 28: David Lipscomb 343
Chapter 29: Alfred Elmore 355
Chapter 30: T.B. Larimore 361
Chapter 31: James A Harding 367
Chapter 32: Conclusion 377
Bibliography 379

Acknowledgments

There have been many fine books of Restoration history written by our brethren, but none is more comprehensive and well written than the works of Earl Irvin West. His four volumes of "The Search for the Ancient Order" especially have been valuable to students of the Restoration Movement. In this present volume we gratefully make many references to the writings of Brother West, as well as such men as J. M. Powell, Dabney Phillips, Garrison and Degroot, F. W. Mattox, William Baxter, H. Leo Boles, Marvin Hastings, Everett Donaldson, J. W. Shepherd, along with some sixty other church historians.

A good portion of the material contained in this book was originally in the form of lecture notes. Having determined to produce the material as a book required returning back to the original sources in order to give credit for references made. While a great deal of time and effort was expended to this end, and the number of references might at times seem tedious, I am sure that my efforts were short of the desired goal. I apologize to any that might have been neglected.

V. Glenn McCoy
August 30, 1998

PART I
THE NECESSITY OF RESTORATION

RETURN TO THE OLD PATHS
INTRODUCTION

Too few members of the Lord's church today are aware of the Restoration Movement and the tremendous debt that is owed to those men who called us back to the New Testament pattern. In this book we tell the story of some of the spiritual giants who suffered and sacrificed in order to preach the pure gospel and restore the church of the New Testament. We owe it to these pioneers, as well as to ourselves, to honor and cherish their memory. As we read about their labors, sufferings, and sacrifices, we may feel a little embarrassed as we compare the ease of modern day preaching with that of the pioneer preachers. Much of our spiritual heritage came to us as a result of men who were willing to give their all. They did what had to be done, and their examples inspire us.

The stories about which we will read have the common thread of a plea for return. Return to the "old paths." Return to God and his Book. Return to the authority of Christ. Return to the church of Christ. Return to preaching and practicing the New Testament plan of salvation. Return to scriptural worship. Return to a life that honors Christ.

The men about whom we will study were by no means perfect. Indeed they were men with "feet of clay." They made mistakes. Many times they had to admit they were wrong and turn in a different direction. As they worked their way out of the darkness of denominationalism, they often stumbled. It is important, however, to emphasize that we do not recognize these pioneer preachers as our authorities in religion. The only authority that we are concerned about comes from the Lord by his Word. While we honor these men for their work, we do not justify our religious practices because of their teachings. If we cannot give a "thus saith the Lord," we have no business practicing it.

> Thus saith the Lord, stand in the way and see, and ask for the old paths, where is the good way, and walk therein (Jeremiah 6:16).

CHAPTER 1
SEED PRODUCES AFTER ITS KIND

November 24, 1922 the tomb of King Tut in Egypt was discovered and opened. Among the contents of the tomb was a sealed bottle containing seeds. Those seeds had been bottled up for over three thousand years, but when they were planted they produced healthy plants.

In the eighth chapter of Luke, Jesus related the familiar parable of the sower. In verse eleven he stated, "The seed is the word of God." Seed will always produce after its kind. Apple seeds will produce apples, corn seeds will produce corn, and watermelon seeds will produce watermelons. When the spiritual seed was sown in the first century, Christians only were produced and the church of Christ came into being. Furthermore, it doesn't matter in what century the seed is planted, for it will always produce the same result.

WHAT IS THE RESTORATION PLEA?

Unfortunately, the church that Jesus established in the first century did not remain faithful. It fell into a state of apostasy. After a few centuries the resulting body hardly resembled the church that Jesus had established. It was necessary for men of faith, courage and vision to call people back to the original pattern, to plead for a restoration. God provided the means of that restoration. He gave people of all ages a plan to follow. "Hold fast the pattern of sound words which you have heard from me, in the faith and love which are in Christ Jesus" (2 Tim. 1:13). As long as they have the Bible, the divine pattern, the compass, they can find their way back to the church that is presented in the New Testament, the church the way God intended it to be.

The plea for restoration was a plea to return to God's original plan as revealed in the scriptures. Paul, the apostle, prophesied that a great apostasy would occur. "Let no one deceive you by any means; for that day will not come unless the falling away comes first, and the man of sin is revealed, the son of perdition, who opposes and exalts himself above all that is called God or is worshipped, so that he sits as God in the temple of God, showing himself that he is God." (2 Thess. 2:3-4). "But the Spirit expressly says that in latter times some will depart from the faith, giving heed to deceiving spirits and doctrines of demons, speaking lies in hypocrisy, having their own conscience seared with a hot iron, forbidding to marry, and commanding to abstain from foods which God created to be received with thanksgiving by those who believe and know the truth." (1 Tim. 4:1-3). As man fell away from the divine pattern by his failure to heed God's Word, so he can return by the same Word that he previously neglected.

GENERAL AREAS OF DEPARTURE

The departures from the original are documented in history. These departures from the truth appeared gradually over a period of several centuries. In general, they are:

1. The corruption of the church government and organization: Churches in the New Testament period were autonomous in form, and each was overseen by elders, as men were qualified to hold that position. However, during the apostasy, men strayed from the simplicity of the authorized organization of the church, resulting in the development of a religious hierarchy.

2. The change in the form and subjects of baptism: According to the scriptures, baptism is the burial in water of those believers who have repented (Acts 8:35-38). The purpose of baptism is the remission of sins (Acts. 2:38). Unfortunately, over time the purpose

was changed and infants became subjects of baptism and the practice of sprinkling took the place of biblical baptism.

3. The worship of the church was contaminated with the additions and changes of men: The historian Mosheim stated, "The Christian worship consisted in hymns, prayers, the reading of the scriptures, a discourse addressed to the people, and concluded with the celebration of the Lord's Supper." (18, p. 1) Men were not content with the simplicity of the New Testament worship. Various elements were added during the falling away, including the worship of images, prayers to Mary, the playing of instrumental music, and the use of adornments such as holy water, the rosary, and the crucifix. One cannot go the scriptures to find authority for any of these. Jesus said, "But in vain they do worship me, teaching as their doctrines the precepts of men" (Matt. 15:9).

RESTORATION OF THE NEW TESTAMENT CHURCH

Since seed will always produce after its kind, it follows that if any would desire to produce the New Testament church today, it can only result from the same seed being sown as was sown in the first century. This principle can be illustrated through the popular game of baseball. Let us use our imaginations and visualize the game of baseball completely disappearing from the face of the earth. No one plays the game, reads about it, or talks about it for one hundred years. At the end of that time, someone finds the rulebook and decides to play the game that has long been forgotten. The rules are followed explicitly. Teams are formed with nine to a side, the field is set up with first base, second, third, and home plate. A bat is constructed and a ball of the correct dimension is produced. Everything is duplicated exactly as directed by the rulebook. We ask the question, what kind of game would they be playing? Obviously, it would be the game of baseball, the same as we play today. How could this be? They used the same rulebook. Whenever and wherever the rulebook is used and followed, it will produce the game of baseball.

So it is with the church. When the church went into apostasy, the "rule book" was virtually ignored for centuries. However, when men decided to return to the Bible in search for the pattern of the New Testament church, they found it. They followed the pattern that resulted in the restoration of the organization, worship, and work of the church that we read about in the New Testament.

In this study we want to look at some of the men who called the people back to the Book. We will not hold these men up as religious authorities, nor as men to be revered. Indeed, these were men who had to work their way from darkness into light. They were only right when they were consistent with the Word. Often times they had to change their positions as they were corrected by further study of the Scriptures. We gratefully view these men as courageous pioneers who charted a course for others to follow.

OVERVIEW OF RESTORATION HISTORY IN THE UNITED STATES

With the coming of the 1800's, there were various forces at work in the denominations, pointing to a discarding of man-made creeds, and a return to New Testament Christianity. Few religious groups were able to escape the demand for reform or restoration within their own religious bodies. James O'Kelly was a Methodist when he began to call for restoration. Both Abner Jones and Elias Smith were Baptists. Barton Stone was a Presbyterian. Thomas and Alexander Campbell were from the Seceder Presbyterian Church. Raccoon John Smith came from the Baptists as did Jacob Creath, Sr., Jacob Creath, Jr., and John T. Johnson. (By 1830 it is estimated that 10,000 Baptists turned to the Restoration.) Walter Scott was raised as a Presbyterian. Alyette Rains was raised by Presbyterian parents, but became a Universalist. David Purviance and Thomas Allen were also Presbyterians.

Without question, if we were to select the two best known preachers from the Restoration Movement, it would be Barton W. Stone and Alexander Campbell. But, there were so many others who also played important roles. Thomas Campbell and Walter Scott would be included if we were to name the four most influential men of the Restoration. However, it is unfair to even suggest that the hundreds of others who gave themselves sacrificially in preaching the primitive gospel were not also extremely important to this great work.

DIVISION COMES

The Restoration Movement grew rapidly until the 1850 census showed it to be the fourth ranking church in size in the nation. From 1850 to 1860 those who joined together to restore the New Testament church were the fastest growing religious group in America. (1, p. 11) Unfortunately, the unity and growth of the movement was hampered following the Civil War. Innovations such as the American Christian Missionary Society that began in 1849 started to divide the Christians. The use of instrumental music had its first recorded use by any congregation in the Restoration in Midway, Kentucky in 1860. This became the cause of even more division.

Those who could not work and worship in congregations where either the Society or instruments were accepted were forced out of their congregations to start over again. Those who objected to these innovations strongly enough to separate themselves were in the minority. As a rule, those who accepted the instrument of music in worship kept the church building and those who objected were forced to meet in rented halls, homes, or school buildings. However, their convictions were strong and they continued to plead for a continuation of the Restoration on the same basis as did the pioneer preachers: "Where the Bible speaks, we speak. Where the Bible is silent, we are silent." Today, those who were once in the minority, churches of Christ, now outnumber the Christian Church and the Disciples of Christ combined.

THE U.S. CENSUS OF 1906

The U.S. census of 1906 was the first time the Christian Church (Disciples) and the churches of Christ were listed separately.

This is not to say that this is the date of the division. For about twenty years prior there had been little fellowship between the two groups. The U.S. census only recognized what had already happened. There was some difficulty in getting the congregations of the church of Christ to respond. Many did not have their own buildings to meet in, and many did not have elders or a regular minister. Earl West estimates that only about one-third of the congregations of the churches of Christ was all that reported. (1, p. 12) Following are the results of the census:

Churches of Christ

1. Number of congregations: 2,649
2. Number of states with a Church of Christ: 33
3. Number of congregations in the south: 1,979
4. Most congregations in one state: Tennessee with 631 (Second was Texas with 627.)
5. Total number of members: 159,658
6. Number of church owned buildings: 1,974 (Total value of $2,555,372)
7. Congregations meeting in rented halls: 693
8. Number of preachers: 2,100
9. Number of Christian colleges: 8 (a total of 1,024 students.)

Christian Church

In contrast, the Christian Church (Disciples of Christ) had 8,293 local congregations with a total of 982,701 members and 6,640 preachers. The numbers are significant, but more significant was the recognition that a division of those who pleaded for restoration had occurred. (1, p. 12)

One of the most valuable lessons to be learned from this study is to discover the underlying causes of this break. These causes can be narrowed down to a fundamental attitude toward the Scriptures. This attitude would allow anything in faith and worship that is not specifically condemned in the Word. This study is also valuable because of the historical background it furnishes to present day issues. A study of the Restoration Movement and those men who were at its forefront should provide inspiration to those who continue the plea. (1, p. 12)

We will look at the history of the Restoration through the eyes of those men who were the most active in it. We need to look at the issues upon the basis of the Scriptures themselves. We will begin our study with the falling away of the church, and then look at those who tried to reform the apostate church, and eventually focus our attention on the Restoration as it took place in America.

CHAPTER 2
THE GREAT APOSTASY

    The church was established and organized as Jesus wanted it to be. After the apostles were gone changes began to occur over a period of time. These changes made the church a different body than Jesus established. F. W. Mattox and E. M. Borden both list A. D. 150 as the approximate time when a major departure in church government occurred as elders were selecting head elders or bishops. (5, p. 111) DeGroot and Garrison state that gradual changes through the first three centuries altered the faith and fellowship of the earliest churches into a federation of episcopal dioceses, headed by bishops, claiming direct authority from the apostles.

    Gradually, especially through the fourth and fifth centuries, the bishop of Rome rose to a place of pre-imminence among the bishops and became the chief. Borden lists A.D. 606 as the crowning date for the first pope, Boniface III. A priesthood came into existence that was not even close to the New Testament pattern. Formalized patterns and sacraments were developed which the apostate church claimed were necessary for salvation, and these could only be performed by the priests to whom power and authority had been given.

    The first human creed designed to govern all Christians came in A.D. 325 and is known as the Nicene Creed. This came from the first world-wide council at Nicaea, near Constantinople. The council was called together by the Roman Emperor Constantine. This creed was the first human creed to receive general acceptance by the church leaders throughout the Roman Empire. Any "Christian" who

11

would not subscribe to this creed was branded a heretic.

It is amazing how far and how quickly the apostate church strayed from the New Testament pattern for the true church. Once it no longer required authority from the Scriptures for what it taught and practiced there were few restraints. Deviation after deviation began to raise its ugly head. Some of these are: (42, p. 4)

1. Distinction made between elders - A. D. 150.
2. Baptism for the dead - A. D. 154.
3. Holy water introduced in second century but not in general used until later.
4. Hallowing of priestly garments (A. D. 257). Stephen, bishop of Rome, took the priestly garments of the Jewish priesthood and adopted it for the church.
5. Prayers for the dead - A. D. 300.
6. Sign of the cross was practiced - A. D. 300.
7. Idols introduced.
8. Lighting of candles instead of individual prayers - A. D. 320.
9. Nuns and monks appeared - A. D. 341.
10. Elaborate program for invoking "saints" introduced.
11. The Lord's Supper was changed into a mass and celebrated daily - A. D. 394.
12. The phrase "Mother of God" was applied to Mary by the council meeting at Ephesus.
13. Extreme unction (anointing of the newly dead or those about to die) - A. D. 526.
14. The actual formal establishment of the doctrine of purgatory (a second chance for dead sinners from which one could escape through money paid to priests who offer prayers for them) by Gregory I - A. D. 593.
15. Latin became the official language for prayer and worship, imposed by Gregory I – A. D. 600.

16. Near deification of Mary as "queen of heaven." Prayers made to Mary, dead saints, angels imposed by Gregory I - A. D. 600.
17. The title "pope" or "universal bishop" was given to Boniface III by emperor Phocas - A. D. 606.
18. Instrumental music was introduced in church worship in A. D. 607 by Pope Vitalia. However, it created such a furor that it was removed and re-introduced much later.
19. Roman Catholicism became the official religion of the empire. All other religions were banned. Dissent from the orthodox catholic faith or refusal to submit to the authority of the high clergy was equivalent to treason against the state.
20. Constantine ordered the kissing of the pope's foot - A. D. 709.
21. The pope was given temporal power by the order of Pepin, king of the Franks - A. D. 750.
22. Worshipping of the cross, images, and relics - A. D. 786.
23. Hagiolatry, worshipping of departed saints - A. D. 788.
24. Holy water (water mixed with a pinch of salt and blessed by priest) used - A. D. 850.
25. Tradition accepted as authority along with the Bible in A. D. 869. "Down to 869, the Sacred Scriptures were accepted alone as authority in the Church. At that time, a council meeting in Constantinople issued a decree recognizing tradition. This referred to preserved tradition, however, and not oral." Even then, tradition was not accepted on an equal basis as the Bible for authority. It was not until 1546 at the Council of Trent that this took place. (40, p. 9)
26. College of Cardinals established - A. D. 890.

27. Baptizing bells first done by Pope John XIII to the great bell of St. John Lateran in Rome in A. D. 965.
28. Dead "saints" canonized by authority of Pope John XV - A. D. 998.
29. Celibacy of the priesthood decreed by Pope Gregory VII (also known as Hildebrand) - A. D. 1079.
30. Rosary invented by Peter the Hermit (counting of beads in prayer).
31. The Seven Sacraments were defined by Hugo, a Parisian Monk, and Peter Lombard, bishop of Rome - A. D. 1130 (Authorized by the council of Trent in 1545).
32. The sale of indulgences in sin began in 1190. (Pope Leo X financed a good part of the building of St. Peter's Cathedral in Rome by this means. This was one of the 95 included in the thesis of Martin Luther that was nailed to the door of the Wittenburg, Germany church in A. D. 1517.)
33. Confession of sins to the priest for the purpose of forgiveness of sins (auricular confession) was imposed by Pope Innocent III - A. D. 1215.
34. Transubstantiation was established by Pope Innocent III as church doctrine - A. D. 1215 (Chysosteon had taught it in A. D. 385 and Augustine in the fifth century.)
35. The worship or adoration of the wafer in the mass was ordained by Pope Honorius since it was said to be the actual body of Jesus - A. D. 1220.
36. The Bible was forbidden to be read by laymen and was placed on the list of Forbidden Books by the Council of Constance - A. D. 1229.
37. The Pope was given absolute authority over a temporal state covering a great part of central

Italy. This included armies, diplomats, and tax collectors. Civil powers were required to cooperate with the church in hunting down and exterminating heretics.
38. Sprinkling was approved for baptism by Council of Ravenna - A. D. 1311.
39. The cup was forbidden to the masses - A. D. 1414.
40. Simony was introduced - A. D. 1517. (The clergy paid dues to the pope for the office they held. The priests reimbursed themselves by charging high prices for their services. Leo X made more than a million dollars a year from the sale of 2,000 offices.)
41. Tradition was declared by the Council of Trent to be equal in authority with the Bible – A. D. 1545.

All of the practices listed above are a far cry from that which characterized the simple New Testament church that Jesus established in A. D. 33. These departures identified the apostate church as something other than the church that Jesus established. It had become a man-made institution that no longer taught or practiced the truth. This fact did not go unnoticed by all. Beneath the surface of the church's apparent absolute power over the lives and thinking of the people, there ran an underground of revolt and dissent. Occasionally a voice of courage would find a way to break through the surface and speak out against the evils of the corrupt church.

CHAPTER 3
FORERUNNERS OF THE REFORMATION

Various types of dissent and attempted reform appeared from the twelfth century through the fifteenth century. Among these were the following:

Peter of Bruys desired to restore Christianity to its original form and simplicity by rejecting infant baptism, transubstantiation, prayers for the dead, and costly churches. He was punished for his efforts by being burned alive.

Henry of Lusanne attacked especially the corruption of the Roman Catholic clergy. He was punished by being cast into prison where he died.

Arnold of Brescia headed a revolt that drove the pope from Rome and established a commune which ruled the city for several years. Eventually he was hanged.

Others tried unsuccessfully in this early period to reform the corrupt church, which by this time had no resemblance to the church that Jesus established. Following these courageous men were others who were early forerunners of the Reformation. These had a greater impact for reform on the Catholic Church. We mention only a few:

PETER WALDO

Peter Waldo and the Waldenses sect: Peter Waldo was a twelfth century merchant of Lyons who adopted a life of apostolic poverty in A. D. 1173, and organized the Poor Men of Lyons to spread the vernacular scriptures. Waldo financed a French translation of the New Testament. When the Church refused permission for this ministry they declared themselves independent of the hierarchy. Persecution drove them into the rugged valleys of the Alps between France and Italy where they survived for centuries. They formed a church and allied themselves with the Protestant Reformation in the sixteenth century. (3, p. 33)

JOHN WYCLIFFE

John Wycliffe (ca. 1330-1384) and the Lollards: Wycliffe was a professor at Oxford and one of the leading theologians of the 14th century. He wrote and spoke out against abuses by the Catholic hierarchy. He was arrested by the papal authorities and examined for his criticisms, but friends in high places protected him. His treatment by the bishops and the pope only increased his indignation. His reply to ecclesiastical censures was a succession of forceful attacks upon both Catholic practice and doctrine. He set his followers to translate the Bible into English. Wycliffe was the first to give us a complete version of the Bible in English. He believed in the supremacy of Scripture over tradition. He believed the common man should learn directly from Scripture. Those who agreed with Wycliffe formed a group which was called "Lollards." This may have been a term of derision meaning "lazy" or "loafers." (5, p. 225)

By the time Wycliffe died, December 31, 1384, his ideas had spread considerably. John Huss, the Czech reformer was one who accepted his ideas. The Catholic Church had such a vengeance against Wycliffe that thirty one years after his death the council of Constance condemned him as a heretic and ordered his body dug up and burned. His ashes were cast into the Severn River. "In 1401 the 'heresy of Wycliffe was made a capitol offense in England and those who possessed any of his writings made subject to punishment by death.'" (5, p. 225)

JOHN HUSS

John Huss (ca. 1369-1415) and the Hussites: John Huss was born at Husinec, Bohemia. He studied at the University of Prague and received a degree of Master of Arts, and a second degree of Bachelor of Divinity. He was ordained a priest and divided his time between the pulpit and the university. He served twice as rector of the University of Prague while still in his thirties. He became a part of a group that advocated reform in the Roman Catholic Church. In the beginning he worked in harmony with church authorities in trying to bring about reform. He was even invited on several occasions by the Archbishop of Prague to preach before the assembly of the clergy and propose a remedy for the evils of the time. (5, pp. 225-227)

When he openly advocated the views of Wycliffe, an estrangement set in between Huss and the clergy. Aroused by Huss' adversaries, the papal court issued several decrees and finally in 1411 issued a sentence of excommunication against him.

In 1412 papal emissaries were sent to Prague to raise money for the intended war with the King of Naples by granting indulgences in sin to contributors. Huss waged a campaign against them and this was the last straw for the Roman Catholic Church. Aggravation of the sentence was declared and the pope was ready to suspend divine service in the city of Prague. Huss then left Prague.

Later he decided to present himself before the general council in Constance in hopes that he would be granted an opportunity to justify his activities and his teaching. Soon after his arrival in Constance he was imprisoned. Since he would not recant, he was condemned as an obstinate heretic and burned at the stake July 6, 1415. After his death the Hussites continued to form a strong body of dissent up to and following the Reformation.

THE ALBIGNESES

The Albigneses became prominent in Southern France about A. D. 1170. They were opposed to traditions being recognized as authority in religion. They were opposed to the doctrines of purgatory and image worship. They recognized the authority of the New Testament and circulated it to the full extent of their ability. Pope Innocent III called for a crusade against them. They were annihilated in a great slaughter. (8, p. 51)

JOHN WESSEL

John Wessel (1420-1498) was a reformer who was less known than John Wycliffe and John Huss. However, like Wycliffe and Huss, he attacked Catholicism in some of its principle features. Many of the beliefs that Wessel advocated were later taught by Luther. (8, p. 51)

JEROME SAVONAROLA

Jerome Savonarola (1452-1498) was a Catholic priest who lived in Florence, Italy. His studies led him to deny the authority of the Pope and make a bitter fight against the immorality of the clergy. "When the Pope found that he could not bribe the powerful preacher with the offer of a cardinal's hat, nor reduce him to silence by repeated admonitions, he excommunicated him." 8, p. 52 Savonarola pronounced this excommunication "void." He was finally arrested. While in prison he wrote a tract on the fifty-first Psalm in which he set forth his ideas of justification. He was tried, condemned, and burned alive on May 23, 1498 in front of the very church where he had preached for so long.

CHAPTER 4
THE PROTESTANT REFORMATION

These early attempts to reform the Roman Catholic Church were soon repressed by the iron hand of the church and the government. However, certain forces were in action during this period which were serving to prepare the way for a widespread movement known as the Protestant Reformation. There were several things that helped to bring this about.

THE RENAISSANCE

The Renaissance was an intellectual awakening in Europe to a new interest in literature, art, and science. This marked a change from medieval to modern aims and methods of thought. The minds of the people had become darkened with superstition, ignorance, and bigotry. This renewed interest in learning served to lift the veil of ignorance and superstition from the minds of the people. Independence of thought was the result.

As the amount of information increased there was also an increase in dissatisfaction with the prevailing religious condition. The Catholic clergy's long monopoly of literature and teaching was broken by the rise of a new class of laymen who could now read for themselves.

THE PRINTING PRESS

Another extremely important factor that paved the way for the Reformation was Gutenberg's invention of the movable type printing press in 1455. This made it possible to print books much faster and more economically than ever before. Prior to the printing press, Bibles were laboriously copied by hand. This resulted in the cost of a Bible being prohibitive for most. If a working man were fortunate enough to purchase a Bible it would cost him a year's wages. The Bible was the first book that was printed on the new press. This greatly improved method brought the Scriptures into common use and led to their translation and circulation into the major languages of Europe. When the people read the New Testament they recognized that the Roman Catholic Church was far from the pattern of the New Testament church.

NATIONALISM

Also, there was a growing spirit of Nationalism which affected the thinking of the people who began to cry for greater freedom in religion. Patriotism caused many to resent having a power in a foreign country rule over their own national churches. They disliked the idea of the pope, in another country, appointing their church officers. Some refused to contribute for the support of the pope and the building of elaborate and costly church buildings in Rome.

The efforts toward Reformation were bitterly resisted by the strong arm of persecution, but the ideas were too great and the number of participants too large to crush forever.

MARTIN LUTHER
(1483-1546)

Without question, the most prominent figure of the Reformation was Martin Luther. In fact, he is known as the father of the Reformation. Luther set out to be a lawyer, but after reading a copy of the Bible for the first time, he changed his plans against his father's will. He entered a monastery at the age of twenty-one and studied in earnest. He later said, "If ever a monk got to heaven by monkery, I would have gotten there." (8, p. 55) Luther became a priest at Wittenburg and also taught in the University in 1508.

Selling of Indulgences

Construction of St. Peter's Cathedral in Rome was underway and Pope Leo X was eager to complete it. A number of agents from the pope were sent out to sell indulgences in sin as a means of raising money. A man by the name of John Tetzel, who proved to be a super salesman of this evil practice, made his way into Germany. Luther vigorously opposed the whole unbiblical system. In October of 1517, he posted on the church building door at Wittenburg, ninety-five oppositions, or theses, in which he condemned the practice of selling indulgences in sin. He challenged anyone to debate with him. This, of course, caused a reaction, both favorable, and unfavorable, all over Germany. A great controversy followed.

Defied Roman Catholic Authorities

On June 15, 1520, Leo X issued a papal bull that gave Luther sixty days to change his course. On December 10 of that year, Luther burned the pope's decree at the city gate. By this act he threw off his allegiance to the Roman Catholic Church. In 1520 he published three pamphlets in which he opposed the Catholic priesthood. He called upon the nobles to throw off the bondage of Rome and take over the lands and wealth that was held by the Catholic Church. He challenged the authority of the Pope and condemned the sacramental system. He also set forth his views on salvation.

On January 3, 1520, Pope Leo issued a bull of excommunication. Four months later, the "Holy" Roman Empire declared Luther an outlaw, but he found protection in the castle of Frederick, Elector of Saxony. Luther was summoned to the Diet of Worms by Emperor Charles V in 1521. At the trial, when the assembly called upon him to retract his statements, he said, "Unless I am persuaded by means of the passages which I have quoted, and unless they thus render my conscience bound by the word of God, I cannot and will not retract... Here I stand, I cannot do otherwise, so help me God." (8, p. 56)

On his way from Worms he was seized by a masked horseman who appeared to be a kidnapper, but who turned out to be a friend, trying to save the life of Martin Luther. The rescuer took him to Wartburg Castle where he remained in safety for almost a year. It is amazing that Martin Luther escaped capital punishment at the hands of the church he tried desperately to reform. He died a natural death at the age of 63 on February 18, 1546, while on a visit to his birthplace at Eisleben.

> In the earlier years of Luther's attempt to establish the Reformation church, he adhered rather faithfully to the principle of sola scriptura. This led him to defy the pope, abolish the mass, teach the principle of justification by faith, abrogate the celibacy of the clergy, restore the preaching office, and discard compulsory fasts and many other Romish practices. At one time he favored the practice of immersion, and sought in other ways to recreate without compromise the original New Testament church. But national, political, and economic pressures eventually conspired to swerve him from his course of action. (65, p. 14)

Martin Luther was a man of intelligence and great courage. He boldly attempted to reform many wrongs that he saw in the Roman Catholic Church, but he failed to go all the way back to the original pattern in the New Testament. When Luther died, his followers did not continue the campaign for reform, but allowed the body of doctrine established by Luther to be the accepted system.

HULDREICH ZWINGLI
(1484-1531)

Huldreich Zwingli was born in 1484 into the family of an influential farmer who was also a chief magistrate in the town of Wildhaus in Switzerland. His uncle was a parish priest who took a great interest in Huldreich and encouraged him to obtain a thorough education. This Zwingli did, attending the Universities of Basel and Bern as well as the University of Vienna. In 1506 he became the parish priest in the town of Glarus. During this time he corresponded with Erasmus. Erasmus encouraged Zwingli to study the New Testament in the Greek language. Reading the New Testament in the original language developed in him an interest in first century Christianity and the church as the Lord intended it to be. This study made him very much aware of the need for reform in the church of which he was a priest.

Criticized Selling of Indulgences

Like Luther, Zwingli began his work of reform by criticizing the practice of selling indulgences in sin. In 1516 Zwingli was made a parish priest at Einsiedein. In this city was located the "black virgin." This was a statue of Mary to which pilgrims came annually to adore. There were a number of superstitious stories connected with it. Zwingli began to oppose this blind faith that was being placed in an inanimate statue. About this same time he began to study Hebrew which gave him a better background for a study of the Old Testament.

In 1519 he was called to be a priest of the church in Zurich and here he adopted a new kind of sermon. Contrary to custom he began to preach a series of sermons on the books of the Bible. It was at this time that he first heard of the work of Martin Luther. He read with great interest everything that Luther wrote.

Resigned Papal Pension

By 1520 Zwingli had learned too much to give blind allegiance to the pope. He resigned his papal pension and began to criticize publicly the Roman Catholic system. He preached that tithes being paid to the pope were not of the authority of God. He stated that anything given should be on a voluntary basis. In 1520 he prepared a sixty-seven point theses in which he differed with the

Catholic Church. He published his oppositions, and offered to debate them publicly. He even suggested that the city court could act as the debate judge.

Zwingli became a very popular preacher in Zurich. He broke completely with the past, making his sermons biblical and expository in nature. In these sermons he condemned many practices that had no biblical authority. He condemned the Catholic doctrine of mass and the invoking of the saints. He declared that the clergy ought to be able to marry in order to live holy lives. In 1519, while still a Roman Catholic priest, he took a widow, Anna Reinhard, as his wife without benefit of a marriage ceremony. This was a common practice for the priests in those days. A public marriage between Zwingli and Anna Reinhard was later performed in 1524.

Significant Reforms

Zwingli also believed church services should be conducted in the language of the people. He taught that monastic orders should be abolished. Pictures of idols were removed from the church buildings. Under Zwingli instrumental music ceased to be used in worship. Organs were removed from the churches. The Lord's Supper became a memorial service. The doctrine of transubstantiation was completely repudiated as having no biblical authority.

Zwingli and Luther were in disagreement as to how the Scriptures were to be used as authority. Zwingli was far more advanced than Luther in this area. He would allow in church services only what the Bible authorized. On the other hand, Luther would allow a religious practice unless it was specifically condemned in the Scriptures. (5, p. 255)

Union with Luther Failed

Since the followers of both Luther and Zwingli were in danger of extermination by the Catholics due to their reform efforts, it was in the interest of both parties to unite their forces. Representatives from Luther and Zwingli met in Marburg in 1529 in the castle of Philip of Hesse in an effort to work out their differences. The representatives found that the two leading reformers were in agreement in most areas. Luther had made a list of fifteen things on which he felt agreement was essential. There was agreement on fourteen of the fifteen items. The one point upon which they differed was in regard to the Lord's Supper. Both agreed that the priests could not perform a miracle to change the elements into the actual body and blood of Christ. However, Luther insisted that the actual body and blood of Christ were present in the elements. The two reformers themselves met to discuss this one point. (5, pp. 256-257)

Luther's argument was somewhat unusual. He said that when an iron was heated until it was red hot it was still iron, but, the heat was within it. He said in the same way there is within the bread and the wine the actual body and blood of Christ. Zwingli contended that the bread and the wine were not the literal body and blood of Jesus, but rather, these elements represented the body and the blood. Therefore, the body and blood were not actually present.

Luther took chalk and wrote on the table "This is my body." He insisted that Jesus meant what he said. Zwingli agreed that Jesus said that but when he said that, his body was unbroken. And when he said "this cup is my blood," he did not mean that it was his literal blood, for after having called it blood he then said, "I will drink henceforth no more of this fruit of the vine," showing that it was still fruit of the vine even after he had called it blood.

Luther could not agree with Zwingli. He declared that Zwingli had a "different spirit." Because of this he was not willing to fellowship with him, and thus, the effort toward a merger failed. The doctrine of the Lord's Supper as set forth by Luther is known as "consubstantiation" and is still held by modern Luther theologians. (5, pp. 255-256)

Killed in Battle

War broke out in 1531 between the followers of Zwingli and the Catholics. Zwingli, as the chaplain, went with the army against the Catholics. In the course of the battle he was killed.

Zwingli had moved in the right direction in re-establishing a pure New Testament church by accepting the principle that nothing could be permitted in religion that could not first be proved by the Scripture. We are indebted to Zwingli for establishing this noble concept upon which others could build in an effort to restore New Testament Christianity. However, like Luther and Calvin, Zwingli believed in the combination of church and state.

It was not long after Zwingli died that John Calvin came to the forefront as the leader of the Reformation in Switzerland. The forces of Zwingli merged with the followers of Calvin to create the Reformed Churches of Switzerland.

JOHN CALVIN
(1509-1564)

John Calvin was born and educated in France. He moved to Switzerland where he became the successor of Zwingli. The principal doctrines set forth by Calvin were as follows: original sin, predestination (a predetermined number for heaven and hell), Christ died only for those ordained for heaven, direct operation of the Holy Spirit (saving a man against his will), and the impossibility of the saved to fall away. He opposed the use of instrumental music in worship.

Calvin's doctrines were taken by John Knox into Scotland and this resulted in the establishment of the Presbyterian Church in that country.

Dictator of Geneva

In 1541 Calvin had so many followers in Geneva that the town council turned the city over to Calvin and he became the virtual dictator of the city. It was during this time that Calvin was responsible for having a man named Michael Servetus burned at the stake. Michael Servetus had written a book on "Errors of the Trinity" with which Calvin disagreed.

Calvin had such complete control over the city that he had

his way entirely. He had a very effective spy system. The religious leaders pronounced excommunication on all who refused to follow Calvin's theology and the secular arm of the government carried out the act. "Under this system, during the period of 1542-1546, there were fifty-seven executions and seventy-six banishments from the city of Geneva because of 'heresy.'... There were laws that prohibited swearing, requiring even the innkeepers to report any such offense. The inns were required to keep a Bible handy and to allow no dice, cards, or gambling. Indecent songs were banned, and no one was permitted to be out after 9:00 p.m. except the spies. Calvin officially held no position, except membership in the twelve man city council, but he was the minister of the church and the master of the city." (5, p. 259)

As we consider the theology of Calvin in the light of the Scriptures, we see many serious errors in his teaching. From the viewpoint of efforts in the direction of a restoration of the New Testament church, we regret that he influenced the thinking of so many people into accepting doctrines that were contrary to New Testament teaching. It is also most regrettable that many never progressed past the theology of John Calvin.

WILLIAM TYNDALE
(1484-1536)

Another great reformer of this period was William Tyndale. His work led the way to the overthrow of the power of Rome in England. He was born in Worcester about 1484. It became his chief desire in life to give the common people the Bible in their own language. He said to a religious teacher of his time, "If God spare my life many years, I will cause a boy that driveth the plow to know more of the Scripture than you do." (58, p. 83)

The story of the sacrifices and persecutions that Tyndale suffered in order to translate the Bible into English is inspirational. He endured much in order to remove the Roman yoke from the necks of the people. Tyndale was an educated man, receiving an M. A. degree in 1515 from Oxford. He also attended Cambridge where he became interested in reading the Greek New Testament. He resolved to translate the New Testament into English to correct the deficiencies and ignorance of the Roman Catholic clergy. The Bishop of London refused to help in this project. Tyndale then left England in 1525 and went to Wittenburg where he met Martin Luther.

New Testament in English

Tyndale was driven from Cologne when his translation was partly printed. He fled to Worms where in 1525 he published his first edition of the New Testament (without his name). It was widely distributed in England before the Catholic authorities discovered it and burned it. As a hunted man, Tyndale moved frequently. In 1534 he printed a revised edition of the New Testament, employing a dignified style which later formed the basis for the King James Version of 1611.

Betrayed

In 1535 he was betrayed by a man who posed as his friend and invited him to his home for dinner. Upon arriving at the home, his would-be host had him arrested. On Friday, October 6, 1536, he was strangled at the stake and his body then burned to ashes. At the stake, with fervent zeal and a loud voice, he cried: "Lord, open the king of England's eyes." (58, p. 88) His main contribution was that he was the first to translate the New Testament into English from the Greek text of Erasmus.

HENRY VIII
AND THE CHURCH OF ENGLAND

Henry VIII, who ruled 1509-1547, began his reign as a loyal Catholic and won the title "Defender of the Faith" from the pope by writing against Martin Luther. However, in his concern to have a male heir to the throne he sought a papal annulment of his marriage to Catherine of Aragon, who had been his wife for eighteen years. The reason Henry wanted the annulment was so he could marry Anne Bolyn. Of six children that he and Catherine had, only one, Mary, survived infancy. Unsuccessful in getting the marriage annulled, Henry obtained from the English Parliament an act declaring himself to be "supreme head" of the Church of England.

No doctrinal changes were made during the reign of Henry VIII. It was simply the Roman Catholic Church with a new name and a new head. However, in 1538 it was ordered that an English translation of the Bible be placed in each church for the people. This was definitely a step in the direction of bringing about a change.

Other marriages were in turn arranged for Henry with five other women; only the second of these, Jane Seymore, produced the desired male, Edward VI.

A Time of Reform

Edward VI was only nine years old when his father, Henry VIII died. Edward VI ruled from A.D. 1547 to 1553. The government was in the hands of advisors, primarily the Duke of Somerset. These men had definite Protestant views and pushed a program of reform. This included the first Book of Prayer in 1549. This was removed and replaced in 1552. Also adopted was the Forty-Two Articles. These were both largely the work of Bishop Cranmer. With some revisions, these two documents became the basic doctrinal standard for the Church of England (Anglican Church).

Mary Takes the Throne

Mary, 1553-1558, succeeded Edward VI to the throne since she was the oldest child of Henry VIII and Catherine of Aragon. Like her mother before her, Catherine was loyal to the Roman Catholic Church and the pope. She repealed the Protestant legislation and put the Catholic Church and the pope back into authority in England. Mary initiated a period of violent persecution against the Protestants. This produced a strong anti-Roman Catholic sentiment and earned for her the name of "Bloody Mary." Two hundred and eighty-eight people suffered martyrdom during her reign rather than place themselves under papal authority.

Bishop Cranmer

Since Bishop Cranmer had been a leader in the Protestant movement, when Mary came to power she demand from Cranmer a retraction of the things that he had said against the Roman Catholic Church and her practices. It was under threat of his very life that he recanted his anti-Catholic statements in writing. This was not enough to satisfy those in power. Cranmer was ordered to make that retraction before the people in a public assembly. At that point Cranmer refused and in fact took back his apology: As he was facing death he said the following:

> And now I come to the great thing that so troubleth my conscience, more than any other thing that I said or did in my life; and that is my setting abroad of writings contrary to the truth, which here now I renounce and refuse as things written with my hand contrary to the truth which I thought in my heart, and written for fear of death, and to save my life it might be; and that is all such bills which I have written or signed by my own hand since my degradation; wherein I have written many things untrue. And forasmuch as my hand offended in writing contrary to my heart, it shall be first burned. And as for the pope I refuse him as Christ's enemy and anti-Christ with all his false doctrine. (58, p. 132)

They dragged Cranmer from the assembly and burned him at the stake. He is reported to have placed the hand that had signed the statement into the fire first and watched it burn. Six months before the death of Cranmer, two other Protestant leaders, Hugh Latimer and Nicholas Ridley were also burned alive. Many of the "Marian exiles," those who escaped the bloody persecution under Mary, found refuge in Geneva and came under the influence of John Calvin.

Protestantism Reinstated

During the reign of Elizabeth, 1558-1603, the daughter of Henry VIII and Anne Bolyn, Protestantism was again re-instated. The papal supremacy was once more rejected, and Elizabeth was declared "Supreme Governor of the Church of England." (8, pp. 66-67)

The Church of England was planted in America by Colonists in Virginia and remained under the jurisdiction of the Bishop of London until the time of the Revolutionary War. Severing its connections with the mother church at the time when the United States became free of England, The Church of England became known as the Protestant Episcopal Church in America. Its name was taken from its episcopal form of church government, being ruled by bishops, as opposed to the presbyterian form of government, or rule by elders of the local congregation.

CHAPTER 5
RESULTING MOVEMENTS

A number of separate movements came out of the pre-Reformation Protestant tradition of the Hussites. Included in this number are the Anabaptists, the Socinians, the Waldensians, and the Bohemian Brethren who inherited the pre-Reformation Protestant tradition of the Hussites. These differed in many ways, but they all adhered to the principle of religious liberty. They believed that membership in the church should be wholly voluntary and that differing with the Roman Catholic Church was not a crime against the state. The three main principles common to all of these elements are as follows:

1. Faith versus works. (Salvation is the gift of God, not a payment by God for meritorious works done.)
2. The Priesthood of all believers. (The individual has the right of access to God without having to go through another human being.)
3. The scriptures versus ecclesiastical tradition. (The Catholic church believed in scripture, but the church was its own infallible interpreter. So, it was impossible to appeal to the scriptures to correct any practice that the church had approved.) (3, p. 36)

The movements of Luther and Zwingli were the two

most important of this period, but they were not the only reform movements. Others came from these two that differed in many ways. Luther's position that anything could be retained in the church that was not specifically condemned in the Scriptures was not accepted by all. This and other disagreements caused many followers to leave him and go further into Reformation. Zwingli wanted to include only that which the Scriptures permitted, but not all agreed with him, especially his belief in the combination of church and state.

ANABAPTISTS

One of the most significant groups growing out of the Luther and Zwingli movements was the Anabaptist group. The word "Anabaptist" suggests "baptism on top of baptism" or rebaptism. The Anabaptists rejected the validity of infant baptism and held that those baptized as infants would have to submit to believer's baptism. This was perceived as baptism on top of baptism. The Anabaptists were persecuted at times by the Catholic Church as well as the followers of Luther and Zwingli.

The Anabaptists were loosely knit and differed in their views among themselves. Some of them were close to the New Testament pattern, while others were extremely radical. In general, they believed the church was composed of believers only. They believed that infant baptism was an invention of man and altogether invalid. They did not agree on the method of practicing baptism. Sprinkling was commonly practiced by the Anabaptists in the early 1500's. On Easter Sunday, 1525, Balthaser Hubmaier (1480-1528) and 300 other men were "baptized" out of a milk dish filled with water. A little later, after further study, most of the Anabaptists changed their practice to baptism by immersion.

Anabaptists believed in the separation of church and state, and in this they parted company with Zwingli. Most rejected predestination and emphasized freedom of will. In general, they believed in the autonomy of the local congregation and each congregation being allowed to elect its own leaders.

In addition to Balthaser Hubmaier there was another leader

by the name of Conrad Grebel (1498-1526) who had worked with Zwingli from 1520-1525. At first Zwingli accepted the view that infant baptism was not acceptable, but he later wavered on this point. When Grebel accused him of not going all the way in restoring New Testament teaching on the subject Grebel challenged Zwingli to a debate. Although Zwingli did poorly in the debate he was able to exert enough influence on the City Council of Zurich to persuade them to unite against the Anabaptists.

In 1526 the town council decided to punish all Anabaptists by putting them to death by drowning. Many fled the city of Zurich for their very lives. Hubmaier and others went over into Western Europe, establishing churches which reflected their views. Hubmaier was captured and burned at the stake by Imperial command. His wife was put to death by drowning by the authority of the Roman Catholic leaders.

Melchoir Hoffman became a leader of the radical wing of the Anabaptists. He taught that Christ was going to return to earth and establish an earthly kingdom in 1533 in Strasbourg, Germany. When Hoffman's prophecy failed, a man by the name of Matthys became the leader of this wing of the movement. He decided that instead of Strasbourg the city of Munster would be the location of the new kingdom. However, in his attempt to take over the city by force, he was killed. Matthys was succeeded by John Leyden. He married the widow of Matthys along with sixteen other women. Polygamy was conveniently approved since there were so many more unmarried women than men in Munster.

Anabaptists flooded into the city of Munster from all over Western Europe. The city was soon controlled by them. All who would not accept the views of the Anabaptists were forced to leave the city. John Leyden proclaimed himself to be the king and stated that he would rule until Christ came. These extreme conditions moved the Protestants and Catholics to unite in an effort to stamp out the Anabaptist movement. The city of Munster was taken from the Anabaptists by force. Many of the people were ruthlessly murdered in 1536. Anabaptists in many places were drowned or executed in horrible ways. (5, p. 264-265)

MENO SIMONS

For a time it appeared that the entire movement of the Anabaptists was doomed for extinction. One man, Meno Simons, saved the movement by a more intelligent approach to the movement and the Scriptures. Meno Simons had been a Catholic priest in the Netherlands. He studied the Anabaptist views, turned his back on the priesthood, and affiliated himself with the group. Eventually he became the leader. In the Netherlands they took the name "Brethren" to avoid the widespread hostility against the Anabaptists. The "Brethren" soon adopted the name "Mennonites" after the first name of the leader. (5, p. 265)

After the terrible episode in Munster, Meno Simons believed he was called by God to protect the movement. He emphasized church membership on the basis of personal conversion that was sealed by adult baptism. He taught against the followers holding civil offices or bearing arms. He also taught that there could be no state control of the church. Many Anabaptists in Holland moved to America and established the Mennonite church.

Because of mistreatment in England, many English Protestants went to the Netherlands where they came in contact with the Anabaptists. They returned to England, and by 1611 there were many Anabaptists in that country. Independent congregations began to call themselves simply "Baptists." The second generation of reformers had not received "baptism" as children so they refused the name Anabaptist, denying that they had been baptized again.

From the influence of Meno Simon's movement, congregations were established in Germany and took the name Dunkards or Tunkards. Some of them came to America and brought with them the practice of triune immersion and foot washing. The Quakers, Mennonites, Amish Mennonites, Dunkards and Baptists all had their origin in the Anabaptist movement.

PURITANS AND SEPARATISTS

The early "Puritans" were those who wanted to remain in the Church of England in order to reform it to be more holy. The early leader of the Puritans was Thomas Cartwright (1535-1603). In 1569 he advocated the appointment of elders in each congregation, the election of ministers by their people, the abolition of such offices as archbishops and archdeacons, and the reduction of the clergy. Some call the Puritans associated with Cartwright "Presbyterian Puritans." Cartwright and his fellow Puritans opposed all separation from the Church of England.

The "Separatists" carried reform even further by removing themselves from the Anglican Church. The first recognized leader was Robert Browne. He was first a Presbyterian Puritan under the influence of Cartwright. He then adopted Separatist principles and established an independent congregation in Norwich in 1581. As a result of his preaching he was imprisoned several times. To avoid persecution, Browne and his followers fled to the Netherlands. Eventually Browne returned to the Church of England. Separatism then waned, but soon reappeared.

BAPTIST CHURCH

Historically, the Baptist church did not exist until after the Anabaptist movement of the 16th century from which its name is derived. "A Separatist movement of far reaching ultimate consequences had its beginnings early in the reign of James I when John Smyth, a former clergyman of the establishment, adopted Separatist principles and became 'pastor' of a gathered congregation at Gainsborough.... The hand of opposition being heavy upon them, the members of the Gainsborough congregation, led by Smyth, were self-exiled to Amsterdam, probably in 1608... At Amsterdam Smyth... on the basis of his own study of the New Testament became convinced that the apostolic method of admitting members to church fellowship was by baptism on profession of repentance towards God and faith in Christ. In 1608 or 1609 he therefore baptized himself by pouring, and then the others of his church, forming the first English Baptist

Church, though on Dutch soil." (66, p. 408-409) Thomas Helwys was "baptized" on that occasion by Smyth. In 1612 Helwys returned to London and founded what is recognized as the first Baptist Church in England. This group rejected Calvinism. The branch of the Baptist Church that accepted Calvinism began in London in 1633.

In 1639, the first Baptist church in America was established in Providence, Rhode Island by Roger Williams. When the Baptists came to America from Europe and scattered about the colonies, they disagreed among themselves and formed more than twenty major branches of that church. (5, p. 265)

QUAKERS

The Quakers came to be noticed in England about 1650. Their leaders were George Fox and James Nailer. Nailer brought discredit to the group. He was described as a "half mad fanatic." One writer described the Quakers as "a new sect who shows no respect to any man, magistrate or other, and seem a melancholy, proud sort of people and exceedingly ignorant." (5, p. 283) They are said to have disturbed other churches during their services by calling their preachers false prophets and lying witnesses. Nailer was finally arrested, whipped and branded.

George Fox repudiated the fanatical tendencies of Nailer, although he brought reproach upon himself by refusing to remove his hat in the presence of magistrates or officials. His followers, however, developed a deep personal piety. They opposed war and refused to take oaths. They objected to sacraments and all ministerial orders. The Quaker movement in England was a development from within the Anabaptist movement, which in turn, had come out of the Reformation movement. (5, p. 283)

DUTCH REFORMED CHURCH

In 1567 the Duke of Alva began a persecution in the Netherlands of the followers of Calvin and Zwingli as well as the

Anabaptists. This drove many Dutchmen to England where they were received with kindness and allowed to worship according to their convictions. This was the beginning of the Dutch Reformed Church. (5, p. 280)

PRESBYTERIAN CHURCH

John Calvin is associated with the Presbyterian church although he never founded a distinct denomination. His doctrinal system, known as Calvinism, is usually associated with the Presbyterian Church. There are a number of non-Presbyterian churches that also hold Calvinistic views.

John Knox was the driving force that took Calvinism to Scotland. He was so influential that the Scottish Parliament threw out the Episcopals (Church of England). The first book of discipline was written in 1560, but it was not until 1592 that the Scottish Parliament made Presbyterianism the established faith in Scotland. (26, p. 43) The Westminster Association was in session from July 1, 1643 to February 22, 1649, framing the Westminster Confession of Faith which became the doctrinal basis of English and American Presbyterianism.

The Presbyterian Church was formed in England in 1572 by Thomas Cartwright. He had written several pamphlets against the Church of England and it's Episcopal form of government. These were widely distributed and resulted in the formation of the Presbyterian Church in England. Francis Makemie is called the "Father of American Presbyterianism." He organized the Presbyterian Church in Maryland in 1684. Throughout the history of Presbyterianism there have been 17 major divisions. (26, p. 43) The word "Presbyterian" was used to describe the church because of the form of government they utilized, namely, rule by elders. This differentiated them from the Church of England or Anglican Church where priests were dominant. (5, p. 281)

FAILURE OF PROTESTANT REFORMATION

The Protestant Reformation did not succeed for four reasons. First, they did not go far enough back to the pattern for the original church that Jesus had started. They tried to reform rather than start over. Secondly, they developed rigid systems of theology that became standards for orthodoxy and grounds for division. Thirdly, the followers rarely improved upon the leader once the leader was gone. And, finally, they established state churches, which was a carry-over from the Catholic Church.

CHAPTER 6
EARLY BEGINNINGS OF THE RESTORATION MOVEMENT IN GREAT BRITAIN

CONGREGATIONS DEDICATION TO RESTORATION

The late Dabney Philips, historian of the Restoration Movement stated, "It has been established that in 1669 during the reign of Charles II, there were eight congregations of the Lord's Church in Northwest England." An old book of business minutes dated in 1669 has been found that reveals that they called themselves by the name Church of Christ, practiced baptism by immersion, celebrated the Lord's Supper each Lord's Day and had elders and deacons. (2, p. 14)

In 1735, John Davis, a young preacher in the Fife district of Scotland was preaching New Testament Christianity twenty-five years before Thomas Campbell was born. "It is said that in March, 1818, a church of Christ in New York sent a circular letter to various congregations, apparently 'of the same faith and order.' Among the replies received were some from Glasgow, Edinburgh, Manchester and Dublin, where it was said there were churches guided only by the Word of God, and consequently wearing the name of Christ, baptizing believers, and observing the Lord's Supper weekly. In the Glasgow letter, it is interesting to note this statement: 'Such churches as ours have existed in Scotland, at Edinburgh and Glasgow, from 30 to 40 years.' A congregation in Kirkcaldy began as far back as 1798, and small churches existed about 1804 in Ireland, near Dungannon, and another at Coslane, near Chester. It is known that much ground work had been done by such men as Archibald McLean and his coadjutors.'" (40, p. 21)

In the 18th century and early in the 19th century there sprang up in the British Isles a considerable number of small and independent movements who used language associated with those who were trying to restore New Testament Christianity. These groups were aimed in a more precise way than any of the preceding, to return to the exact practice of the New Testament church. This included doctrine, ordinances, methods of worship, organization, and the name itself.

BELIEFS HELD IN COMMON

One historian claims to have listed 40 of these independent movements. They all remained small and many soon vanished but in the aggregate their influence was considerable. Many called themselves "Church of Christ" or "Brethren." Their common beliefs included the following:

1. Churches were cluttered up with human additions.
2. Creeds were too complicated and went beyond the Word.
3. Worship was too formal.
4. The clergy was too professionalized, too authoritative in lording it over the church, and too eager for worldly advantages.
5. They were democratic, and stressed the independence of the local congregation.
6. They repudiated any connection between the church and state.
7. Union was no part of the program in any of these.
8. Their one desire was to be right with God. (3, p. 46)

JOHN GLAS AND ROBERT SANDEMAN

One of the earliest and most interesting of these movements was the one started by John Glas, a Presbyterian minister who left the Church of Scotland in 1728. The leadership of this movement was carried on by his son-in-law, Robert Sandeman. The resulting churches were more frequently called "Sandemanian" than "Glasite" and sometimes "Old Scotch Independents." There were probably never more than 20 to 30 churches in Great Britain and fewer in the United States, all of them being in New England. The English chemist, Michael Faraday, was a member of a Sandemanian congregation. The father-in-law of Shelly was at one time a preacher in his youth for a Sandemanian group.

John Glas withdrew from the Church of Scotland primarily because he was convinced it was wrong in the following ways:

1. The church was connected with the state.
2. The church had synods and law making bodies to fix standards of doctrine for the church and to exercise discipline over it. The church of the New Testament had none.
3. Each congregation of the Church of Scotland was not autonomous, or self ruled, with the right to conduct its public worship, choose its minister and discipline its own members.

One biographer of John Glas gave an example of his intent to follow only the Word. Glas' group agreed to observe the Lord's Supper once per month, much more frequently than did the Church of Scotland. They then came to realize they had as much scripture for once a month as the Church of Scotland had for less often. From a study of the New Testament they concluded that they should observe the Lord's Supper every week as the early church did, if they were going to be directed by the Scriptures only.

On the same basis they chose a plurality of elders. On examination of First Timothy, chapter three, and Titus, chapter one, they found no mention of a university education or an understanding of the ancient languages as required credentials to be an elder. Therefore, they dropped these requirements to be consistent with being directed by the Word.

Robert Sandeman was a theological thinker and a writer. In 1755 he wrote a book in reply to a book by John Hervey in which it was proposed that man must have a change of heart produced by a direct act of the Holy Spirit before faith is possible. Hervey had written that man must have a special act of enabling grace to make it possible for him to be saved. In his 600-page book, Sandeman argued that faith comes first, based on evidence, and the change of heart is the result of faith. The book had a second printing in 1759 and a third in 1803. This was about a year before Barton W. Stone established the church of Christ in Kentucky. (6, p. 24)

In Alexander Campbell's time there were those who claimed that Campbell and Walter Scott depended heavily on Sandeman's writings. One writer, W. H. Whitsitt, in a book called The Origin of the Disciples of Christ (1888), called the Disciples "an off-shoot of Sandemanianism." This was answered by G. W. Longan in 1889 in his Origin of the Disciples of Christ. He stated that Campbell only agreed with 4 of 15 points in which the critic had analyzed Sandeman's distinctive teaching. The "off-shoot" theory was easily disproved, but there were some similarities that were not purely coincidental. These included the emphasis upon restoring the practices of the primitive church, the plurality of elders, weekly observance of the Lord's Supper, and refusing to call Sunday the Sabbath.

Campbell personally answered the charge that he was substantially a Sandemanian by answering that he had spent a winter studying Sandeman's book and all the replies and defenses. He regarded him as a "giant among pygmies" in the great debate on faith, but he rejected his system as a whole. Campbell disagreed with Sandeman's lack of a plea for unity, but at the same time he agreed with his goal of restoring primitive Christianity.

The Sandemanians did not have enough evangelistic zeal to cause them to grow and to keep themselves alive. Unfortunately, Glas and Sandeman did not see the problem with the Presbyterian practice of "baptizing" by sprinkling. However, some of their associates in Scotland led by Archibald McLean arrived at the conclusion that the baptism taught in the New Testament was only for believers and the mode was immersion. They came to be called "Old Scotch Baptists" because of their stand on baptism.

Sandeman came to America and established a congregation in Danbury, Connecticut and spent the rest of his life there. In about 1817 a member of this congregation, Lewis Osborne, came to disagree with infant baptism as practiced by that congregation. He refused to have his child "baptized." He went to New York to meet with Henry Ehret. (Years later Henry's son, Isaac, would become a very influential man in the liberal wing of the church, being the editor of the Christian Standard.) In New York, Osborne was immersed by Henry Ehret. Upon his return, he baptized his wife and two others. The four became the nucleus of a restoration congregation in Danbury, Conn. in 1817. Twenty-three years later, in 1840, Alexander Campbell visited there and found their property was in the name of the "Reformed Baptist Society." His visit resulted in the changing of the title of the property and the affiliation of this congregation with other Restoration churches. (3, p. 267)

Robert Sandeman died in Danbury, Connecticut on April 2, 1771. The following epitaph was engraved on his tombstone:

> Here lies until the resurrection, the body of Robert Sandeman, a native of Perth, North Britain, who in the face of continual opposition from all sorts of men, long and boldly contended for the ancient faith; that the bare work of Jesus Christ without a deed, or thought on the part of man, is sufficient to present the chief of sinners spotless before God; to declare this blessed truth as testified in the Holy Scriptures, he left his country-- he left his friends, and much patient suffering finished his labors at Danbury, 2nd April 1771, aged 53 years. (29, pp. 58-59)

ROBERT AND JAMES HALDANE

Also among the independents, there was a small movement by two brothers, Robert and James Haldane, that deserves consideration. They were wealthy laymen of the Church of Scotland who were disgusted by the sterility and formalism of the established church. They were also alarmed at the teaching that was coming from the ministers that was not consistent with the New Testament.

The Haldane brothers spent their money freely in promoting an evangelical revival in Scotland. They brought the famous English evangelist, Roland Hill, to hold meetings in Scotland and even built a tabernacle in Edinburgh to be the center of his work.

They led in the organization of Sunday schools and encouraged lay preaching as well as the establishment of institutes for training young men to preach. They were ardent for the extension of Christianity. An attempt was made to send a mission to India but the East India Company frustrated the efforts of the brothers. They financed the bringing of twenty-four African children from Sierra Leone with the intent of educating them in England and then sending them back to Christianize their own people; however, Anglican authorities took that project off their hands. They organized the "Society for Propagating the Gospel at Home" which was an agency for promoting the evangelistic cause, but they could not find a place for their activities within the state church, the Church of Scotland.

In 1799, out of frustration, they withdrew from the Church of Scotland and organized an independent church in Edinburgh, Scotland. James Haldane, then thirty-one, became its minister and continued to fill that pulpit for fifty years. The following was practiced by the church:

1. Congregational independence as in the New Testament.
2. Weekly observance of the Lord's Supper.
3. Their conviction was that true reformation of the church required exact conformity to apostolic teaching and practice.

In 1805 James A. Haldane published a volume which had a title of great length, A View of the Social Worship and Ordinances Observed by the First Christians, Drawn from the Scriptures Alone; Being an Attempt to Enforce Their Divine Obligation, and to Represent the Guilty and Evil Consequences of Neglecting Them. The title of Chapter one was, "There is Reason to Presume that the New Testament Furnishes Instructions Concerning Every Part of the Worship and Conduct of Christian Societies, as Well as Concerning the Faith and Practice of Individuals." The title of Chapter two was "All Christians are Bound to Observe the Universal and Approved Practices of the First Churches Recorded in Scriptures."

In the early years the Haldanes believed in infant baptism, but independent study led them to reject infant baptism, sprinkling, and human creeds. In Haldane's book he defended infant baptism, but two years later the Haldanes became convinced that the practice of the New Testament church was otherwise, so they changed and became immersionists. In Fool of God, the writer tells us that Alexander Campbell often went to hear Haldane preach. (27, p. 45) "It is amazing that within nine years these two brothers organized 85 congregations. They preached frequently near where Thomas Campbell lived in Ireland and in Glasgow, Scotland where Alexander was a student in the University of Glasgow." (2, p. 16)

One of the ministers associated with the Haldanes was Greville Ewing. He advocated congregational independence and weekly observance of the Lord's Supper. Alexander Campbell spent a year in Glasgow as a student and became a close friend with Ewing. Near the end of that year, Campbell broke with the Seceder Presbyterian Church of which he was a member and his father Thomas was a minister. The Haldanes and Ewing no doubt had a lot to do with that decision made by Alexander Campbell.

It is impossible to say how many congregations associated with the Haldane brothers were in Great Britain and in America because they did not call themselves by the Haldane name. They were an independent group whose goal was to restore the exact pattern of the primitive church in teaching, worship and structure. They also practiced closed communion.

PART II
RESTORATION IN AMERICA

CHAPTER 7
EARLY BEGINNINGS OF RESTORATION IN THE NEW WORLD

THE CALL TO THE NEW WORLD

The American colonies were mission fields. In England people were urged from the pulpits to carry religion to the colonies for five reasons.

1. They reasoned that countless thousands of natives could not be saved unless Christian people went and converted them.
2. Protestant colonies were needed to off-set Spain's already impressive empire in the New World.
3. It was the patriotic thing to do to expand the power and possessions of Protestant England. (Mexico, Central and South America were already secured for Spain and the Catholic Church. Catholic France had reached out to Canada.)
4. Settlers, without land in England and no hope for any, could have houses and land in America.
5. Colonies in America would better England's economic condition by commerce and relieving the pressure of over-population.

Even though the mission effort was a failure, the other goals were achieved.

HEAVY HAND OF THE CHURCH OF ENGLAND

Those who came to the New World seeking religious freedom found that if they dissented with the Church of England they were likely to encounter some type of persecution. Tragically, four Quakers were hanged on Boston Common in 1661. Quakers and Baptists were persecuted in most of the colonies until about 1700. In Rhode Island, where Roger Williams had established the first Baptist Church around 1639, the Baptists had secure standing and were free from persecution. The Quakers controlled the government in Pennsylvania enough to allow persecuted groups from elsewhere to come into Pennsylvania and enjoy religious liberty.

The Church of England ruled affairs in the colonies with an iron hand. For example, in March of 1624 in Virginia, the assembly held that all citizens must attend Anglican Church services on Sunday. Whoever missed once without an allowable excuse was fined one pound of coffee. A month's missing brought a fine of 50 pounds. Every person was told "to yield ready obedience" to the "cannons of England under pain of censure."

No man was allowed to sell his tobacco until the minister from the Anglican Church gave permission. The minister's portion was from the first and best tobacco. Clergymen were kept busy hunting and punishing all types of heresy.

THE ACT OF CONFORMITY

In 1632, in Virginia, the "Act of Conformity" was enacted "in order to preserve the purity of doctrine and the unity of the church, that all ministers be conformable to the orders and constitution of the Church of England, and not to teach anything else publicly or privately." The same act directed the governor and counsel to enforce the law rigidly and non-conformists were to leave the colony. (1, P. 1)

Quakers were persecuted and described as "unreasonable and turbulent sort of people who, contrary to the laws, daily gathered assemblies and congregations of people, teaching and publishing lies." Captains of ships were fined 100 pounds sterling for bringing Quakers into the state of Virginia. Quakers were imprisoned without bail. (1, P. 2)

Persecution also raged against the Baptists who came to Virginia in 1714. By the time of the Revolutionary War, they were quite numerous. In January of 1768, four were arrested and Patrick Henry rode 50 miles to defend them. In a dramatic way, Henry said, "These men are charged with what? ...preaching the gospel of the Son of God." He waived the indictment above their heads, raised his head and hands to the sky and exclaimed "Great God!" The men were immediately dismissed. (1, P. 2)

CHURCH OF ENGLAND LOSES FAVOR

In spite of persecution, the non-conformists increased in number. At the same time they were gaining favor with the colonists. The established Church of England was becoming very unpopular. By the time of the Revolutionary War, two-thirds of the people favored the dissenters, yet they were forced by law to pay the clergy. It was 1786 before Thomas Jefferson's Bill for Religious Freedom was passed, but it was 1801 before the final vestige of church and state union was abolished.

James Madison, who would later become the President of the United States, commented strongly about the condition of the church in New England in the following way:

> Poverty and luxury prevailed among all sects; pride, ignorance and knavery among the priesthood, and vice and wickedness among the laity. That is bad enough, but it is not the worst I have to tell you. That diabolical, hell-conceived principle of persecution rages among some, and to their eternal infamy, the clergy furnish their quota of imps for such purposes.

There are at this time in the adjacent counties, not less than five or six well-meaning persons in close jail for publishing their religious sentiments, which, in the main, are very orthodox. (1, p. 3)

THE METHODIST CHURCH

As early as 1729, John Wesley in England, noting the formality and tyranny of the Church of England, proposed forming societies within the church which were dedicated to the purifying of the corrupt elements within the church. This did not remove them from the Anglican Church. Wesleyan preachers were still Anglican. Wesley lived and died a member of the Church of England. He was buried in his Anglican robes.

Wesleyan Societies, as they were known, came to be established by persons demanding a holier life on the part of members of the church. These Wesleyan Societies came to the New World and spread throughout the colonies. As the sentiment against England and the Church of England grew, the Wesleyan Societies grew in favor by the colonists who were crying for liberty. They did not carry with them the stigma of the oppressive Church of England.

The problem of ordination to perform marriages, funerals, and baptisms came up. The common belief of apostolic succession prevailed among Anglican clergymen in those days. No minister was ordained who was not himself ordained by an ordained minister. The Wesleyan preachers were not ordained. The Anglican clergymen who were ordained, refused to ordain the Wesleyan preachers. By the close of the Revolutionary War, the English clergy for the most part returned to England, but Wesleyan preachers stayed in the colonies. From England, John Wesley sent three ordained Anglican priests, led by Thomas Coke, to the New World. In their possession was a document written by John Wesley and destined to be known as the "Magna Carta of American Methodism."

Not long after, Coke and the group met with Wesleyan preachers and many others at the Christmas Conference in Baltimore,

Maryland in 1784. It was at this conference that Francis Asbury was ordained as a superintendent of the church. It was also here that the discipline for the Methodist Episcopal Church was accepted and for the first time, the title Methodist Episcopal Church was accepted as the name for the Wesleyan Societies. The Societies were then trying to be a church separate and distinct from the Church of England.

The name chosen did not set well with many of the preachers, nor did the type of church government. Even John Wesley had admitted that the church government was not apostolic, but that it was the most practical under the circumstances. A compromise was reached which denied the doctrine of apostolic succession, and the Methodist church was born.

In order to move away from the Church of England they established a government that was a mixture of monarchical and democratic principles. The democratic portion satisfied the freedom loving colonists, and the monarchical phase satisfied those who favored the government of the Church of England. Although the bishops were given more administrative power than the bishops of England, the legislative power was vested in the regular conferences which were soon controlled by the lay people.

JAMES O'KELLY
(1735-1826)

James O'Kelly was of Irish descent. Although no records have been found of his birth, he is believed to have been born in Virginia. One historian believes that he was born in Ireland. There was strong opposition to Francis Asbury, superintendent of the Methodist Church in America. The primary one leading that opposition was James O'Kelly. As a Methodist, he labored hard in his ministry, was a man of zeal, an advocate of holiness, given to prayer and fasting, and an able defender of Methodist doctrine. He strongly opposed Negro slavery and spoke against it in private and from the pulpit.

Before he became a Methodist, O'Kelly married Elizabeth Meeks in 1760. They had two sons, John and William. O'Kelly's son William was 12 when the first Methodist preachers came into

Cedar Creek County of Virginia in 1775. William and his mother were converted. William wanted to be a preacher but his father discouraged him. William grew up and got into politics. He was for several years a member of the State Legislature of North Carolina.

O'Kelly was not long in getting interested in religion. He listened carefully to the Methodist preachers who came into his area. He also listened to the sermons read which had been written by John Wesley back in England. O'Kelly was impressed by the fact of the all sufficiency of the Scriptures. Wesley had said, "We will be downright Christians" and this pleased O'Kelly. It was about the middle of the Revolutionary War that O'Kelly began to preach for the Methodists.

The influence of Francis Asbury was seen everywhere. In Southern Virginia and North Carolina where O'Kelly traveled and preached, the general impression was that Asbury was a tyrant. Asbury's rule was "pay, pray, and obey" and this did not set well with all laymen. Tension especially mounted between O'Kelly and Asbury. One historian said that O'Kelly was too much Irish to tolerate Asbury, who was too much English. (1, p. 8)

It was a time of crisis when the Virginia Conference of the Methodists met on May 18, 1779. O'Kelly and others wanted separation from the Church of England. Asbury said Wesley wanted an episcopal type of government as the Church of England. O'Kelly brought some disfavor on himself and probably hurt his influence for more important matters when he advocated that preachers be required to rise at 4:00 or 5:00 in the morning. O'Kelly declared that it was a shame for preachers to be in bed after 6:00 a.m. The subject of baptism came up as to whether it should be sprinkling or immersion. Unfortunately, O'Kelly favored sprinkling and did so to his death.

For the next five years, O'Kelly found himself at odds with Asbury continually. By the time of the famous Christmas Conference in Baltimore, December 25, 1784, O'Kelly was recognized as a leader against Asbury's views. A week after the Conference, O'Kelly and twelve others were ordained as elders by Thomas Coke who was designated by John Wesley.

Separation from Methodists

On November 1, 1792, there was another crisis when the General Conference met in Baltimore. O'Kelly introduced a motion that a preacher be given the right of appeal to the conference if he did not like his assigned preaching appointments. The debate was intense for three days. Asbury left the conference. Finally, O'Kelly lost. When this happened, O'Kelly and his followers announced they were through with the conference.

Among those standing with O'Kelly were Rice Haggard, John Allen, John Robertson, and William McKendree. McKendree later went back to the Methodists, Allen became a physician and gave up preaching. In the end, O'Kelly and Haggard were the two to carry on with the principles of reform. A short time later O'Kelly and others met at Reese Chapel in Charlotte County, Virginia. They submitted a petition to the Methodists asking for union based on certain amendments. The Methodists refused. Another meeting in Chesterfield County, Virginia was held on August 1, 1793. They petitioned Asbury to meet in a conference and examine the government of the Methodist Episcopal Church in light of the scriptures. Asbury refused to meet.

Republican Methodists Change Name

Another conference was held in Powhaton County, Virginia on December 25, 1793. At this conference the group decided to sever all ties with the Methodist Episcopal Church. They took the name "Republican Methodists" to indicate their freedom. (1, pp. 7-10)

The next general meeting of the O'Kelly group was its most important. The meeting was held August 4, 1794, at Old Lebanon in Surry County, Virginia. A committee of seven had been appointed to devise a plan of church government. Finally, they decided to lay aside every manuscript and go by the Bible alone. Rice Haggard stood up, holding his Bible, and said, "Brethren, this is a sufficient rule of faith and practice. By it we are told that the disciples were called Christians, and I move that henceforth and forever the followers of Christ be known as 'Christians' simply.'" (1, p. 10) Following Haggard, a man from North Carolina stood up and moved that they take the Bible itself as their only creed. This break with the conference is generally known in church history as "The O'Kelly Secession." There were more than 6,000 people that were part of this secession. (6, p. 29)

Based on these two motions the O'Kelly movement devised what became known as the "Five Cardinal Principals of the Christian Church." These five principles are as follows:

1. The Lord Jesus Christ is the only head of the Church.
2. The name "Christian" to the exclusion of all party and sectarian name.
3. The Holy Bible, or the Scriptures of the Old and New Testament our only creed, and a sufficient rule of faith and practice.
4. Christian character, or vital piety, the only test of church fellowship and membership.
5. The right of private judgment and the liberty of conscience, the privilege and duty of all. (1, p. 10)

In 1801 the "Republican Methodists" changed their name to the "Christian Church" in order to be identified with the name given to individual disciples in Acts 11:26, 26:28; I Peter 4:16. By 1809 some estimate that O'Kelly's group had a membership of 20,000.

The significance of O'Kelly's action lies in the main direction he was looking. Although they fell short of the desired goal, theirs was a movement with the emphasis on overthrowing human elements in religion, as well as a plea to be guided only by the scriptures. Certainly, weaknesses appear in the "Five Cardinal Principles" and O'Kelly's unbiblical position on the mode of baptism, but the fact that they were attempting to bring about a restoration of the New Testament church is also evident.

ELIAS SMITH
(1769-1846)

While the Restoration was working among the Methodists in Virginia and North Carolina, it was also working among the Baptists in Vermont and New Hampshire.

Elias Smith was born June 17, 1769 at Lyne, Connecticut in New London County. He died in 1846. His father, Stephen was a Baptist and remained so until one year before Elias died when a church of the restoration principles was established near him in Woodstock, Vermont.

Elias Smith was just a boy when the Revolutionary War was going on. He could hear the canons of the British warships and see them flame as they lay in Long Island Sound. He grew up with a desire for liberty and this extended itself into religion as well, as Smith was compelled to oppose the tyranny of human creeds.

As a child he worried a lot about his sins. His spelling book contained a form of a prayer in it. Smith would take this and sneak out to the barn where he would weep and pray. His mother was a "New light Congregationalist" and had young Elias sprinkled against his will. He ran from being sprinkled but his uncle chased him and brought him back to submit to what they called "the seal of the covenant."

Baptized by Immersion

In 1789, while living in Connecticut, Smith became greatly concerned over his baptism. He gave considerable study to the subject and finally convinced himself that believers were the only people qualified to be baptized. He also concluded that immersion was the proper method of baptism.

The Baptist Church in Woodstock, Connecticut was holding a monthly meeting and William Grow was preaching. It was at one of these meetings that Mr. Grow baptized him in Queechy Creek in the name of the Father, Son, and Holy Spirit in accordance with Matthew 28:18-20. According to Baptist teaching, Smith was now a Christian, but he was not yet a Baptist. There were four things required of him to be a Baptist:

1. First, he must give a reason of his hope in Christ.
2. Secondly, he must be baptized.
3. Thirdly, he must give his consent to the Articles of Faith and the Church Covenant.
4. Finally, he must be voted in. (1, p. 12)

All of this Smith did and became a member of the Second Baptist Church in Woodstock, Connecticut. Regarding those Articles of Faith, years later Smith wrote, "The Articles of Faith to which I consented contained what Baptists call 'particular election,' or that Christ died for the elect and that such a number should be saved… I assented to them because the minister and the church thought that they were true. Since that time, the minister and the members have rejected the abominable doctrine of partiality and now stand in gospel liberty." (1, p. 12)

In 1789 Smith began preparation to be a preacher in the Baptist Church. William Grow supplied him with a book of sermons and a Cruden's Concordance. In 1801 he moved to Salisbury, New Hampshire. By now he had begun to have some misgivings about certain doctrines in the Baptist Church, particularly Calvinism. Because he preached views which were contrary to Baptist teaching, he fell in disfavor among many Baptists. In his reaction against Calvinism he, for a time, embraced Universalism, but after an intensive study he turned from that extreme. Smith later wrote about this period in his life.

When in my 24th year, I believed there would be a people bearing a name different from all the denominations then in this country; but what would they be called, I then could not tell. In the spring of 1802, having rejected the doctrine of

Calvin and Universalism, to search the scriptures to find the truth, I found the name which the followers of Christ ought to wear; which was Christians (Acts 11:26). My mind being fixed upon this as the right name, to the exclusion of all the popular names in the world, in the month of May, at a man's house in Epping, New Hampshire, by the name of Lawrence, where I held a meeting I spoke upon the text, Acts 11:26. I ventured for the first time, softly to tell the people that the name, Christian was enough for the followers of Christ without addition of the words, Baptist, Methodist, etc. (1, p. 13)

Smith Met Jones

In 1802 Smith and a group began meeting as "Christians" only. Smith wrote, "When our number was some short of 20 we agreed to consider ourselves a Church of Christ... and agreed to consider ourselves Christians without the addition of any 'unscriptural name.'" (1, p. 14) By 1804 there were 150 members. It was in June of 1803 that Abner Jones, another former Baptist, met Smith for the first time. Until then, Smith thought he was alone in his attempt to restore New Testament Christianity.

In 1808 Smith published a paper called Herald of Gospel Liberty which ran until 1817. He claimed it was the oldest religious journal in the world. It began with 274 subscribers and at the highest point had 1,500. Financial hardship caused him to terminate the paper.

An article published in the Herald of Gospel Liberty by William Guiry, December 18, 1808 seemed to summarize the position of the paper and the man behind it, "After we became a separate people, three points were determined on the following: First, no head over the church but Christ. Second, no confession of faith, articles of religion, rubric, cannons, creeds, etc. but the New Testament. Third, no religious name but Christians. (1, p. 16)

ABNER JONES
(1772-1841)

Abner Jones was a contemporary of Elias Smith. He was born April 28, 1772, and died in 1841. Although the two did not know each other until 1803, both of them were working in the same direction, a restoration of the New Testament church.

Until he was 20 years old, Jones was not religious. In the spring of 1793 he was converted and baptized by Elisha Ransom and became a Baptist. Shortly after, Jones began to study and preach some as a Baptist. In his study he was soon led to dissent with the Calvinism of the Baptists and they, in turn, gave him the cold shoulder. He became determined more than ever to study the Bible and preach just what it taught.

Established "Free" Churches

Jones became a doctor and practiced medicine from 1797-1798. He then closed his practice and went into preaching full-time. It was in 1801 that he organized what he called the first "free church" in the New World. This was in Lyndon, Vermont. It rejected human names. The members insisted solely upon the name "Christian." At this time, Alexander Campbell was a boy of thirteen in Ireland.

It was 1802 when he organized congregations at Hanover and Piermont, New Hampshire. From there on, his life was given to preaching and establishing these "free churches" in New England.

The Christian Connection

The New England seed sowers remained aloof from the Campbell and Stone movements. A segment of the Smith and Jones groups would later merge and be known as the "Christian Connection." Years later most of the "Christian Connection" merged with the Congregationalists. Abner Jones' primary contribution to the restoration cause was that he established the first free Christian Church in New England. O'Kelly, Elias Smith, and Abner Jones were looking away from denominationalism and were seeking a New Testament pattern for Christian unity.

It is regrettable that they were unable to make their journey all the way back to the New Testament for the pattern there. However, we must remember they were traveling an uncharted course. They were thinking their way through. It remained for others to carry on.

CHAPTER 8
BARTON WARREN STONE

While there were many good men who were active in the Restoration Movement in the United States, the two men recognized as the most prominent are Barton W. Stone and Alexander Campbell. Stone was sixteen years older than Campbell and began the work of Restoration before Campbell did.

Barton Stone was born December 24, 1772, in Port Tobacco, Maryland. The first seven years of Stone's life were spent in this region of Maryland. His father died when Barton was three years old, and in 1779 his mother moved the family to Pittslyvania County, Virginia on the border of North Carolina.

The Revolutionary War was raging in 1781 and young Barton could hear the guns of the battle at Guilford Courthouse between the forces of General Green and Lord Cornwalis some 30 miles away. His brothers marched off to fight while Barton and his mother hid their horses to keep them from being taken by the soldiers. Of this period Stone later wrote, "From my earliest recollection I drank deeply into the spirit of liberty, and was so warmed by the soul-inspiring draughts that I could not hear the name of "British" or "Torries" without feeling a rush of blood through the whole system." (1, p. 19)

Stone considered his education complete after four or five years of study even though he had learned little of grammar, geography, or the sciences. He said that he had difficulty in learning because of his fear of the school teacher. The students were punished for the least offense. His teacher was such a tyrant and frightened Barton so much that when he was called on to recite his lessons, he was speechless. After a short while he was turned over to a teacher with a much kinder disposition. From him he learned reading, writing and arithmetic. As an adult he wrote against such abusive teachers.

A RELIGIOUS VOID IN THE NEW WORLD

When the war ended, most of the clergy for the Church of England returned to England. Their salaries had mostly been abolished due to the fact that the church was no longer supported from taxation. There was a religious void for the people. Only ten percent of the people were church members. Representatives from various religious groups came in to the area. From the Baptists young Stone learned about immersion. He was very interested in their experiences. In his autobiography Stone wrote:

> Immersion was so novel in those parts that many from a distance were incited to come to see the ordinance administered. I was a constant attendant and was particularly interested to hear the converts giving in their experience. Of their conviction and great distress for sin, they were very particular in giving an account, and how and when they obtained deliverance from their burdens. Some were delivered by a dream, a vision, or some uncommon appearance of light; some by a voice spoken to them, "Thy sins are forgiven thee," and others by seeing the Savior with their natural eyes. Such experiences were considered good by the church, and the subjects of them were received for baptism and into full fellowship. Great and good was the reformation in society. Knowing nothing better, I considered this to be the work of

God and the way of salvation. (28, p. 117)

The Methodists came and preached. Stone liked their sincerity and piety. Of the Methodists he wrote:

> Their appearance was prepossessing - grave, holy, meek, plain and humble. Their very presence checked levity in all around them - their zeal was fervent and unaffected, and their preaching was often electric on the congregation and fixed their attention. The Episcopalians and Baptists began to oppose them with great warmth. The Baptists represented them as denying the doctrines of grace and of preaching salvation by works. They publicly declared them to be the locusts of the Apocalypse, and warned the people against receiving them. Poor Methodists! They were then but few, reproached, misrepresented; and persecuted as unfit to live on the earth. My mind was much agitated, and was vacillating between these two parties. For some time I had been in the habit of retiring in secret, morning and evening, for prayer, with an earnest desire for religion; but, being ignorant of what I ought to do, I became discouraged, and quit praying, and engaged in the youthful sports of the day. (28, p. 118)

Stone was also turned off by religious controversies and soon lapsed into religious indifference. Stone, having a thirst for knowledge, turned his attention to reading anything he could get his hands on.

ENTERS GULFORD ACADEMY

At age fifteen in 1787, his father's estate was divided up and Stone received his share. With his inheritance he was determined to get an education. Thirty miles southwest of Stone's home was the famous David Caldwell School called Gulford Academy in North Carolina. Stone entered at age eighteen in 1790. The school had fifty students with only one teacher, David Caldwell, who was a Presbyterian preacher. The dominant influence of the school was definitely religious. When James McGready came and preached to the school, thirty of the fifty young men "got religion" and joined the Presbyterian Church.

Stone was so intent on learning that he did not want to get involved with the religious students. He, along with some of the other boys, even made fun of them, to his later regret. McGready came again to hold another revival. Stone had decided to leave the school to go elsewhere and was making preparation to leave, but a storm prevented him. One of the students convinced him to go hear McGready preach. Stone heard McGready preach and was very impressed. As a result became intensely interested in religion. Years later, Stone wrote of his reaction to the McGready meeting:

STONE TRIES TO "GET RELIGION"

The meeting over, I returned to my room. Night coming on, I walked out into an open field, and seriously reasoned with myself on the all-important subject of religion. What shall I do? Shall I embrace religion now or not? I impartially weighed the subject, and counted the cost. If I embrace religion, I must incur the displeasure of my dear relatives, lose the favor and company of my companions - become the object of their scorn and ridicule - relinquish all my plans and schemes for worldly honor, wealth and preferment, and bid a final adieu to all the pleasures in which I had lived, and hoped to live, on earth. Are you willing to make this sacrifice to religion? No, no, was the answer of my heart. Then the certain alternative is, you must be damned. Are you willing to be damned - to be banished from God - from heaven - from all good - and suffer the pains of eternal fire? After due deliberation, I resolved from that hour to seek religion at the sacrifice of every earthly good, and immediately prostrated myself before God in supplication for mercy. (28, p. 121)

However, Stone's dilemma was how to get religion. In his own words, Stone said:

> According to the preaching and the experience of the pious in those days, I anticipated a long and painful struggle before I should be prepared to come to Christ; or, in the language then used, before I should get religion. This anticipation was completely realized by me. For one year I was tossed on the waves of uncertainty - laboring, praying and striving to obtain saving faith - sometimes descending, and almost despairing, of ever getting it. The doctrines then publicly taught were that mankind was so totally depraved that they could not believe, repent nor obey the gospel - that regeneration was an immediate work of the Spirit, whereby faith and repentance were wrought in the heart. (28, p. 122)

Stone heard McGready preach again a year later. McGready convinced him of sin but left him with no hope. McGready's strong Calvinistic views, as well as the wrath of God that he emphasized disturbed Stone greatly. Stone later wrote, "He left me without one encouraging word." He was depressed and dejected for several weeks. He went home to get some comfort from his mother and explained what had happened to him and how miserable he was. She, in the meantime, had joined the Methodist Church. She encouraged Barton to do the same. He did not choose to do so. Stone returned to school, still depressed over his spiritual condition and his inability to "get religion."

SEEKS TO BECOME
A PRESBYTERIAN MINISTER

In 1791 Stone went to Alamance and heard William Hodge of North Carolina preach on the subject "God is Love." Hodge was a New Light Presbyterian and did not follow the standard hard line of McGready. On hearing of the love of God, at last Stone felt there was hope for him.

When Stone got home from the meeting he went into the woods alone to read the scriptures, to pray, and to think. He considered scriptures such as: "God is love," "I am come to seek and to save that which is lost;" "He that cometh unto me I will in no wise cast out;" Stone said, "I loved him -- I adored him -- I praised him aloud in the silent night." He said, "I now saw that a poor sinner was as much authorized to believe in Jesus at first as at last -- that now as the accepted time and day of salvation." (28, p. 11)

Stone joined the Presbyterian Church and determined to be a preacher. In 1793 he applied to the Orange Presbytery for a license to preach. The subject that was assigned to Stone was "The Attributes of God and the Trinity." William Hodge was selected to supervise his preparation. Stone passed his examination successfully but his license would come later. Apparently, the practice was to apply for a license, pass the examination at one session of the presbytery, and wait another six months until the next session when he would receive the license. He would be ordained at a still later time.

During this wait, two things happened that effected him. First, he had grave doubts about the Calvinistic doctrine which he was committing himself to preach; and second, he ran out of money. He decided that perhaps he should give up the idea of preaching. Without waiting for his license, Stone went down into Washington, Georgia and got a job teaching language for one year in an academy operated by Hope Hull, a Methodist minister. In fact, Hull had supported James O'Kelly in his early opposition to Francis Asbury. During this time away, Stone again decided to be a minister. He returned to North Carolina in 1796 and received his license from the Orange Presbytery.

MOVE TO CANE RIDGE

After getting his license, Stone went into eastern North Carolina to do mission work in a hard area. He became discouraged and moved to Wythville, Virginia and preached for several months at a Presbyterian meeting-house called "Grines Meeting House." He then moved on to Tennessee. Stone passed through Nashville, Tennessee and noted that it was "a poor little village hardly worth notice."

A friend told Stone about Kentucky, so he found his way eventually to Cane Ridge. Cane Ridge is located about thirty miles north of present day Lexington, Kentucky. This area was explored by Daniel Boone and given its name because of the thick stand of cane in that area.

Robert Finley, a Presbyterian preacher, led a group of pioneer settlers from Pennsylvania and North Carolina to the canebrakes of Bourbon and Nicholas counties. He organized Presbyterian churches at Cane Ridge and Concord. Meeting- houses were erected at both places. A blue ash log building was constructed at Cane Ridge in 1791. The building at Cane Ridge is still standing, but the one at Concord was destroyed a few years ago by a windstorm. Finley also established a log cabin seminary about 1/4 mile from the Cane Ridge meeting house. Here Finley trained ten or twelve Presbyterian preachers. Three of these men, Richard McNemar, John Dunlavy, and John Thompson were signers of the "Last Will and Testament of the Springfield Presbytery." Robert Trimble, later an associate justice of the United States Supreme Court was also a student there. Finley began serving the Cane Ridge and Concord congregations in 1793. On October 6, 1796 he was deposed as the "pastor" because of "habitual inebriety." Another account of the dismissal of Finley lists the cause as "insubordination," rather than his drinking. (68, p. 17) Finley, in his teaching, did not follow the straight Presbyterian line and probably had a great deal of influence on those who went through his seminary.

ORDAINED

The dismissal of Finley by the presbytery had left a vacancy in both pulpits when Barton W. Stone, twenty-four years of age, appeared on the scene in the late fall of 1796. Stone was apparently selected at the "supply pastor" to the congregation at Cane Ridge as well as the one ten miles away at Concord. He was not ordained at this time, but worked with these congregations on the basis of the license granted to him by the North Carolina Orange Presbytery. It may well be that these two congregations made their own arrangements directly with Stone rather than through the Presbytery. Between the two places Stone preached regularly. He was quite successful in his work, adding thirty new members at Cane Ridge and fifty new members at Concord. (69, p. 17) Stone left the area for a while and when he came back, these two congregations issued a call through the Transylvania Presbytery for their preacher to locate with them and he became a candidate for ordination. In preparation for ordination, Stone re-examined the "Westminster Confession of Faith."

> At this time Stone was still having serious doubts about the Trinity, Reprobation, Predestination, and other matters in the Westminster Confession of Faith. Prior to going before the Presbytery, he took aside Dr. James Blyth and Robert Marshall and told them of his difficulties. They asked him how far was he willing to receive the Confession. Stone told them, "As far as I see it consistent with the Word of God." (6, p. 49)

The Transylvania Presbytery met in 1798 at Cane Ridge to consider Stone's ordination. Stone was asked, "Do you receive and adopt the Confession of Faith as containing the system of doctrine as taught in the Bible?" He replied for all to hear, "I do, as far as I see it consistent with the Word of God." Surprisingly, the Presbytery accepted his qualified adoption of the Confession of Faith. It appears that Stone's respect for the Bible was increasing while at the same time his respect for human creeds was decreasing. Stone was definitely looking in the right direction.

Stone was out of sympathy with all five points of Calvinism: Inherited Sin, Total Depravity, Irresistible Grace, Predestination, Unconditional Election, and the final Perseverance of the Saints. He believed that God did love the whole world, and that the reason he did not save all was due to unbelief. Saving faith is produced by testimony revealed on the pages of Holy Writ. When we read the Bible, believe and obey it, we become children of God. This was his firm belief and conviction. Stone delivered his soul with reference to Calvinism in these words: "Let me here speak when I shall be lying under the clods of the grave. Calvinism is among the heaviest clogs on Christianity in the world. It is a dark mountain between Heaven and earth, and is amongst the most discouraging hindrances to sinners in seeking the Kingdom of God and engenders bondage of gloominess to the Saints. Its influence is felt throughout the Christian world, even where it is least suspected. Its first link is total depravity..." (6, p. 49)

A TIME OF RELIGIOUS REVIVAL

Kentucky at this turn of the century was on the verge of a great religious revival. Stone made a special trip to Logan County, Kentucky in 1801 to hear James McGready who was preaching in a revival meeting. While he was impressed with McGready as a speaker, he had grave concerns about his message. McGready preached the Presbyterian doctrine of Calvinism that man was totally depraved and had no ability to believe except through miraculous regeneration. If these doctrines were true, how could this be reconciled with the persuading of men to believe and repent? Why preach to men to believe if they were totally depraved and could not? For the next few years this dilemma was to cause Stone great anxiety. As Dabney Philips put it, Calvin's god was Stone's devil. It seems that it would have been easier for Stone if he had no religious training at all than to have to unlearn that which he was taught already.

MARRIES ELIZABETH CAMPBELL

Stone made plans to have a religious revival at Cane Ridge similar to the one McGready conducted in Logan County. However, before the great meeting, there was something else that Stone needed to do. He traveled two hundred miles to Greenville, Kentucky and on July 2, 1801, married Elizabeth Campbell. The new couple headed back to Cane Ridge as soon as the wedding was over. They built a cabin a few miles east of the Cane Ridge meeting house on the one hundred and five acres he had purchased two years earlier. Sadly, Eliza Campbell Stone died in 1810 after nine years of marriage. She left Stone with a son and four daughters. The following year in 1811, Stone married Celia Bowen. By Celia he fathered fourteen more children, a total of nineteen.

THE GREAT CANE RIDGE REVIVAL

The revival began on the third Lord's Day in August, 1801. The roads around Cane Ridge were literally crowded with wagons, carriages, horsemen, and footmen, moving to the camp- ground. Estimates as to the number in attendance go as high as twenty to thirty thousand. Four or five preachers would be speaking at the same time in different parts of the encampment. Methodists, Baptists and Presbyterians cooperated in the preaching. During the meeting emotions ran high, resulting in a "display of acrobatic conversions." There were five general types of "bodily agitations" that were prevalent: (1) The falling exercise. This was the most common. The subject would cry out in a piercing scream, then fall flat on the ground and lying for several minutes, as though dead; (2) The jerks. In this exercise, various parts of the body would jerk violently to one side and then to the other; (3) The dancing exercise. This would begin with the jerks and then pass on to dancing. Usually, they would dance until they fell exhausted to the ground; (4) The barking exercise. This was really the jerks, but when a person's body jerked suddenly and violently, it caused a big grunt which appeared to be barking to the observer; (5) The laughter and singing exercises were just what the terms signify. This emotional upsurge continued for a week. It would have continued longer but the food gave out and the meeting was forced to close in spite of the fact that there had been "three thousand conversions." (6, p. 50)

OPPOSITION FROM THE PRESBYTERIANS

In the great Cane Ridge revival, Stone and others preached free salvation, based on faith and repentance. Also, preachers from different churches worked together in such a way that Stone was impressed with the value and need for unity. Although desirable, the goal was never reached. When Stone stressed the fact that sinners had the power to turn to Christ, a number of strong Calvinistic preachers opposed him. Among those who stood by him were Richard McNemar, John Thompson, and John Dunlavy, who were preaching for churches in Ohio, Robert Marshall who was preaching for a church in Kentucky, and David Purviance who was a ruling elder in the Cane Ridge Church. Stone's doctrine of the universality of the gospel and faith as a condition of salvation did not set well with the Presbyterians. The orthodox Presbyterians soon branded Stone a heretic.

In the Cane Ridge meeting these men preached to affirm the

love of God for the whole world, confirmed the mission of the Son of God to save the lost and proposed that man must believe, repent, and obey the gospel to be saved from his sins. Their preaching was in clear contrast with the doctrine of the Presbyterian churches and the Westminster Confession of Faith in which their orthodoxy was defined. The Washington Presbytery met and censored those Presbyterian ministers who took part in the Cane Ridge meetings. Richard McNemar, who was preaching for the Turtle Creek Presbyterian Church in Brown County, Ohio was the first to be called before the Washington Presbytery to give an account for the anti-Calvinist things that were taught at Cane Ridge. He was charged with heresy and his case was referred to the Kentucky Synod that met at the First Presbyterian Church in Lexington, Kentucky in September of 1803. (69, p. 19) In the proceedings the Synod sustained the action of the Washington Presbytery in censoring him. McNemar was put through such an ordeal that Stone and the others met to formulate a plan because they knew that they would be next. On Saturday, September 10, 1803, they submitted their objections to the Synod because of the treatment of McNemar and declared themselves withdrawn from it. The report added that the "Confession of Faith was an impediment to revival." In Stone's autobiography he commented on his and his colleagues' views:

> The distinguished doctrine preached by us, that God loved the world --the whole world, and sent his son to save them, on condition that they believed in him --that the gospel was the means of salvation --but that this means would never be effectual to this end, until believed and obeyed by us --that God required us to believe in his son and had given us sufficient evidence in his word to produce faith in us, if attended by us --that sinners were capable of understanding and believing this testimony, and of acting upon it by coming to the Savior and obeying him and from him obtaining salvation and the Holy Spirit. (25, p. 45)

CALVINISM

The Calvinism of the day declared that a man was depraved and could do nothing to be saved. He had to wait and if God saw fit to call him, he would do so, but if God did not see fit, the man was lost to the glory of God. The following is a summary of the five points of Calvinism as written by W. J. Seaton, minister of the Inverness Reformed Baptist Church:

1. T - Total Depravity (i.e., total inability) - "Man is totally unable to save himself on account of the fall in the Garden of Eden being a total fall."
2. U - Unconditional Election - "If unable to save himself, then God must save. If God must save, than God must be free to save whom he will."
3. L - Limited Atonement (i.e., particular redemption) - "If God has decreed to save whom he will then it is for that Christ made atonement on the cross."
4. I - Irresistible Calling - "If Christ died for them, then the Holy Spirit will effectually call them into salvation."
5. P - Perseverance of the Saints - "If salvation then from the beginning has been of God, the end will also be of God and the saints will persevere to external joy."

McClintock and Spnge's Cyclopedia of Biblical, Theological and Ecclesiastical Literature, Volume II, pages 39-46 give the following definition of Calvinism:

OF INHERENT DEPRAVITY:
All men are conceived in sin, and born the children of wrath, indisposed to all saving good, propense to evil, dead in sin, and the slaves of sin; and without the regenerating grace of the Holy Spirit, they neither are

willing nor able to return to God.

OF ELECTION AND IRRESISTIBLE GRACE:
Election is the immutable purpose of God, by which, before the foundations of the world were laid, he chose, out of the whole human race, fallen by their own fault from their primeval integrity into sin and destruction, according to the most free good pleasure of his own will, and of mere grace, a certain number of men, neither better nor worthier than others, but lying in the same misery with the rest, to salvation in Christ. Moreover ... some are non-elect, or passed by, in the eternal election of God, whom truly God, from most free, just, irreprehensible, and immutable good pleasure decreed to leave in the common misery... to condemn and eternally punish them, to the manifestation of his own justice.

OF PERSEVERANCE:
God ... does not wholly take away his Holy Spirit from his own, even in lamentable falls, nor does he permit them to glide down that they should fall from the grace of adoption and the state of justification; or commit the 'sin unto death,' or against the Holy Spirit; that, being deserted by him, they should cast themselves headlong into eternal destruction. So that not by their own merits or strength, but by the gratuitous mercy of God, they obtain it, that they neither fatally fall from faith and grace, nor finally continue in their falls and perish. (51, p. 19)

In contrast to Calvinism, Stone and his group said that God loved man and wanted all men to be saved. They believed the gospel was God's power to save because it contained sufficient evidence to produce faith in the heart of the honest inquirer. If the sinner would believe and obey this gospel, he could be saved. This, in 1804, was as far as Stone appears to have gone in his thinking, but it was far enough to make the Calvinistic Presbyterians consider him a heretic.

THE SPRINGFIELD PRESBYTERY

When Stone and the others withdrew from the Presbyterian Synod of Kentucky they set up their own Presbytery called the Springfield Presbytery. They also sent out letters to the congregations explaining why they had withdrawn from the Synod. They wrote an explanation for their actions in a document called "An Apology for Renouncing the Jurisdiction of the Synod of Kentucky." Marshall, Stone and Thompson each wrote a section that expressed their abandonment of all authoritative creeds but the Bible.

For six years Stone had preached as a Presbyterian for the Cane Ridge and Concord congregations in Kentucky. He called them together and informed them that he could not conscientiously preach Presbyterianism any longer. In their presence he tore up their financial obligation to him. Without salary and having freed his slaves, Stone worked on his farm to support his family but continued to preach to large and interested audiences. Sometimes he worked on his farm at night so that he could continue his preaching. He was popular among the people and would remain with the Cane Ridge congregation until 1811.

The Springfield Presbytery had a short life. It lasted only nine months, but in that short time fifteen congregations were set up, seven in Ohio and eight in Kentucky. In this short time Stone and the others realized that the Springfield Presbytery was not right, that it "encouraged a party spirit" and they made plans to dissolve it. On June 28, 1804, they published the "Last Will and Testament of the Springfield Presbytery." It contained only 800 words but it is recognized as one of the most unique documents in religious literature. Some consider June 28, 1804, as the date marking the beginning of the Stone movement in the Restoration. Notice that it was written eight years before the Campbells were baptized. Here is the "Last Will and Testament of the Springfield Presbytery" in its entirety:

THE LAST WILL AND TESTAMENT OF THE SPRINGFIELD PRESBYTERY

The Presbytery of Springfield, sitting at Cane Ridge, in the county of Bourbon, being through a gracious Providence, in more than ordinary bodily health, growing in strength and size daily; and in perfect soundness and composure of mind; and knowing that it is appointed for all delegated bodies once to die; and considering that the life of every such body is very uncertain, do make and ordain this our Last Will and Testament, in manner and form following, viz.:

Imprimis. We will, that this body die, be dissolved, and sink into union with the Body of Christ at large; for there is but one Body, and one Spirit, even as we are called in one hope of our calling.

Item. We will, that our name of distinction, with its Reverend title, be forgotten, that there be but one Lord over God's heritage, and his name One.

Item. We will, that our power of making laws for the government of the church, and executing them by delegated authority, forever cease; that the people may have free course to the Bible, and adopt the law of the Spirit of life in Christ Jesus.

Item. We will, that candidates for the Gospel ministry henceforth study the Holy Scriptures with fervent prayer, and obtain license from God to preach the simple Gospel, with the Holy Ghost sent down from heaven, without any mixture of philosophy, vain deceit, traditions of men, or the rudiments of the world. And let none henceforth take this honor to himself, but he that is called of God, as was Aaron.

Item. We will, that the church of Christ resume her native right of internal government - try her candidates for the ministry, as to their soundness in the faith, acquaintance with experimental religion, gravity and aptness to teach; and admit no other proof of their authority but Christ speaking in them. We will, that the church of Christ look to the Lord of the harvest to send for laborers into his harvest; and that she resume her primitive right of trying those who say they are apostles and are not.

Item. We will, that each particular church, as a body, actuated by the same spirit, choose her own preacher and support him by a free will offering, without a written call, or subscription - admit members - remove offenses; and never henceforth delegate her right of government to any man or set of men whatever.

Item. We will, that the people henceforth take the Bible as the only sure guide to heaven; and as many as are offended with other books which stand in competition with it, may cast them into the fire if they choose; for it is better to enter into life having one book, than having many to be cast into hell.

Item. We will, that preachers and people, cultivate a spirit of mutual forbearance; pray more and dispute less; and while they behold the signs of the times, look up, and confidently expect that redemption draweth nigh.

Item. We will, that our weak brethren, who may have been wishing to make the Presbytery of Springfield their king, and wot not what is now become of it, betake themselves to the Rock of Ages, and follow Jesus for the future.

Item. We will, that the Synod of Kentucky examine every member, who may be suspected of having departed from the Confession of Faith, and suspend every such suspected heretic immediately; in order that the oppressed may go free, and taste the sweets of gospel liberty.

Item. We will, that Ja___ ____, the author of two letters lately published in Lexington, be encouraged in his zeal to destroy partyism. We will, moreover, that our past conduct be examined into by all who may have correct information; but let foreigners beware of speaking evil of things which they know not.

Item. Finally, we will, that all our sister bodies read their Bibles carefully, that they may see their fate there determined, and prepare for death before it is too late.

Springfield Presbytery L.S.

June 28th, 1804.
Robert Marshall
John Dunlavy
Richard McNemar -Witnesses
B. W. Stone
John Thompson
David Purviance

HIGHLIGHTS OF THE "WILL"

The "Last Will and Testament" was a plea for men to hold to the Bible alone as the standard of faith and practice. They determined to be known only as Christians. Rice Haggard had urged the adoption of this name ten years earlier to the O'Kelly movement and was present at this meeting to suggest it again. Furthermore, they determined that the title "Reverend" should be forgotten. Preaching was to be done without the philosophy and traditions of men. Congregational autonomy was to be the rule.

It was necessary to let the Springfield Presbytery die because they realized that while they were advocating a return to the simple New Testament church, they were inconsistent by having the

Presbytery. The New Testament had no command or example for such confederations as modern church sessions, presbyteries, synods, or general assemblies. As long as they continued in them they were missing the mark as they attempted to duplicate the original.

While Stone and his group were looking to restore New Testament Christianity, the denominations were not happy with them. Evil reports were circulated about them. The term "New Lights" was hurled at them. This term of derision was used about any off-brand group in religion, but the name stuck and for years Stone's group was called the "New Light" Christian Church by some.

BAPTISM EXAMINED IN LIGHT OF SCRIPTURES

Independent Bible study caused the Stone group to abandon the practice of infant baptism and sprinkling. It is interesting to hear Stone as he relates his early views on baptism and the progression of his thinking as he moved from sprinkling and infant baptism to believers' baptism by immersion, and finally that baptism was ordained for the remission of sins.

Having learned the truth about baptism, Stone and his associate preachers first baptized each other by immersion and then baptized their congregations. All of this was five years before Thomas Campbell issued the "Declaration and Address." Earl West said that Stone's investigation of the subject of baptism continued until eventually Stone convinced himself that immersion was for the remission of sins and should be administered only to the penitent believer. He stated later that his thinking on baptism was greatly clarified by Alexander Campbell. Insight into Stone's position on baptism is gained from Stone's autobiography:

> About this time the subject of Baptism began to arrest the attention of the churches. On this I will state what took place while I was a Presbyterian preacher. Robert Marshall, one of our company, had then become convinced of the truth of the Baptists' views on this subject, and ceased from the practice of

pedobaptism; and it was believed he was on the eve of uniting with the Baptists. Alarmed lest he should join them, I wrote him a lengthy letter on the subject, laboring to convince him of his error. In reply, he wrote me another, in which he so forcibly argued in favor of believers' immersion, and against pedobaptism, that my mind was brought so completely to doubt the latter, that I ceased the practice entirely. About this time the great excitement commenced, and the subject of baptism was for awhile, strangely, almost forgotten. But after a few years it revived, and many became dissatisfied with their infant sprinkling, among whom I was one.

    The brethren, elders, and deacons came together on this subject; for we had agreed previously with one another to act in concert, and not to adventure on any thing new without advice from one another. At this meeting we took up the matter in a brotherly spirit, and concluded that every brother and sister should act freely, and according to their conviction of right -- and that we should cultivate the long-neglected grace of forbearance towards each other -- they who should be immersed, should not despise those who were not, and vice versa. Now the question arose, who will baptize us? The Baptists would not, except we united with them; and there were no elders among us who had been immersed. It was finally concluded among us, that if we were authorized to preach, we were also authorized to baptize. The work then commenced, the preachers baptized one another, and crowds came, and were also baptized. My congregations very generally submitted to it, and it soon obtained generally, and yet the pulpit was silent on the subject. In Brother Marshall's congregation there were many who wished baptism. As Brother Marshall had not faith in the ordinance,

I was called upon to administer. This displeased him and a few others.

The subject of baptism now engaged the attention of the people very generally, and some, with myself, began to conclude that it was ordained for the remission of sins, and ought to be administered in the name of Jesus to all believing penitents. I remember about this time we had a great meeting at Concord. Mourners were invited every day to collect before the stand, in order for prayers, (this being the custom of the times.) The brethren were praying daily for the same people, and none seemed to be comforted. I was considering in my mind, what could be the cause. The words of Peter, at Pentecost, rolled through my mind. "Repent and be baptized for the remission of sins, and you shall receive the gift of the Holy Ghost." I thought, were Peter here, he would thus address these mourners. I quickly arose, and addressed them in the same language, and urged them to comply. Into the spirit of the doctrine I was never fully led, until it was revived by Brother Alexander Campbell, some years after. (25, pp. 60-61)

THE SHAKERS INVADE THE RESTORATION

For a time things went very well and churches sprang up over a wide territory but then a fad known as "Shakerism," a semi-religious, socialistic movement from New York, was introduced in Kentucky by three missionaries named Bates, Mitchem, and Young. They made havoc of the faith of some of the Restoration converts and were successful in getting Richard McNemar and John Dunlavy to defect to their strange beliefs. Stone and the others were eventually able to stabilize the onslaught of false teaching but not without great loss.

The Shakers insisted that Anna Lee, their founder, was the

Christ and had power to save. She claimed new revelations superior to the Bible. The Shakers maintained that Christ had already come the second time. They taught that marriage was forbidden, and those already married should dissolve their marriage. They also taught that Shakers would never die. They taught that the resurrection and judgment were then underway. Stone spoke of the coming of the Shakers in his autobiography:

> The churches and preachers grew and were multiplied; we began to be puffed up at our prosperity. A law of Synod, or Presbytery, forbade their people to associate with us in our worship, on pain of censure, or exclusion from their communion. This influenced many of them to join us. But this pride of ours was soon humbled by a very extraordinary incident. "Three missionary Shakers from the East came amongst us -- Bates, Mitchem, and Young. They were eminently qualified for their mission. Their appearance was prepossessing -- their dress was plain and neat -- they were grave and unassuming at first in their manners - very intelligent and ready in the Scriptures, and of great boldness in their faith.
>
> They informed us that they had heard of us in the East, and greatly rejoiced in the work of God amongst us -- that as far as we had gone we were right; but we had not gone far enough into the work -- that they were sent by their brethren to teach the way of God more perfectly, by obedience to which we should be led into perfect holiness. They seemed to understand all the springs and avenues of the human heart. They delivered their testimony, and labored to confirm it by the Scriptures -- promised the greatest blessings to the obedient, but certain damnation to the disobedient. They urged the people to confess their sins to them, especially the sin of matrimony, and to forsake them all immediately -- husbands must

forsake their wives, and wives their husbands. This was the burden of their testimony. They said they could perform miracles, and related many as done among them. But we never could persuade them to try to work miracles among us.

Many such things they preached, the consequence of which was similar to that of Simon Magus. Many said they were the great power of God. Many confessed their sins to them, and forsook the marriage state; among whom were three of our preachers, Matthew Houston, Richard McNemar, and John Dunlavy. Several more of our preachers, and pupils, alarmed, fled from us, and joined the different sects around us. The sects triumphed at our distress, and watched for our fall, as Jonah watched the fall of Nineveh under the shadow of his gourd. But a worm at the root of Jonah's gourd killed it, and deprived him of its shade, and brought on him great distress. So the worm of Shakerism was busy at the root of all the sects, and brought on them great distress; for multitudes of them, both preachers and common people, also joined the Shakers. Our reproach was rolled away.

Never did I exert myself more than at this time, to save the people from this vortex of ruin. I yielded to no discouragement, but labored night and day, far and near, among the churches where the Shakers went. By this means their influence was happily checked in many places. I labored so hard and constantly that a profuse spitting of blood ensued. Our broken ranks were once more rallied under the standard of heaven, and were soon led on once more to victory. In answer to constant prayer, the Lord visited us and comforted us after this severe trial. The cause again revived, and former scenes were renewed.

The Shakers now became our bitter enemies, and united with the sects in their opposition to us. They denied the literal resurrection of the body from the grave: they said the resurrection of the body meant the resurrection of Christ's body, meaning the church. They, the elders, had constant communication and conversation with angels and all the departed saints. They looked for no other or better heaven than that on earth. Their worship, if worthy of the name, consisted in voluntary dancing together. They lived together, and had all things common, entirely under the direction and control of the elders. They flourished greatly for some years, and built several superb villages; but afterwards began to dwindle till they became nearly extinct. John Dunlavy, who had left us, and joined them, was a man of a penetrating mind, wrote and published much for them, and was one of their elders in high repute by them. He died in Indiana, raving in desperation for his folly in forsaking the truth for an old woman's fables. Richard McNemar was, before his death, excluded by the Shakers from their society, in a miserable penniless condition, as I was informed by good authority. The Shakers had a revelation given them to remove him from their village, and take him to Lebanon, in Ohio, and to set him down in the streets, and to leave him there in his old age, without friends or money. Soon after he died. Matthew Houston is yet alive, and continues among them.

Their doctrine was, that the Christ appeared first in a male, and through life was preparing the way of salvation, which he could not accomplish till his second appearance in a woman, Anne Lee, who was now the Christ, and had full power to save. (25, pp. 64-65)

John Thompson and Robert Marshall had earlier returned to Presbyterianism. Now Richard McNemar and John Dunlavy had fallen to Shakerism. Stone felt very much alone. Stone was a mild man who did not like controversy, but he could rise to the occasion and he did not let all his woes discourage him from carrying on in preaching the gospel and establishing churches of Christ.

SIMILARITIES OF THE STONE AND CAMPBELL VIEWS

It was inevitable that Stone and Campbell would eventually meet for they were without question the two foremost religious thinkers of their times. They first met in 1824 at Georgetown, Kentucky. Campbell was thirty-six. Stone was fifty-two. At first it seemed the differences between them were too great, but after they had talked at length, they found these could be reconciled. Stone's comments about Campbell show us his generosity and humility: "I will not say there are no faults in Brother Campbell, but that there are fewer, perhaps in him, than any man I know on earth; and over these few my love would throw a vale, and hide them from view forever. I am constrained and willingly constrained to acknowledge him the greatest promoter of this reformation of any man living. The Lord reward him." (1, p. 32) Stone wrote of the similarity of their views:

> The reformed Baptists have received the doctrine taught by us many years ago. For nearly thirty years we have taught that sectarianism was anti-Christian, and that all Christians should be united in one body of Christ -- the same they teach. We then and ever since, have taught that authoritative creeds and confessions were the strong props of sectarianism, and should be given to the moles and bats -- they teach the same. We have from that time preached the gospel to every creature to whom we had access, and urged them to believe and obey it --

that its own evidence was sufficient to produce faith in all that heard it, that the unrenewed sinner must, and could, believe it unto justification and salvation -- and through the Holy Spirit of promise, and every other promise of the New Covenant was given. They proclaim the same doctrine. Many years ago some of us preached baptism as a means, in connection with faith and repentance, for the remission of sins and the gift of the Holy Spirit -- they preach the same and extend it farther than we have done. We rejected all names but Christian -- they acknowledge it most proper, but seem to prefer another. (1, p. 32)

DIFFERENCES

Garrison and Degroot point out that, although the similarities were great, there were some differences in the early years which were significant. Until 1830 Stone's position on baptism was not nearly as firm as was Campbell's. Afterwards, Stone's position was firmed up. Stone had previously confessed that he was inconsistent in his position that baptism was for the remission of sins, but was not necessary for church membership. Campbell stood firmly that baptism was essential for the forgiveness of sins and membership in the church. (3, pp. 209-210)

They also differed in methods of winning converts. Stone's group did not have an effective presentation of the gospel with clarity for what was required of the sinner. Even after years of Restoration preaching, the mourner's bench was still used. In the "Christian Messenger" it mentioned the "crowds of mourners came forward weeping and praying for mercy." On the other hand, Campbell's group led by Walter Scott presented clearly the plan of salvation: believe the evidence about Christ, repent of sins, be baptized. Upon the fulfillment of this, God would grant remission of sins and grant the blessings that follow it. There was no place for "agonies of uncertainty" as to whether one was accepted by God. All of this clarity and certainty seems to have come as a surprise to Stone's group of "Christians."

"Campbell and Stone differed on the Godhead, atonement, and the nature of Christ, but these issues presented no serious problem because they did not flow down to the rank and file. They differed on the name, Stone preferring "Christian" and Campbell expressing a preference for "Disciple." (68, p. 67)

John Rogers, early associate of Barton W. Stone, pointed out three major differences that the "Christians" had with Campbell. These were the largest obstacles that the Stone group had to overcome in effecting the union.

1. They feared that Campbell was not sound on the subject of spiritual influence. That he did not believe in heart-religion. That religion with him was more intellectual than spiritual.
2. They had difficulties on the question of baptism for remission of sins -- they thought in believing in baptism for remission, they denied their own Christian experience and doomed all the pious pedo-baptists to ruin.
3. They could not see the fitness, and propriety of taking the Lord's Supper every Lord's day. They argued it would become common, and lose its sacredness and efficacy." (68, p. 67)

Campbell taught that the Holy Spirit operated on the hearts of sinners only through preaching or reading of the Word. The "Christians" did not limit the work of the Spirit on the sinner to Word.

Dean Mills states that there were difficulties over baptism for the remission of sins on the part of some of the "Christians" which were never solved. Some in Ohio and Indiana rejected the concept and ultimately opposed the union. Barton Stone appears to have preached the doctrine of baptism for the remission of sins before Campbell did. He did this in a meeting in Millersburg, Kentucky in

1821. His introduction of this doctrine "dampened" the meeting, according to John Rogers. Stone attempted to preach baptism for the remission of sins elsewhere but he met resistance and seems to have put the doctrine in the background for a few years. (68, p. 68)

Stone and Campbell seem to have disagreed on the matter of fellowshipping those who were not immersed for the remission of sins. Stone said that he was as fully convinced on the issue as was Campbell, but he wanted to approach this issue with more tolerance. Stone remained cordial to the unimmersed, but he admitted that he would not consider them "Christians in the full sense of the term." (68, p. 69)

Regarding frequency of the Lord's Supper, Stone agreed with Campbell that "whenever the church shall be restored to her former glory, she will again receive the Lord's Supper on every first day of the week." Several of the "Christian" ministers did not agree with Stone. (68, p. 69)

While foot washing was not practiced by those associated with Campbell, there were some advocates of foot washing among the "Christians." Stone believed this to be a family matter and not for the church assembly. Stone said that when Jesus washed the feet of the disciples it was a family affair, the family of Jesus. He believed it to be in the same area as lodging strangers. However, some among the Christians did not agree with Stone and practiced foot washing as a church ordinance. (68, p. 70)

THE CHRISTIAN MESSENGER

Through the years Barton Stone kept busy in his preaching and his influence was great. He established congregations in Kentucky, Southern Ohio, Tennessee, and Northern Alabama. By 1811 one source said there were 13,000 in the movement that was associated with Stone. 17, p. 103 T. M. Allen, a convert and contemporary of Stone established at least seventeen congregations in Missouri and Kentucky during his lifetime. (9, pp. 224-225)

Between 1819 and 1828 Stone continued preaching, also receiving additional income from teaching school. In 1826 he began publishing a monthly periodical called the "Christian Messenger." Its motto was "Let the unity of Christians be our polar star." John T. Johnson became his associate editor in January of 1832, and continued until it closed at the end of 1834 when Stone moved to Illinois. The very first issue of the "Christian Messenger" dated December 25, 1826, began with these words:

> To illustrate lengthily the importance of the object contemplated in this work would be unnecessary. Of this the public will judge, to whom the work is now presented. It is universally acknowledged, by the various sects of Christians, that the religion of Heaven, for centuries past, has fallen far below the excellency and glory of primitive Christianity. The man, who honestly investigates the cause of this declension, and points the proper way of reformation, must certainly be engaged in a work, pleasing to God, and profitable to man. This is our design; and to accomplish this desirable and, shall our best exertions be enlisted and engaged. (31, p. 1)

For the fourteen years that the "Christian Messenger" was published, B. W. Stone and other editors were always listed as "Elders of the Church of Christ." In the absence of any central organization among the congregations, the "Christian Messenger" became the chief instrument of whatever unity they had. As editor, Stone was the outstanding elder statesmen. His critics wanted to tag him as "head of the church," but he would have none of that, for he was one member of many. He made no such claim for himself. (3, pp. 122-123)

"CHRISTIANS" AND "REFORMERS" UNITE

Up to this time, Stone's group had insisted upon the name "Christian" to the exclusion of all others. Those associated with Alexander Campbell took the name "Reformers" or "Reformed

Baptists" or "Disciples." The two groups would exist side by side in various towns, especially in Kentucky. The similarities between the two groups far outweighed their differences, and after 1830 leaders of both groups began to consider the possibility of unity.

Stone wrote in 1831 "The question is going the round of society, and is often proposed to us, 'Why are you and the Reformed Baptists one people?' Or, 'Why are you not united?' We have uniformly answered, 'In spirit we are united.'" Campbell replied, "I think the question of union and cooperation is one which deserves the attention of all them who believe the ancient gospel and desire to see the ancient order of things restored." (41, p. 33) But since both movements stressed the autonomy of each local church, the desired unity would have to come gradually. The first such merger that we have on record took place between the "Christians" and "Reformers" in Millersburg, Kentucky, near Cane Ridge. They began by meeting together occasionally, and then realizing that there were few differences between them in faith and practice, they united in April 24, 1831. But the union of the two groups was soon to become much larger in scope.

John T. Johnson (1788-1856), associated with the Campbell movement, probably did more to bring about a merger between the "Christians" and the "Reformers" than any other single individual. Johnson was a lawyer who had served two terms in the United States Congress. His brother, Richard M. Johnson, became vice-president under Martin Van Buren. John T. Johnson was converted to the principles of the restoration movement and left politics to plead for the restoration of the ancient gospel. Alexander Campbell commended his decision, "Sir, in descending from the forum and legislative hall to proclaim the crucified Savior, you have ascended far above all earthly crowns." (41, p. 33).

Johnson and Barton W. Stone both lived in Georgetown, Kentucky, and were good friends. In November of 1831 Stone preached in a meeting at Johnson's Great Crossings church. Realizing the similarities of their positions, the two discussed the possibilities of unity. Two other leaders, Raccoon John Smith and John Rogers also joined the discussions. The four men agreed to call a general meeting and see if the members of the two fellowships desired unity. These men arranged a joint meeting of the two groups that took place December 23-26, 1831 at Great Crossings near Georgetown, Kentucky. At this four-day session they were not able to take care of everything, and the meeting was so encouraging that the two groups decided to have another four day meeting at the Hill Street church building in Lexington, Kentucky. The culmination of the meeting was on New Year's day, January 1, 1832. The meeting house was crowded early. Smith was to speak for the "Reformers," and Stone for the "Christians."

JOHN SMITH
SPEAKS FOR THE "REFORMERS"

Raccoon John Smith, the first to speak, delivered one of the best speeches of his life. He appealed for the unity of the two groups. Smith demonstrated his ability as a public speaker by the clever use of the term "New Lights" in the dramatic conclusion of his speech. "New Lights" was a term used by some to describe the Christians associated with Stone. Smith's plea was to leave behind the names that distinguished the Campbell group from the Stone group and all be united on the basis of the Bible as the only light that was needed. The following is Smith's complete speech:

> God has but one people on the earth. He has given to them but one Book, and therein exhorts and commands them to be one family, a union such as we plead for - a union of God's people on that one Book - must then be practical.
> Every Christian desires to stand complete in the whole will of God. The prayer of the Savior and the whole tenor of his teaching, clearly show that it is God's will that his children should be united. To the Christian, then, such a union must be desirable.
> But an amalgamation of sects is not such a union as Christ prayed for, and God enjoins. To agree

to be one upon any system of human inventions would be contrary to his will, and could never be a blessing to the Church or the world; therefore the only union practicable or desirable must be based on the Word of God, as the only rule of faith and practice.

There are certain abstruse or speculative matters - such as the mode of the Divine Existence, and the Ground and Nature of the Atonement - that have, for centuries, been themes of discussion among Christians. These questions are as far from being settled now as they were in the beginning of the controversy. By a needless and intemperate discussion of them much feeling has been provoked, and divisions have been produced.

For several years past, I have tried to speak on such subjects only in language of inspiration; for it can offend no one to say about those things just what the Lord, himself, has said. In this scriptural style of speech all Christians should be agreed. I will not linger to build a theory on such texts, and thus encourage a speculative and wrangling spirit among my brethren. I will present these subjects only in the words which the Lord has given to me. I know he will not be displeased if we say just what he has said. Whatever opinions about these and similar subjects I may have reached, in the course of my investigations, if I never distract the church of God with them, or seek to impose them on my brethren, they will never do the world any harm. While there is but one faith, there may be ten thousand opinions; and hence, if Christians are ever to be one, they must be one in faith, and not in opinion. While for the sake of peace and Christian union, I have long since waived the public maintenance of any speculation I may hold, yet not one Gospel fact, commandment, or promise, will I surrender for the world!

> Let us, then, my brethren, be no longer Campbellites, or Stoneites, New Lights, or Old Lights, or any other kind of lights, but let us all come to the Bible and to the Bible alone, as the only Book in the world that can give us all the light we need. (5, pp. 344-345)

STONE SPEAKS FOR THE "CHRISTIANS"

The speech of John Smith captured the hearts of the people who heard it. B. W. Stone made his way to the podium, and with his heart filled with love. He began by saying: "I will not attempt to introduce any new topic, but say a few things on the subject presented by my beloved brother." After speaking for some time with a tone of tenderness, he then said:

> Controversies of the Church sufficiently prove that Christians never can be one in their speculations upon those mysterious and sublime subjects, which, while they interest the Christian philosopher, can not edify the Church. After we had given up all creeds and taken the Bible, and the Bible alone, as our rule of faith and practice, we met with so much opposition that I was led to deliver some speculative discourses upon these subjects. But I never preached a sermon of that kind that really feasted my heart; I always felt a barrenness of soul afterward. I perfectly accord with Brother Smith that those speculations should never be taken into the pulpit; but that when compelled to speak of them at all, we should do in the words of inspiration.
> I have not one objection to the ground laid down by him as the true scriptural basis on union among the people of God, and I am willing to give him now and here my hand. (69, p. 14)

Those in the building watched as Barton W. Stone and Raccoon John Smith shook hands, and then all over the building the representatives from the two groups warmly shook hands in fellowship. Many wept openly and a hymn was sung.

SMITH AND ROGERS SPREAD THE NEWS

Raccoon John Smith and John Rogers were sent to the scattered congregations to carry the good news and to urge the two groups in each community to unite as one congregation. John T. Johnson was put in charge of handling funds to support Smith and Rogers in their work. T. M. Allen, the noted pioneer preacher who did a great work in Kentucky and Missouri, suggested that the unified Stone / Campbell groups be called the Church of Christ after the merger. In 1844, twelve years after the merger, John Rogers wrote concerning the general spirit that prevailed at the time of the union.

> No one ever thought that the Reformers, so called, had come over to us, or that we had gone over to them; that they were required to relinquish their opinions or we ours. We found ourselves contending for the same great principles of Christianity, and we resolved to unite our energies to harmonize the church, and save the world... I entered into it upon principle. I think immense good has grown out of it, that had it never taken place, our cause in Kentucky would be far in the rear of the position it now occupies. (1, p. 33)

The religious journals among the brotherhood supported the union. Stone's Christian Messenger and Campbell's Millennial Harbinger were the strongest voices. The Christian Examiner, edited by J. G. Norwood and Jacob Creath, Jr. had assisted early on but just as the union was being consummated it ceased publication. This was succeeded by Walter Scott's Evangelist, originating from Ohio but was circulated widely in Kentucky. It too was a forceful advocate for union.

THE NEW ENGLAND CHRISTIANS

What about union with the New England Christians? In 1832 Campbell made an extensive tour into the East and strengthened the disciples in Richmond, Baltimore, Philadelphia and New York. No mention was made of the New England Christians that resulted from the work of Elias Smith and Abner Jones. On his next trip to the East in 1836, he went into Vermont and saw some of the Christians there and preached for them several times. He talked to members and elders and described them as being candid and intelligent and willing to be taught the way of the Lord more perfectly. However, nothing came of this and there was no union of the New England Christians and the Disciples.

James DeForest Murch said that the churches in the New England area were strongly influenced by Unitarian and Universalist views, and as a result, they refused almost in their entirety to come into the union that took place in Lexington. As a result of the 1836 trip by Campbell into New England, a congregation dedicated to Restoration principles was established in 1843 in Boston. "A few churches in Massachusetts, notably Haverhill (founded in 1803), Lynn and Worcester, Massachusetts joined the Restoration movement. An independent church at Danbury, Connecticut, visited by Campbell, decided to join the movement and became the strongest church of the Disciples in New England. In Vermont, Campbell's visit eventuated in the churches in Pawlet and West Rupert, but the cause did not grow. Dr. Charles J. White was largely responsible for maintaining and perpetuating these congregations. Two small churches in the region of Lubec, Maine, were the sole representatives of the movement in that state." (53, p. 126)

In 1845 J.J. Harvey suggested a union with the New England Christians. Campbell rejected the proposition on the ground that they were Unitarians. Barton W. Stone had expressed his willingness to unite with them earlier. Many of these Christian Connection congregations eventually merged with the Congregational Church.

STONE'S LIFE BEGINS TO WIND DOWN

When this great unity meeting took place in 1832, Barton Stone was already sixty years old. He was only twenty-four when he was licensed to preach for the Presbyterians. He was thirty-two when the Springfield Presbytery was dissolved and the first congregation of the Restoration Movement was established by Stone. He was fifty-four when he began the Christian Messenger in 1826. Stone was sixty-two in 1834 when he moved to Jacksonville, Illinois, the land of the Kickapoo Indians in the "far west." Here he gave his time to preaching tours, but he was slowing down.

At sixty-four Stone became seriously ill but recovered adequately to continue preaching. At sixty-seven his hearing went bad, and at sixty-nine he suffered a stroke of paralysis and almost died but recovered sufficiently to make preaching tours in Ohio, Kentucky, and Indiana. In 1843 at seventy-two Stone wrote his autobiography. His last sermon was preached on October 21, 1844, at the Bear Creek church in Boone County, Missouri. Apparently, he realized this was his final sermon. As he preached he was unusually solemn. He exhorted the sinner to obey the Lord and encouraged the Christians to be faithful. The audience wept, realizing that this great man would not be with them much longer. There were thirteen responses to the invitation.

STONE PASSES AWAY

Barton Stone spent a day or two with his son, Barton, Jr. who was a physician, and left quite sick for his home in Illinois. However, he traveled no further than Hannibal, Missouri, where he spent his last days with his daughter, Amanda, and her husband, Captain S. A. Bowen.

On Thursday, November 7 he sent for Jacob Creath, Jr., but Creath was sick and could not arrive until November 9, 1844. He and Stone sang a song and had prayer. Creath asked Stone if he had any fear of death. Stone's reply was, "Oh no, Brother Creath, I know in whom I have believed and in whom I have trusted, and I am persuaded that he is able to keep that which I have committed to him. I know that my Redeemer lives. All my dependence is in God and in his son Jesus Christ." Stone then quoted some scripture and commented on them. Stone turned for a moment to his family and exhorted them to be faithful. Creath had to leave at this point. Stone called after him, "God bless you, my brother. I hope to meet you in heaven." Jacob Creath, Jr. wrote to the Millennial Harbinger and described his final meeting with Barton Stone. His letter was published in the December issue, 1844. (1, pp. 34-35)

Stone was put in a chair by his friends. Dr. David Morton asked him what he thought of the doctrine he had been preaching. He replied that he believed it on the whole to be true, although some mistakes had been made. The rest of the time he spent smoking his pipe and conversing upon the love of God. He then reclined his head on the shoulder of his son, Barton, Jr. and passed away at age seventy-two on November 9, 1844.

He was first buried at Hannibal, Missouri. Shortly thereafter, the remains of Baron Stone were moved to Jacksonville, Illinois, and buried in a locust grove on the Stone farm. When that property was sold, his remains were exhumed and moved to the Antioch Church Cemetery. In 1847 the Cane Ridge Church of Christ arranged to have Stone's casket moved to the church cemetery. (69, p.20). The stone marker at Cane Ridge bears this inscription:

> "The Church of Christ at Cane Ridge and other generous friends in Kentucky, have caused this monument to be erected in a tribute of affection and gratitude to Barton W. Stone, minister of the gospel of Christ and the distinguished reformer of the 19th century."

The old Cane Ridge meeting house stands today with a superstructure built over it to protect it. Originally, the meeting house was constructed of ash logs. It was fifty feet long, thirty feet wide, fifteen feet high. It had a dirt floor and contained two doors and three windows on each side. There was no chinking between the logs and no fireplace. There was a gallery for slaves with a ladder to enter through a door size window from the outside.

A POET

It was not generally known that Barton Stone was a poet and left a number of poems. He composed a stanza eulogy in memory of his beloved Eliza Stone who died May 30, 1810. A portion of it is as follows:

> But mortal tongues can't speak the songs,
> To saints immortal this belongs,
> I'll now forsake those shining throngs
> And leave my dear Eliza.
> A mansion too for me is there,
> Soon with Eliza I'll appear,
> And with her, in the banquet share,
> And part no more forever.
> Come brothers, sisters, children dear,
> O, dry your sorrows, banish care.
> And seek, with me, to enter where
> Eliza now is feasting.
> To Canaan's happy land I go,
> Where streams of pleasure ever flow;
> Soon shall I quit this vale of woe
> And dwell in bliss forever. (25, pp. 312-313)

Stone's wife and infant child were buried side by side. Stone wrote of the willow tree over their graves:

> Beneath this grassy turf lies innocence and love;
> The willow bends its flexible boughs above;
> Nor is her son, deep-sleeping by her side;
> Forgotten by the mourner, far-spread wide;
> It waves its boughs o'er his infantile head,

And sweeps the tomb, and murmurs o'er the dead.
(25, p. 317)

CHAPTER 9
THOMAS CAMPBELL

Thomas Campbell has been described by some as the architect of the Restoration Movement. He must be given credit for some of the clearest thinking and most important contributions of this period. He was highly educated both for the ministry as well as secular school work. He was described as a man of culture and learning with a strong mind and a kind heart.

Thomas was born in County Down, Ireland. As a young man he set out as a teacher, but before long he had the customary experience which led him to believe he was called of God to preach. He belonged to the Anti-Burgher group of the Seceders. Through the help of John Kinley who promised to pay his expenses, Campbell attended Glasgow University for three years, finished the prescribed courses, and then went to Whitburn where he studied under Professor A. B. Bruce in the Anti-Burgher school. Thomas finished his course there, took the examination, and was given a license to preach.

In Antrip, Ireland, Thomas met and married a French Huguenot girl named Jane Corneigle who attended where Thomas preached. His ministerial duties included visiting the membership twice a year to examine the families' Bible knowledge. In his own family, Thomas practiced daily family worship and encouraged his membership to do the same. Families were expected to keep the

Lord's day holy and upon returning home from worship, members were quizzed on the main points of the sermon.

Thomas preached in several places and in 1798 moved to Rich Hill. Thomas started a school and Rich Hill to supplement his income. He preached and operated this academy for nine years at a combined salary of $250 a year. In this atmosphere of learning Alexander, Thomas' son, had his mind filled with large selections of literature. It was the rule in the Campbell family that each child should memorize a verse of scripture during the day and then recite that passage at evening worship. Almost daily Alexander studied the Bible along with Brown's catechism. He memorized rich passages in Greek, Roman, French, and English literature.

Thomas Campbell had a high regard for the Bible and this fact made an early impression upon Alexander's mind. He would come into his father's library and notice frequently that the Bible and a concordance were upon the stand being studied while many other books were in the library shelves untouched. Gradually his father was turning more to the Bible and away from creeds and doctrines of men.

OLD LIGHT, ANTI-BURGER, SECEDER, PRESBYTERIAN

Thomas Campbell was a minister of the Old Light Anti-Burgher Seceder Presbyterian Church. This particular group developed in an interesting manner. By 1690 the Presbyterian Church was firmly established in Scotland with the Westminster Confession of Faith being ratified. The Presbyterian Church became the state church of Scotland. After 1707 there were two major parties within the Presbyterian Church, the Moderates and the Evangelicals.

In 1731 the Evangelicals led by Ebenezer Erskine strongly objected to a new method of filling vacancies. Erskine was promptly expelled from the ministry of the church. The next year, 1732, he and others formed the Associate Presbytery and the Secession branch of Presbyterianism was born. The Seceders grew and by 1800 there were 200 congregations in Scotland, but more division was to follow.

In 1789 the Seceders divided into Burghers and Anti-Burghers on the question of oaths. The Burgesses of the towns required oaths binding the people to support the religion practiced in that realm. Those who considered the oath unlawful were the Anti-Burghers.

The year 1799 saw more division. Both branches of the Seceder Church divided again into New Lights and Old Lights on the question of whether the Solemn League and Covenant should be made a term of communion. Amidst all this religious division, Thomas Campbell worked for unity and even appeared before the Synod to plea for a union of the two Burgher sects, but to no avail. However, in 1820 after Thomas was in America the two sects united after seventy-five years of division. (3, p. 127)

Campbell was led more and more to depend on the Bible. Once the governor-general of Ireland offered him a position as private tutor with a large salary and a fine home. Campbell refused to accept the position because he believed that the move would be harmful to the spiritual welfare of his children.

TO AMERICA

As a minister Thomas worked very hard. Before long he developed stomach trouble that gave him considerable pain. The doctors could not do anything to improve Campbell's health so they finally recommended an extended trip. Several families around Rich Hill had already gone to America. Alexander had told his father he was going to America when he got old enough, so Thomas, when faced with the necessity of a trip overseas, naturally turned to America. Thomas' family was to stay behind and follow him when he got settled in the New World. In 1807 Campbell left Londondery, Ireland for America on the ship Brutus. He was forty-five years old at the time. Having spent the first half of his life in Ireland, he would spend the next half in America.

Just before his departure Thomas wrote a letter to his family which gives us a good indication where his emphasis was. He wrote: "live to God: be devoted to him in heart, and in all your undertakings. Be a sincere Christian, imbibe the doctrine, obey the precepts, copy the example, and believe the promise of the gospel." (21, p. 24) He left behind his wife Jane and six children. Alexander, now eighteen years old had agreed to continue teaching at the academy at Rich Hill. Thomas did not know when he left Ireland, but it would be two years before he would see his family again.

Upon arriving in Philadelphia, thirty-five days later, Campbell found the Anti-Burgher Synod of North America in session. He had brought a letter of recommendation from the Presbytery of Market Hill, Ireland, and was cordially received. He was assigned preaching responsibilities in Washington County, Pennsylvania. The assignment was in the southeastern section of the state where many of his friends from Ireland had located. The Synod gave the newly arrived preacher $50 for the necessary equipment and provisions for the journey to get to his new work. Before departing for his assignment, Thomas wrote a letter to his family in Ireland, part of which is as follows:

> What a debtor am I to the grace of God. See that you follow the directions I gave you at my parting, whether by word or by writing. Be a comfort to your mother: love, cherish and pity one another. Love the Lord your God, love His Son, Jesus Christ, and pray to the Lord constantly for me your poor father, who longs for you all and who cannot rest, if the Lord will, till he has prepared a place of residence for you all, where I trust we shall spend the rest of our days together in His service. (2, p. 24)

The next two years of Thomas Campbell's life have been traced through the minutes of the Chartiers Presbytery, for his name appears there quite often. The minutes of Saturday, May 16, 1807, tells that Campbell was received for the first time into the fellowship of this group. At the session of June 30 and July 1, 1807, Thomas Campbell was given appointments to preach at Buffalo on the second and third Sundays of July, at Mount Pleasant on the fourth, and on the first Sunday of August at Pittsburgh. Campbell was kept busy preaching Sunday after Sunday.

PERSECUTION FROM THE SECEDERS

A man who reads the Bible with an open and intelligent mind will sooner or later absorb much to make him dissatisfied with the human elements in religion. If that man has faith and courage, he will dare to speak out, sooner or later against what is wrong. As Campbell filled his appointments, he found himself teaching things contrary to the creed of the Presbyterian Church, but things which he felt were in harmony with the scriptures. It was only a matter of time until opposition would arise.

The first sign of trouble came at the regular meeting of the Chartiers Presbytery held at the Mt. Hope meeting house on October 27, 1807. The order of business came around to the question of filling appointments. It was found that a Mr. John Anderson had not kept his appointment at Buffalo on one recent Sunday, at which time he was to assist Thomas Campbell in administering the Lord's Supper. When Anderson was called upon to give an account of his action, he replied that he knew Campbell to be a teacher of false doctrine because he had heard him say before that there was nothing but human authority for creeds and confessions of faith. The Presbytery asked if anyone else had known of Campbell teaching these doctrines. Mr. William Wilson responded that he did. (4, p. 133)

In Robert Richardson's Memoirs of Alexander Campbell, he lists the fact that Thomas Campbell administered the Lord's Supper to members of other groups of Presbyterians who were not Seceders, but Garrison and DeGroot 3 point out that this charge does not appear in the minutes of the meeting of the Presbytery as a ground for the complaint against him, although it probably was a part of the problem. The one that was mentioned about having nothing but human authority for confessions of faith, etc. was one of two charges which eventually increased to seven. Included were these seven charges:

1. Campbell had refused to include any sort of mystical experience as giving assurance that he had Christ.
2. He denied the use of creeds as terms of communion.
3. He maintained that lay elders should pray and exhort in public worship when no minister was at hand.
4. He believed that Christians should have the opportunity of "an occasional hearing" of other ministers of other groups where "the public worship is not corrupted with matters of human invention."
5. The fifth charge had to do with atonement. Campbell's explanation appeared to be satisfactory for the presbytery at the time. Two days later they said that he did not remove all suspicion of the error.
6. The sixth charge was that he was a perfectionist, which he denied. No evidence was introduced against him on this charge.
7. He was charged with invading a Mr. Ramsay's parish. Thomas admitted he had preached at Cannonsburg, "but not in a congregation where any of our ministers are settled," not on an appointment by the Presbytery but on a call from "some of the regular and respectable people of that vicinity." (3, pp. 130-133)

SUSPENDED AND APPEALED

After 11 days of meetings by the Presbytery, on March 11, 1808, with only three members present (Anderson, Wilson and Alison) they voted to permanently suspend Thomas Campbell. Campbell appealed this decision to the Associate Synod of North America, the high court of the Seceder Presbyterians. They devoted more than a week to Thomas Campbell's case. On May 24, 1808, the Synod voted the Presbytery's proceedings had been irregular and revoked the sentence of suspension against him. It resolved to conduct its own trial and to consider the charges and answers. (3, pp. 133-139)

On May 26, 1808, the Synod decided on a far less severe verdict. He was to be "rebuked and admonished." On charge number four they required him to abstain from teaching anything about an "occasional hearing" in public or private. On May 27, he was asked if he would give in to them. He did this, but it was against his will. He at first wrote a letter of refusal to agree to submit but then withdrew the letter and accepted their terms. There was bad blood in the Chartiers Presbytery now because the Synod had reversed their decision of suspension against Campbell. F.W. Mattox said the Presbyterians sent out spies to listen to his sermons in order to catch him in unorthodox teaching. When Campbell returned from preaching in Philadelphia, at the end of July, he found that no appointments had been made for him in the jurisdiction of the Presbytery of Chartiers. No reason was offered for their failure to appoint him work. The truth of the matter was that they simply did not accept the action of the Synod. (3, pp. 133-139)

Thomas Campbell had been thrust back into the Presbytery, but the Presbytery would not put him to work, and he was not allowed to make his own appointments. When he insisted on a definition of his standing in the Presbytery, he was told that he was a member of it by the Synod's order, with the clear implication that he was an unwelcome member. There were sharp words of controversy, charges of falsehood, resulting in Thomas denouncing the authority of the Presbytery.

WITHDRAWAL FROM THE SECEDERS

On September 13, 1808, the Presbytery's minutes of that date have this entry: "Thomas Campbell in his own name and in the name of all who adhered to him, declined the authority of this

Presbytery for reasons formerly given, the authority of the Associate Synod of North America and all courts subordinate thereto, and all further communion with them." (3, pp. 133-139) The next day he delivered to the Presbytery the original letter that he had written for the Synod dated May 28, 1808, and then retracted. The Presbytery immediately voted his suspension, to which he made no objection this time for he was already out by his own act. This decision was final and the separation was complete. The Synod was duly informed and at its next May meeting it took the expected action of instructing the Presbytery to erase Mr. Campbell's name from its roll.

In the minutes of the same meeting, May 23, 1809, it is recorded that Mr. Campbell had refunded to the Synod the sum of fifty dollars. This was the amount that had been given to him on his arrival in Pennsylvania two years before. Campbell had seen the evils of division and it became evident to him that the trouble lay with human creeds. Alexander Campbell later wrote of Thomas' desire to be as charitable as possible:

> He objected not so much to the doctrines of the secession creed, but to the assumption of any form of religious theories or opinions, as the foundation of the Church of Christ: alleging that the Holy scriptures, divinely inspired, were all sufficient and alone sufficient for all the purposes contemplated by their author, in giving them. (1, pp. 46-47)

PREACHES WITHOUT PRESBYTERIAN SHACKLES

Thomas Campbell was excluded from the church building of the Presbyterians, but this did not stop him from preaching. "Many Presbyterian families in the community, already restive under the strict terms of the orthodox church, had been watching the scrimmage, cheering on the rebellious Mr. Campbell. When he was left stranded, their homes were thrown open to him for preaching services, and as groups could be assembled he began ministering among them.

His preaching was revolutionary. He held that no church has a divine warrant for holding to any man-written confessions of faith as essential; that at best such confessions were mere opinions of mortal men.... But it was his pronouncement that Christ died for all men, and that any man could believe on him and be saved, which provoked the strongest reaction." (67, p. 5) Large numbers came to hear him, as he found numerous intelligent religious people who were unhappy with the existing churches. His preaching underscored the inadequacy of human creeds, the supremacy of the Bible, and a plea for biblical unity.

One area in which Thomas differed from his former Seceder brethren was in the act of conversion. He did not see that it required an emotional experience. He thought that faith was an intelligent response of the mind to the Biblical evidence presented. At this time Thomas Campbell was the outstanding preacher in his area. He was highly respected by his denominational neighbors, and the announcement that he was leaving denominationalism made a deep impression in the community. A time and place was set for a meeting of all who were interested in finding a scriptural basis for unity.

"Where the Bible Speaks, We Speak"

The house of Abraham Altars, between Mt. Pleasant and Washington, Pennsylvania, was chosen, and here, one of the most famous meetings of the Restoration took place. Campbell addressed the group by reviewing the events that led up to the meeting. He argued strongly against sectarian division and pleaded for Christian unity. He then closed his speech with this famous motto: "Where the Bible speaks, we speak; where the Bible is silent, we are silent." That was in the year 1808. Quite naturally, when Campbell first spoke these words and paused, there was a solemn hush that fell over the assembly. This showed the intensity of the emotions of those present to things that were just said. Campbell sat down. A Scottish bookseller, Andrew Monro, who was a rather sentimental person, was the first to break the silence. The following conversation was recorded in the Memoirs of Alexander Campbell, written by Robert

Richardson: (5, pp. 318-319)

> "Mr. Campbell, if we adopt that as a basis, then there is an end of infant baptism." This remark, and the conviction it seemed to carry with it, produced a profound sensation. "Of course," said Mr. Campbell in reply, "if infant baptism be not found in Scripture, we can have nothing to do with it." Upon this, Thomas Acheson, of Washington, who was a man of warm impulses, rose, and advancing a short distance, greatly excited, exclaimed, laying his hand upon his heart: "I hope I may never see the day when my heart will renounce that blessed saying of the Scripture, 'Suffer little children to come unto me, and forbid them not, for of such is the kingdom of heaven.'" Upon this saying he was so much affected that he burst into tears, and while a deep sympathetic feeling pervaded the entire assembly, he was about to retire to an adjoined room, when James Foster, not willing that this misapplication of Scripture should pass unchallenged, cried out, "Mr. Acheson, I would remark that in the portion of Scripture you have quoted there is no reference, whatever, to infant baptism." Without offering a reply Mr. Acheson passed out to weep alone; but this incident, while it foreshadowed some of the trials which the future had in store, failed to abate, in the least, the confidence which the majority of those present placed in the principles to which they were committed. (5, pp. 318-319)

Earl West points out that the anxiety with which these men expressed themselves must not be construed as division within their ranks. On the contrary, their various statements show an earnest seeking after the way of the Lord. He likened it to men stepping out of intense darkness into light, and the light blinding them for a while. These men were coming out of the darkness of partyism and stepping into the light of revealed truth, and they staggered for a moment to get their bearings. (1, p. 48) From here on the activities of Thomas Campbell and those associated with him were stepped up. Their ideas were taking on more definite form.

CHRISTIAN ASSOCIATION OF WASHINGTON

At a meeting held on August 17, 1809, this small band of men formed themselves into the "Christian Association of Washington." This Association was not to be recognized as a church, but was an organization for the promotion of Christian unity. These men had not yet fully come to a full concept of the Restoration, but they were step by step going in that direction. As soon as the Association was formed it was seen that a building in which they could meet was needed. A log cabin was erected on the Sinclair farm, three miles from Mt. Pleasant on the road to Washington. For a time this building was used for a school. Campbell utilized it in renewing his teaching career.

THE "DECLARATION AND ADDRESS"

It was in this log cabin that Campbell wrote the Declaration and Address. When it was finished, Campbell called a special meeting of the Association and read it before them. The document met their general approval and it was ordered to be printed on September 7, 1809. This famous document contains over 30,000 words. The principal points of it may be summarized as follows:

1. The Unity of the Church: "that the church of Christ on earth is essentially, intentionally, constitutionally one."
2. Christian Fellowship: "that, although there must be separate local congregations, yet they should be one with no schisms and discord."
3. Terms of Communion: "that nothing be required

of Christians as articles of faith but what is expressly taught and enjoined upon them in the word of God."
4. "That the New Testament is supreme authority for Christians in all matters of faith and practice." (2, p. 27)

A second slogan was adopted by Thomas Campbell: "In faith, unity: in opinion, liberty, and in all things, charity." (2, p. 27) When Thomas Campbell and his associates renounced their allegiance to creeds and announced their purpose to be guided by the New Testament alone, they were unaware of what had been done by men such as James O'Kelly, Elias Smith, Abner Jones, and Barton W. Stone. They were all taking steps in the same direction.

BRUSH RUN CHURCH

A church was organized in 1811 at Brush Run on the basis of the "Declaration and Address." It was composed of independent believers, and for several months it worshipped without any affiliation with any denomination. The Brush Run congregation erected a small frame building on the farm of William Gilcrist in the valley of the Brush Run, two miles southeast of West Middletown, Pennsylvania. The building was 18 by 32 feet. The first service was held on June 18, 1811, when the interior was unfinished. (2, p. 28)

THE QUESTION OF BAPTISM

Early on, the subject of baptism was a problem for Thomas. At first he felt this was a question for great patience and was not to be considered a major issue. Alexander later questioned his father as to whether following the Declaration and Address would mean giving up infant baptism. Thomas replied that it was merely an inference in the document. A bit later Thomas admitted there was no specific teaching or precedent in the Bible to authorize infant baptism. However, he saw no reason for an adult "going out of the church merely for the sake of coming in again." Although Thomas had never personally been immersed, he did immerse three others on July 4, 1811 in Buffalo Creek. Thomas stood on a root above the candidates who were in water shoulder high. He then pushed down the heads of the candidates until they were covered with water. As he did this, he repeated over each, "I baptize thee in the name of the Father, and the Son, and the Holy Spirit." (2, pp. 30-31)

THE CAMPBELLS ARE IMMERSED

It was a difficult decision that Thomas made to be immersed, after serving twenty-five years as a Presbyterian minister. His own baptism took place June 12, 1812, when he was baptized by a Baptist preacher named Matthias Luce. It was understood by Matthias Luce, the Campbells, and those baptized with them that they were not being baptized into the Baptist church. They were being baptized into Christ. In all, seven people were baptized on that day in a service that took seven hours. (15, p. 131) Within a few weeks, most of the thirty members of the Brush Run congregation were immersed by Thomas Campbell upon a simple confession of faith. Those who were not baptized concluded that they belonged elsewhere. As expected, opposition against the Brush Run members developed. Once or twice Campbell was disturbed by dissenters while baptizing candidates.

In 1815 Thomas Campbell moved to Pittsburgh, Pennsylvania to operate a successful school. Among the students was Robert Richardson, who later became the biographer of Alexander Campbell.

Thomas began a small congregation in Pittsburgh that met in a school building. In the fall of 1817 Thomas moved to Newport, Kentucky, across from Cincinnati. For almost two years things ran smoothly. Then he began to teach the Bible to a number of slaves on Sunday afternoon in the school house. Some had an unfavorable reaction to this practice. Thomas determined to leave Newport and moved his family to Bethany in the fall of 1819. There he helped Alexander with the "Buffalo Seminary." He lived approximately seven miles from the Campbell "Mansion." Often he made preaching tours into Western Pennsylvania and into the Western Reserve of Ohio.

THOMAS CAMPBELL DIES

At the age of eighty-three Thomas Campbell was still traveling among the congregations, but time began to catch up with him. He became totally blind in the summer of 1847, but his mind remained sharp. Friends and family members read the scriptures and hymns to him. Thomas preached a "farewell sermon" at Bethany on Sunday, June 1, 1851, when he was 88 years old. The subject was "The Two Great Commandments," based on Matthew 22:37-40. W. K. Pendleton took down the entire message in the absence of Alexander.

Thomas lacked one month being ninety-one when he died on January 4, 1854. He manifested the same calm confidence in God at death that had characterized him in life. Immediately prior to his death he told Alexander, "I am going home and will pass over Jordan." His body was placed in "God's Acre" across from the Campbell home in Bethany, West Virginia. On the tombstone is inscribed a brief biography of his life. Some time later Alexander wrote to a relative about his father, saying, "I never knew a man, in all my acquaintance with men, of whom it would be said with more assurance that he walked with God." (2, p. 31)

By 1812 the son began to show his abilities as a preacher. At about this time writers began to say less about Thomas and more about Alexander. One can be sure that this is exactly the way that Thomas wanted it.

CHAPTER 10
ALEXANDER CAMPBELL

A MAN OF MANY ACHIEVEMENTS

Alexander Campbell was born September 12, 1788, in Antrip County, Ireland. He died on a Sunday evening, March 4, 1866, at the age of 77. General Robert E. Lee once stated, "If I were asked to select a representative of the human race to the inhabitants of other spheres in our universe, of all men I have known, I should select Alexander Campbell, then I know they would have a high impression of what our humanity is like." D. S. Burnet, a Restoration leader, remarked, "He was as familiar with God's word as Moses was with God on the mount." President James Madison commented, "He was the ablest and most original and powerful expounder of the scriptures I have ever known." (1, p. 37)

Alexander Campbell was held in every high esteem by the people of his day. One historian remarked that contrary to the way it usually is, Campbell was actually more famous while he lived than after he died. After his death his contributions are largely centered on the Restoration Movement, but his activities during his life were not limited to the field of religion.

He was a multi-talented man. In 1829 he was elected to the Virginia Constitutional Convention. He introduced ideas that later were enacted into law. For example, he advocated free public schools, the election of judges, and the gradual emancipation of slaves. Alexander preached to the joint session of Congress in 1850 on the text of John (3:16, 17). He wrote five hymns, two poems, and edited a hymnal. He was a highly successful farmer. He developed a new strain of sheep, and on one occasion was elected as president of the American Wool Growers Association. Campbell was the Postmaster of Bethany, Virginia for 30 years. He produced a revised version of the New Testament about 1831. The noted poet, Vachel Lindsay (1879-1931), perhaps best remembered for his poem "Congo," wrote the following poem of tribute about Alexander Campbell:

THE SAGE OF BETHANY

> He stepped from out of the Brush Run Meeting house
> To make the big woods his cathedrals,
> The river his baptismal font,
> The rolling clouds his bells,
> The stormy skies his waterfalls,
> His pastures and his wells.
> Despite all sternness in his word
> Richer grew the rushing blood
> Within our fathers' coldest thought
> Imagination at the flood
> Made flowery all they heard.
> The deep communion cup
> Of the whole South lifted up.
>
> He preached with faultless logic
> An American Millennium:
> The social order
> Of realist and farmer
> With every neighbor
> Within stone wall and border.
> And the tongues of flame came down

Almost in spite of him. (22, p. 12)

THE BOYHOOD OF ALEXANDER

With that brief preview into some of the accomplishments of Alexander Campbell, let's now go back to Ireland. Alexander, born in Antrip County, spent his boyhood on a farm near Rich Hill, ten miles from the town of Newry where his father, Thomas, lived while preaching for the Seceder Presbyterian Church at Ahorey. This area is in the northeastern section of Ireland, approximately 30 miles from Belfast. Alexander's education began at Market Hill and continued in an academy taught by his uncles Enos and Archibald Campbell. His father was also an able teacher and assisted in the training of his son.

As a young boy he was not that different from other boys. The story is told that one day Alexander went out under a shade tree to study his French lesson. It was a warm summer day and he fell asleep. A cow came along and devoured his French book. Upon repeating the incident to his father, he received a whipping and was told by his father, "the cow has more French in his stomach than you have in your head." The young Alexander worked as a laborer on the farm. The physical labor helped develop his strong body that served him well in the rigorous schedule of later life. It was not long after the episode with the cow that Alexander began to apply himself more diligently to his studies. (1, p. 38)

A SERIOUS STUDENT

John Locke's Letters of Toleration and his Essay on the Human Understanding were the first books that made a profound impression on Alexander's mind. Under his father's guidance he read extensively in literature, philosophy and religion. He also studied Latin and Greek under his father. His memory became remarkably retentive. On one occasion he memorized 60 lines of blank verse in 52 minutes without missing a word. (1, p. 38)

Alexander Campbell grew up in a home that had respect for the Bible. The Seceder Presbyterian Church required each family to have daily family worship. Thomas and Jane Campbell required each family member to memorize portions of the scriptures during the day to be recited at the evening devotion. All the passages learned during the week were to be repeated again on the Lord's day. Later in life Alexander commented on his parents, "to my mother as well as my father, I am indebted for having memorized in early life almost all the writings of King Solomon, his Proverbs, his Ecclesiastics, and many of the Psalms of his father David." (1, p. 39)

As a teenager Alexander truly became interested in spiritual matters. Like his father, he was expecting some peculiar assurance of forgiveness such as dreams, visions, voices, or emotional tugs, for this was the teaching from every pulpit. He believed Jesus was the Son of God from the time that he could read the scriptures. He trusted the Savior for salvation and said that, "it never entered my head to investigate the subject of baptism, or the doctrines of the creed." (1, p. 40)

A MEMBER OF THE SECEDER PRESBYTERIAN CHURCH

Alexander identified with the Seceder Presbyterian Church in Ahorey, Ireland, where his father was the minister. Thomas desired that his son Alexander become a minister, although Alexander had not yet made that decision. He did give special attention to literature that was available in the ministerial field. Alexander was surprised to find that, although the Catholics were strong numerically, many of them were ignorant, superstitious, and "priest ridden." The more he studied Catholicism and its practical effects upon the people, the more he abhorred it. Episcopalians impressed him as cold, aristocratic, and as loving the fashions of the world, but his keenest disappointment came from his study of the Presbyterian Church, of which he was a member. He found it divided into numerous factions, which became the source of Campbell's life-time opposition to religions division. As a young man Alexander watched with sympathetic interest at his father's efforts to reunite the Seceders in Ireland and Scotland.

A heavy schedule of preaching, teaching and farming

impaired the health of Thomas Campbell and resulted in his leaving Ireland. He left the academy in the hands of Alexander who was 18 years old. When the academy session was finished, Alexander joined the teaching staff of the school that his uncle Archibald Campbell directed at Newry.

SHIPWRECKED

Thomas Campbell lived in America 18 months and was most anxious for his family to join him. An epidemic of smallpox delayed the first attempt to depart Ireland for America, but finally on October 1, 1808, Jane and the six children set sail from Londonderry for Philadelphia on the ship Hibernia. Alexander was the eldest child at 19. The voyage was interrupted when the ship was blown off course and for three days it lay in anchor in the Bay of Islay, an island off the mainland of Scotland. The evening of October 7, 1808, the ship was blown onto a rock and began to take on water. For a while it looked as if all would be lost, as signals of distress went unanswered. It was in the anguish of this hour that the future of Alexander Campbell's life was shaped. Only one motive seemed worthy of his future life, and that was the salvation of mankind. He made the resolution that if he were saved he would devote his life to being a minister of God's word.

All of the passengers on the ship were saved. The islanders were hospitable and took care of their needs. Alexander returned to the ship to salvage as much of their personal belongings as possible, including the books that he valued greatly. After several days on the island, the Campbells went into Glasgow where Alexander found an apartment for the family. The trip to America would have to wait until the following summer.

THE UNIVERSITY OF GLASGOW

In Glasgow, Alexander enrolled as a student in the University of Glasgow where his father had attended 25 years earlier. During his year at the University, Alexander applied himself diligently. He became proficient in Greek, Latin, Hebrew, and in French and English literature, philosophy, logic and church history. He developed study habits that would serve him well through life. He retired at 10 p.m., and rose up regularly at 4 a.m. At 6 a.m. he attended a class in French, from 7 a.m. to 8 a.m. a class in Greek New Testament, from 8 a.m. to 10 a.m. he studied Latin. In the afternoon he studied advanced Greek, plus a class in logic. In addition he attended several lectures each week delivered by other professors.

THE INDEPENDENTS

In Glasgow, Alexander and his family attended a Seceder Presbyterian Church, usually on Sunday mornings. On Sunday evening, they would attend an independent church where Greville Ewing (1767-1841) was the preacher. Ewing was one of the most popular preachers in the city, as evidenced by the size of his audiences numbering from 1,000 to 2,000 at each service. Ewing was an associate of the Haldane brothers, early restoration preachers in Ireland. Greville Ewing was very popular with the university students. He often had students in his home for what was called "discussion groups." It was in these discussion groups that Alexander became acquainted with the works of such men as John Glas, Robert Sandeman, and other religious reformers.

Alexander was intrigued with this independent church and its adherence to Bible teaching. While attending there, Alexander had the opportunity to hear such distinguished preachers as Robert and James Haldane, Alexander Carson (1776-1844), Roland Hill (1744-1833), and John Walker (1768-1833). These men had in common the idea that religious unity could be achieved by adhering strictly to Bible teaching.

The independent church where Ewing preached observed the Lord's Supper every first day of the week. They determined to take the Bible as their only guide in matters of faith. They believed in the possibility of restoring the church of the New Testament by using the Bible as a blue print. Even though Alexander was impressed with the teaching of Greville Ewing, he did not yet feel himself ready to abandon the religious views of his youth and the Seceder church to which the Campbells belonged.

SEPARATION FROM THE PRESBYTERIANS

It was during this period of religious uncertainty that the annual communion period of the Seceder church approached. Alexander had begun to have considerable misgivings about his connections with the Seceder church, but as a matter of principle and habit, he decided to appear before the elders and get the metallic token which every one had to obtain who wished to take the Lord's Supper. He was questioned, not only by the elders, but was sent to another session to be further examined, after which he received the token. There were some 800 prepared to participate in the communion service on the appointed day. Alexander decided to wait until the very last, in hopes of overcoming his doubts about the Seceder church and its practices. When the time came for him to take the communion, "he threw his token upon the plate handed round, and when the elements were passed along the table, declined to partake with the rest." Robert Richardson said, "It was at this moment that the struggle in his mind was completed and the ring of the token, falling upon the plate, announced the instant at which he renounced Presbyterianism forever." (30, p. 190)

During the year that he was a student at Glasgow University, he kept a notebook, in which he entered a number of statements advocating religious reforms. For example, "I see as many marks of wisdom in what is omitted in the Bible as in what is included." Thomas Campbell has a similar idea in mind when he coined the phrase, "Where the Bible speaks, we speak; where the Bible is silent, we are silent." On party names he wrote, "I observe that the scriptures positively testify against the practice of Christians calling themselves by their earthly leaders." (6, p. 85) John Walker, another independent preacher had made a strong impression on the mind of young Alexander. In Alexander's notebook he had written the following statements made by Walker, "The writer who takes the sacred scriptures alone for the standard of his faith and takes the whole of them must expect opposition and dislike, more or less, from all sects and parties. The more clearly we maintain and exhibit the simplicity of the real gospel of Christ, the more we shall be disliked and despised by their earthly leaders." (6, p. 85)

THE CAMPBELLS SAIL TO AMERICA

Eventually, it came time for the Campbells to resume their journey to the New World. Alexander made all the necessary arrangements on the ship Latonia. On August 3, 1809, the vessel departed from Greenock, near Glasgow, and landed in New York City on September 29, 1809. They had been on the high seas for fifty-seven days. After two days of sightseeing in the city, the Campbells traveled by stagecoach to Philadelphia, a trip which required three days. In Philadelphia Alexander hired a wagon and team to take the family to Washington, Pennsylvania where they would be united with Thomas. On Monday morning, October 9, they started on their long trip of some 350 miles.

Thomas Campbell was so eager to see his family, from whom he had been separated for more than two years, that he started on horseback to meet them. He was accompanied by his good friend, John McElroy. After traveling three days there was a happy reunion between Thomas and his family. Mrs. Campbell related to her husband the incidents which had occurred in the family since he had been in the U. S., and Thomas detailed the religious trials and the many persecutions he had suffered at the hands of the Seceder clergy due to his efforts to promote unity on a Bible basis.

As the family journeyed toward the village of Washington, father and son had the opportunity to talk about the changes that had taken place in their respective thinking. Thomas Campbell had in his saddle-bags the proof sheets of a document that he had recently finished with the title of "Declaration and Address." The elder Campbell was eager for his son to read the document and tell him what he thought of it. Alexander devoured every word of it and heartily approved of the principles it set forth. Back in Scotland, Alexander had independently reached many of the same conclusions that his father had set forth in the "Declaration and Address."

ALEXANDER MAKES A COMMITMENT

Alexander indicated to his father at this time that he was going to preach those principles about which Thomas had written for the rest of his life. Furthermore, he would preach them without any pay whatsoever. To this his father replied, "Son, if you do this, I fear that you will wear many a ragged coat." It was a wonderful surprise when each learned that the other no longer held to the old religious group of which they had been a part. The circumstances under which they reached their conclusions were wholly different. Independent study of God's Word brought them together in their thinking. Thomas was more than pleased at his son's decision to preach and urged him to make an intensive study of the Bible for at least six months under his direction. Alexander later related his study schedule for the winter of 1810:

> 8 a.m. to 9 a.m. - Read Greek
> 11 a.m. to 12 p.m. - Read Latin
> 12 p.m. to 1 p.m. - Read Hebrew
> Each day -Commit 10 verses of scriptures to memory and read the same in the original languages. Allow two hours for this.
> Each day -Other reading and studies as occasion may serve. These studies required 4-1/2 hours.
> Church history and other studies constituted the principle part of his other literary pursuits. (30, pp. 278-279)

BEGINS TO PREACH

Not long after the family was settled in their two-story log house, Thomas Campbell preached a sermon at a nearby farmhouse. After the sermon had been delivered, Thomas asked Alexander to give an exhortation, which he did. Alexander preached his first full sermon on July 15, 1810. He was 22 years old. His sermon was based on Matthew 7:24-27. His first effort was successful beyond the expectations of the people who heard him. Some even said, "he can preach better than his father." This sermon was preached at Buffalo, in the home of Major Templeton who was pleased with the Campbells' emphasis on the Bible. This was something new in that community which was largely Calvinistic in its theology. In his ledger, Alexander noted that "this sermon was written out in full and committed to memory." (6, p.87)

His second sermon was preached July 22, 1810, at a place called the "Cross-roads" on the subject of Christian unity. During his first year as a preacher, Alexander preached one hundred and six times.

MARRIES MARGARET BROWN

At the age of twenty-two, Alexander married eighteen year-old Margaret Brown on March 12, 1811. The ceremony took place in the living room of her parents, the John Browns in Buffalo, Virginia. John Brown was a Presbyterian, a successful farmer and a millwright. He owned a gristmill and a saw-mill. The house that the Browns owned eventually became the Campbell Mansion.

Margaret was well-educated, a devoted wife and mother, a good manager of their domestic affairs, and in full sympathy with Alexander's work. Margaret bore eight children and then died in 1827 at the age of thirty-seven of tuberculosis. Two of Campbell's daughters, Lavinia and Clarinda, also died of tuberculosis.

Alexander would later marry Selina Huntington Blakewell, a spinster, in 1828. Alexander was thirty-nine and Selina was twenty-six. They were married for forty years. Before Margaret died she suggested to Alexander that Selina would make him a good wife. Selina bore Alexander six children. This gave Alexander fourteen children in all. it is Interesting to note that Alexander and Selina celebrated their wedding anniversary on March 12, which was actually the anniversary date for Margaret and Alexander.

THE CAMPBELL "MANSION"

The Browns moved to their new home in Wellsburg on the Ohio River, some eight miles away. In order to persuade Alexander from moving out of the area, the Browns gave Alexander and Margaret the "Mansion" plus 300 acres of rich farm land. In 1819 Campbell made the first of numerous additions. When he started the Buffalo Seminary he enclosed the west porch into a hall and added a large school room with a dormitory above. The main part of this structure was cut and framed in Pittsburgh, forty miles away, shipped down the Ohio River to Wellsburg, then carried by oxcart to the Campbell farm. He named his home "Bethany" in 1827. In 1836 Campbell added a new wing to his house to accommodate the increasing number of visitors from all parts of the country and even from Europe. In 1840 the final additions were made, consisting of two small bedrooms to the rear and an additional parlor. The parlor walls were covered with hand crafted paper imported from Paris, France. The same pattern was used in the Hermitage, the home of Andrew Jackson, near Nashville, Tennessee. By this time "Bethany" had become a house of twenty-seven rooms.

THE BRUSH RUN CHURCH

The formation of the congregation at Brush Run was an historic event. It occurred in 1811. Due to the hostile attitude of the religious bodies toward his efforts, Thomas Campbell thought it wise to form an independent church from the nucleus of the Washington Association. The question was considered and agreed upon at the next meeting of the Association. On Saturday, May 4, 1811, another meeting was held for the purpose of organizing a church. At this meeting, Thomas Campbell was appointed elder, and Alexander was licensed to preach. Four men were selected as deacons.

At the next meeting on May 5, 1811, which was the Lord's

Day, the church held its first communion service and Alexander preached on the subject "I am the Bread of Life." It was observed that Joseph Bryant, Margaret Fullerton, and Abram Alters did not commune. When asked why, they replied that they had never been baptized. Some weeks later, they were immersed by Thomas Campbell. Thomas had serious misgivings about baptizing those who had already been recognized as members of the church. However, he had no problem with the act of baptizing those three since they had never been baptized. Thomas had no misgivings about immersion because, as he put it, "it was evident that in the primitive age they went down into the water and were buried in it." But, up to this point, Thomas still defended infant baptism, which he believed put the infant into the church. That is why he made the statement that he saw no reason for "an adult to go out of the church merely for the sake of coming in again." However, something was to soon happen which would change the thinking of Thomas and clarify and solidify the thinking of Alexander.

BAPTISM STUDIED IN DEPTH

On March 13, 1812, a little girl was born to young Alexander and his wife. Her name was Jane, named for Alexander's mother. Soon after this event, Alexander's thoughts turned to baptism. The question arose as to whether the infant should be "baptized" according to the regular Presbyterian practice. Alexander set a period of time aside to give a thorough study on the subject of baptism, and specifically infant baptism. With a strong desire to know the will of God, he abandoned all uninspired authorities and applied himself diligently to the Word. He read all that he could find in English, French, and Greek. In studying the Greek words for baptism, he soon became satisfied that they could only mean "immersion" and "immerse."

Alexander, in his studies, discovered three New Testament truths that previously had not been clear to him. First, only penitent believers were fit subjects for Christian baptism. Second, the baptism of the New Testament was immersion. His conclusion was that the sprinkling of infants did not constitute baptism, because it was the application of an unauthorized form to an incompetent subject. This answered negatively the question about baptizing his little daughter, and also swept away the concept of "rebaptism." To immerse those who had been sprinkled was not "rebaptism" but baptism itself since they were not biblically baptized at the time of their sprinkling. And third, only a simple confession of faith that Jesus Christ was God's was required of one prior to baptism. This simple confession eliminated the unscriptural Baptist requirement of relating an "experience" as evidence of salvation.

The full purpose of baptism was yet to come in Campbell's understanding and teaching. This was developed in the Campbell-McCalla debate in 1823 along with Walter Scott's evangelism that began on a large scale in 1827. Alexander was now fully convinced that the rite of sprinkling, to which he had been subjected in infancy, was wholly unauthorized, and that he was an unbaptized person. He concluded that he could not consistently preach a baptism to others of which he had never been a subject himself. After discussing the matter with his wife, Margaret, she agreed with Alexander's reasoning and also wanted to be immersed.

On his way to talk to a preacher some distance away he stopped and talked to Thomas. He informed his father of his conclusions and of his intention of being baptized. Thomas and his wife came to the same conclusion along with Alexander's sister, Dorothea. To find a preacher in the community who would baptize the Campbells on a simple confession of faith, without having to relate an experience was no small task, but he had made the acquaintance of a Baptist preacher by the name of Matthias Luce who lived thirty miles from Washington. He asked Luce to do the baptizing, but with the stipulation that the baptisms had to be performed precisely according to the pattern given in the New Testament, and that there would be no requirement of a religious experience being related. Furthermore, it was understood that they were not being baptized into the Baptist Church, but into Christ.

IMMERSION OF THE CAMPBELLS

Seven in all were baptized that day, Thomas and his wife Jane, Alexander and his wife Margaret, Dorothea Campbell, James Hanen and his wife. The day was Wednesday, June 12, 1812, and the place was Buffalo Creek. The ceremony took seven hours during which both Alexander and Thomas delivered lengthy comments. Because of the popularity of the Campbells and the novelty of immersion a large crowd gathered to witness the baptisms. An interesting incident occurred during the lengthy baptismal service. Joseph Bryant had come to witness the baptisms, but because of the length of the service, he had to leave to report for muster of volunteers for the war against Great Britain. Bryant was able to attend the muster, travel back to Buffalo Creek, and hear one hour of the preaching and still see all seven baptized. Bryant was one of the three that Thomas had baptized earlier.

The adoption of immersion as an essential item in the Campbell's plan of Christian union radically changed the direction that they were to take from this time forward. No longer was it simply a matter of persuading churches to unite on beliefs that all Christians already held. It would now be necessary to persuade them also to accept immersion. At this time only Baptists believed baptism to be essential. It now seemed more important to seek first the restoration of the New Testament church, and then to work for Christian unity. Within a short period of time all the members of the Brush Run congregation were immersed believers. (30, p. 345)

INVITATION FROM THE REDSTONE ASSOCIATION

The New Testament teaching and practice of immersion brought the Brush Run church into closer and more friendly relationship with the Baptists. He began to receive numerous invitations to preach for many different congregations, and yet he was reluctant to be identified with them. In Campbell's

"Millennial Harbinger" he later wrote: "I had no idea of uniting with the Baptists more than the Moravians or the mere Independents. I had unfortunately formed a very unfavorable opinion of the Baptist preachers as then introduced to my acquaintance, as narrow, contracted, illiberal, and uneducated men. This, indeed, I am sorry to say, is still my opinion of the ministry of that Association at that day; and whether they are yet much improved, I am without satisfactory evidence. (30, p. 346)

The Baptists all pressed Campbell to join their Redstone Association. The matter of joining the Redstone Baptist Association was put before the Brush Run church in the fall of 1813. After much discussion, it was decided to seek admission to the Association with the stipulation that they be "allowed to preach and teach whatever we learned from the Holy Scriptures, regardless of any creed or formula in Christendom." (6, p. 92) This proposition was discussed at the next meeting of the Redstone Association. There was some opposition, led by a man named Pritchard, but the minutes of the association indicate that on September 2, 1815, the Brush Run church was accepted. it is interesting to note that the Campbells did not accept the Philadelphia Confession of Faith. Ordinarily this was a prerequisite before a church could become a part of a Baptist association. Nevertheless, the Redstone Association let the Brush Run congregation into the association without this requirement being met. There may have been several factors involved in the Campbells agreeing to join the Redstone Baptist Association, but one sure thing that it did was to widen the scope for Alexander Campbell to preach to a much wider audience than he could have otherwise done. Shortly after the Brush Run congregation was established a second congregation was also established at Wellsburg. Unfortunately, Wellsburg was quite close to where Pritchard preached. This started a seven year persecution against Alexander Campbell with Mr. Pritchard leading the charge.

THE "SERMON ON THE LAW"

The next Redstone Association convened at Cross Creek, August 30, 1816. Alexander knew that there was a coalition of Baptist preachers led by Pritchard that was against him, and he told his wife before he left home that he did not think they would let him preach. There were some Baptist preachers who wanted to hear him and the people in general wanted to hear him. Pritchard tried to block Campbell, but when a scheduled speaker had to withdraw because of illness, he was selected to take his place. It is unclear whether Campbell spoke extemporaneously or if he had come prepared in the hope that he could deliver his important address.

The sermon that he preached was "Sermon on the Law." For some time Campbell had been thinking on the relationship of the two covenants in the Bible. Baptists were accustomed to disregard the covenants, and to quote from the Old Testament as freely as the New Testament to a sinner. Campbell had come to the conclusion that much of the error in religious practice was due to the lack of understanding of the relationship of the two covenants. More than 1,000 people heard this sermon. Alexander was no sooner underway than Pritchard called out two or three of the preachers, supposedly to attend to a lady suddenly taken sick. Whatever the reason, a disturbance was created which interrupted Campbell's sermon. Finally, however, Alexander was able to proceed. He later learned that the reason Pritchard had called out the preachers was for the purpose of suggesting that Campbell be condemned before the people because he was not preaching Baptist doctrine. One of the Baptist preachers replied to Pritchard, "Elder Pritchard, I am not yet prepared to say whether it be or be not Bible doctrine, but one thing I can say, were we to make such an annunciation, we would sacrifice ourselves and not Mr. Campbell." (1, p. 63)

The "Sermon on the Law" became one of the most famous of the Campbell speeches. In it Campbell showed that the law of Moses was taken out of the way, and therefore, not binding upon Christians. The effect of the sermon was like a bombshell in the Baptist camps. A movement started to charge Campbell with heresy and have him excluded from the Baptist fellowships. At the next regular meeting of the Redstone Association at Peter's Creek in 1817 the subject was brought up, but through the intervention of some friends, it was dropped. Nevertheless, during the next several years the feelings that the Baptists leaders had toward Campbell were never again cordial. The railings against him, for the most part, fell on deaf ears among the people. Campbell believed that this "Sermon on the Law" was the springboard that was needed to put the Reformation he advocated before the world of religion.

BUFFALO ACADEMY

Like his father, Alexander was a natural born teacher. He wanted to prepare young men to preach the word. In 1818 he established the "Buffalo Seminary" in his own home. He provided daily Bible instruction and accompanied this with teaching on languages and sciences. Though the school was well-supported, Campbell closed it after about four years. It disturbed Campbell that most of the young men went into law and medicine, rather than into the ministry.

THE CAMPBELL - WALKER DEBATE

In the spring of 1820 Alexander Campbell was urged to engage in a public debate with a Seceder Presbyterian preacher by the name of John Walker. At first he declined, suggesting that such was not "the proper method of proceeding in contending for the faith once delivered to the saints." Walker had preached a series of sermons in favor of infant baptism. It was a Baptist preacher named Mr. Birch who strongly urged Campbell to debate Walker. Campbell finally agreed to the debate. The place for the discussion was only twenty-three miles from Bethany in the town of Mt. Pleasant, Ohio. Campbell was only thirty-two years old at the time. The debate was on the proper subject for baptism as well as the mode of baptism. Walker was the first speaker, and his speech lasted all of two minutes. Here it is in full:

> My friends, I don't intend to speak long at one time, perhaps not more than five or ten minutes, and will, therefore, come to the point at once. I maintain that baptism comes in the room of circumcision -- that the covenant on which the Jewish church was built, and to which circumcision is the seal, is the same with the covenant on which the Christian church is built, and to which baptism is the seal -- that the Jews and the Christians are the same body politic, under the same lawgiver and husband: hence, the Jews were called the congregation of the Lord -- and the bridegroom of the church says, "my love, my undefiled is one:" consequently the infants of believers have a right to baptism. (6, p. 98)

Campbell arose and after introductory remarks said, "I cannot persuade myself to believe that they who affirm that baptism comes in the room of circumcision really think so: for if they thought so, they would certainly act more consistently than they do." He then named five inconsistencies about this position. If infant baptism occupied the same position in the New Testament that circumcision occupied in the Old Testament, the following should occur:

1. They would baptize none but males.
2. They would baptize precisely upon the eighth day.
3. They would baptize all the slaves or servants that the master or householder possessed, for the Jews circumcised all their slaves, all in their house bought with money.
4. They would not confine the administration of baptism to the clerical order, for both men and women circumcised their own children.
5. They would not confine baptism to the infants of professed believers only, for the most wicked

Jews had the same privileges to circumcision that the most faithful had.

In his last speech, Campbell issued the challenge: "I, this day, publish to all present that I feel disposed to meet Pedobaptist ministers of any denomination, of good standing in his party, and I engage to prove with the pen that infant sprinkling is a human tradition and injurious to the well-being of society, religious and political." (6, p.99) The debate was soon put into book form and was widely distributed and favorably received. Alexander Campbell was then convinced that public discussion of religious question had real merit in promoting "the reformation we plead." The printed page began to occupy an important teaching role in Campbell's thinking.

SIDNEY RIGDON

In the summer of 1821 Alexander was sitting on his front porch resting. He had just finished his noon day meal and was waiting until it was time to return to the classroom at Buffalo Seminary. Two strangers on horseback rode up to the gate, dismounted and hitched their horses, then walked up the path that led to the Campbell mansion. The two strangers introduced themselves as Adamson Bentley and his brother-in-law, Sidney Rigdon, Baptist preachers who lived in Warren, Ohio. They said they had read the debate with John Walker, and they wanted to talk about some matters that Campbell had introduced in the debate. Campbell had them wait until his teaching duties at the seminary were finished. After the evening meal, the discussion began and continued until the next morning. They discussed the full gamut from Old to New Testament. The next morning Rigdon said, "If I have within the past year taught and promulgated from the pulpit one error, I have a thousand." (6 p. 99) At that time, he was the great orator of the Mahoning Association, though in authority with the people, he was second to Adamson Bentley.

Bentley and Rigdon left Bethany to return to the Mahoning Association to advocate the principles taught by Campbell. Campbell cautioned them "not to begin to pull down anything they had built until they had reviewed again and again what they had heard nor, even then, rashly and without consideration." (6, p. 99) Within the next few years the Mahoning Association would prove to be most helpful in the cause of promoting the Restoration Movement. In the summer of 1823 Campbell aligned himself with the Mahoning Association to escape action of the Redstone Association who were out to excommunicate and embarrass him. Between 1827 to 1830 nearly all the Baptist churches in the Mahoning Association left the Baptist Church to seek after a restoration of the New Testament Church.

Unfortunately, in a very few years after Rigdon met with Campbell, he joined with Joseph Smith in the leadership of Mormonism. Johnny Ramsey gives Rigdon credit (blame) for helping to write the Book of Mormon. 20 Louis Talbet in "What's Wrong With Mormonism," states, in reference to those behind the Mormon religion, "There were the Pratts, Parley P. and Orson; and last but by no means least, there was Sidney Rigdon, to whom all serious students of Mormonism give full credit for the organization of the Mormon Church." (35, p. 9)

Sidney Rigdon, Parley P. Pratt, and Orson Hyde had all been active leaders in the Restoration Movement before turning to Mormonism. Rigdon had originally converted Pratt and Hyde to the Restoration position, and Pratt then converted Rigdon to Mormonism. These three men naturally carried over with them some of the ideas and terminology in which they had been trained. The defection of these three preachers carried other disciples over into Mormonism. The entire congregation at Kirtland where Rigdon had been preaching became Mormon. It should be remembered that these disciples had not been in the Restoration Movement very long before they were led away into this digression. With any new movement there seems to be a percentage who are disposed to follow any new thing. Apparently Rigdon fully expected to become the successor of Joseph Smith as president of the Mormon Church, but Brigham Young, to Rigdon's great disappointment, was named to the position. Pratt and Hyde became "apostles." (3, p. 300)

THE CHRISTIAN BAPTIST

In the fall of 1822 Campbell began to think of giving up his Buffalo Seminary. The published debate with Walker had taught him the power of the press to disseminate his views. So, he began thinking of printing a religious journal. About this time he made the acquaintance of Walter Scott. In discussing the idea of the paper with Scott he told him that he wanted to name the paper, "The Christian," but Scott recommended a variation of that name. He thought it would be a means of disarming prejudice to call it the Christian Baptist. In the spring of 1823, Campbell published his "Prospectus" for the proposed paper. In this, Campbell said:

> The Christian Baptist shall espouse the cause of no religious sect, excepting the ancient sect called "Christians first at Antioch." Its sole object shall be the eviction of truth and the exposing of error in doctrine and practice. The editor, acknowledging no standard of religious faith or works other than the Old and New Testament, and the latter as the only standard of the religion of Jesus Christ, will, intentionally at least, oppose nothing which it contains and recommend nothing which it does not enjoin. Having no worldly interest at stake from the adoption or reprobation of any article of faith or religious practice, having no gift nor religious emolument to blind his eyes or to pervert his judgment, he hopes to manifest that he is an impartial advocate of truth. (1, p. 69)

Campbell bought the type, presses, and the rest of the necessary equipment, and erected a building near the creek at the base of the cemetery hill. Here, he began publication of the Christian Baptist, the first issue of which appeared August 3, 1823. The Christian Baptist made many friends, but it also made many enemies. In the seven years the Christian Baptist was published Campbell breathed the spirit of the iconoclast, one who attacks the old established institutions. He was considered by some to be harsh and often bitter in his denunciation of many of the religious practices of the day. Campbell sought to expose the pride, worldliness and paganism in the churches. He turned his attack against the "kingdom of the clergy," because he believed that the clergy, Protestant, and Catholic alike were guilty of deceiving the people and holding from them the truth of the Scriptures. A Virginia Baptist preacher who called himself "Robert Cautious" wrote to Campbell and asked that Campbell not be immoderate in his condemnations, and cautioned him regarding the danger of "running past Jerusalem, as one hastens out of Babylon." (1, p. 69)

Creeds, confessions of faith, and authoritative councils of men were repudiated as the editor launched out alone in his quest for the truth. He pleaded for a return to the apostolic church of the New Testament and for the destruction of denominationalism. He wrote:

> I have no idea of adding to the catalogue of new sects. This game has been played too long. I labor to see sectarianism abolished, and all Christians of every name united upon the one foundation on which the apostolic church was founded. To bring Baptists and Pedo-Baptists to this is my supreme end. But to connect myself with any people who would require me to sacrifice one item of revealed truth, to subscribe any creed of human device, or to restrain me from publishing my sentiments as discretion and conscience direct, is now, and I hope ever shall be, the farthest from my desires, and the most incompatible with my views. (1, p. 70)

NO PLACE FOR THE DOCTRINES OF MEN

How did Campbell propose to restore the New Testament church? He simply advocated that men drop things of human origin in religion, and return to the sacred Scriptures for all that they teach and practice religiously. Accordingly, Campbell said:

> The people must abandon the language, customs and manners of the Ashdod. For this purpose they will meet, and read, and examine the New Covenant writings. They will also look to heaven for wisdom and courage, and as soon as any item of the will of heaven is distinctly apprehended, it will be brought into their practice. (1, p. 71)

The Christian Baptist was read far and near. The editor of the Northern Whig of Belfast, Ireland said concerning the Christian Baptist, "It might do good provided it were written with less bitterness. It is a mixture of pepper, salt, and vinegar, served with a dash of genuine Irish wit, but with a great deal of instruction." (1, p. 106)

It would be hard to even estimate the great good that the Christian Baptist did for the Restoration. It reached into communities where Campbell would never have gone, and into thousands of homes where he would never have been invited. Because of the name Christian Baptist, many Baptists read it and were convinced of the need to reform and restore the ancient order. Some of the great preachers of the Restoration Movement of the 19th century were directly influenced by the Christian Baptist. This list included Raccoon John Smith, J.T. Johnson, Philip S. Fall, Jacob Creath, Jr., and the parents of David Lipscomb, just to name a few. Moses E. Lard looked upon the Christian Baptist as being the masterpiece of Campbell's life. He said, "In originality and utility he has written nothing to excel it." (6, p. 106)

OPPOSITION FROM THE BAPTISTS

With the Christian Baptist having its effect on many Baptists, and the views of Alexander Campbell being made known which were contrary to Baptist doctrine, by 1823 opposition to Alexander

Campbell was steadily mounting. Elder Pritchard and his associates of the Redstone Association were out to get him. They planned a public ex-communication of Campbell at the next meeting of the Redstone that was only a short time away. Campbell found out about this devious plan, however, and on August 31, 1823, he appeared before the Brush Run church and asked for a letter of dismissal for himself and thirty-one others in order to join with the church at Wellsburg where a meeting house had been previously constructed. The Wellsburg church was promptly received into the fellowship of the Mahoning Association at the instigation of Adamson Bentley.

Campbell went to the Redstone Association as an observer and not an official messenger from Brush Run. When his enemies demanded to know why he was not there as a messenger, Campbell stated that the church of which he was a member did not belong to the Redstone Association. In describing the chagrin of his enemies, Campbell said, "Never did hunters, on seeing the game unexpectedly escape their foils at the moment when its capture was sure, glare upon each other a more mortifying disappointment than that indicated by my pursuers at that instant on hearing that I was out of their bailiwick and consequently, out of their jurisdiction. (6, p. 107)

THE CAMPBELL - McCALLA DEBATE

At the close of the debate with Walker, Campbell had issued a general challenge for a public debate with any reputable advocate or defender of infant baptism. W. L. McCalla, a Presbyterian preacher of Augusta, Kentucky, accepted the challenge. Arrangements were made for the debate to be held in Washington, Kentucky, October 1832.

Several days before the debate was to begin, Campbell set out on horseback to make the 300-mile trip. Sidney Rigdon accompanied him to take notes. On the 14th of October, Campbell met McCalla and found him to be very obstinate and a difficult person whose personality was such that a friendship was not possible. The rules for the debate were made according to the desires of McCalla. Campbell selected for his moderator the most popular Baptist preacher in

Kentucky, Jeremiah Vardeman. Vardeman related that on his way to the debate he overtook a man on foot who told him he was on his way to Washington to hear the debate. Vardeman took him to be a zealous Baptist and pretending to be on the other side, said, "Is not our man likely to whip your man Campbell?" The man asked, "Can you tell me if this is the same Mr. Campbell who debated Mr. Walker at Mt. Pleasant, Ohio?" Vardeman said he believed he was. The stranger said, "I heard that debate and all I have to say is that all creation cannot whip that Mr. Campbell." (6, p. 108)

BAPTISM
FOR THE REMISSION OF SINS

The subject of the McCalla debate was the same as the Walker debate, "The Subject and Mode of Baptism." The two men went over the same ground on the covenants, but when it came to infant baptism, Campbell injected the argument that baptism was for the remission of sins, and therefore, could not be for infants since they had no sins. This thought was revolutionary for its day, and Campbell knew the Baptists were against it. Campbell said to them, "My Baptist brethren, as well as the Pedobaptist brotherhood, I humbly conceive, require to be admonished on this point. You have been, some of you, no doubt, too different in asserting this grand import of baptism." (1, p. 65)

Campbell demonstrated his honesty and boldness the evening of the fourth day of the debate after the evening meeting. Campbell said:

> ... having secured the special favor and attention of the Baptist ministry and of the uncommitted public, while I had in one room at the residence of my kind host, Major Davis of Washington, all the principal Baptist preachers of the state, I thought it expedient to introduce myself more fully to their acquaintance. This I did in the following manner: "Brethren, I fear that if you knew me better you would esteem

and love me less. For, let me tell you in all candor, I have almost as much against you Baptists as I have against the Presbyterians. They err in one thing and you in another: and probably you are each nearly equidistant from original apostolic Christianity." I paused and such a silence ensued accompanied with a piercing look from all sides of the room, I seldom before witnessed. (6, pp. 108-109)

Campbell had the opportunity then, after their challenges to pass out ten copies of his Christian Baptist. Included in this issue was his article "The Kingdom of the Clergy" which was a scathing attack on denominational ministers of the day.

WERE THE CAMPBELLS BAPTISTS?

The association of the Campbells with the Baptist church needs some clarification at this point. Alexander had called to their attention the differences between the Campbells and the Baptists during the debate with McCalla. At that time, because of his stand on immersion, most of the Baptists were looking upon him as their champion. Among their differences are these:

1. The Baptists accepted the Philadelphia Confession of Faith as their bond of unity and statute of discipline and operated under it. The Campbells rejected all creeds as anti-Christian and a hindrance to unity on the basis of the Bible alone.
2. The Baptists stood for Calvinism as set forth in the Philadelphia Confession of Faith. The Campbells held Calvinism to be a corruption of Christianity, a curse to the world, a cause of division and a perversion of the truth faith.
3. The Baptists generally had the Lord's Supper

every three months and not more often than once a month. The Campbells taught that the church should break bread every Lord's Day and that monthly communion was a departure from the original order.
4. The Association Baptist church believed that each congregation should have only one elder (or bishop). The Campbells felt that if a congregation did not have a plurality of elders (or bishops) that congregation had digressed from primitive policy.
5. Although it appeared that the Baptists and Campbells agreed on baptism they actually did not. To the Baptists immersion was an ordinance required for church membership but to the Campbells it was done in order to obtain remission of sins. These basic differences indicate that Alexander Campbell never truly considered himself a "Baptist." (5, p. 336)

Campbell's association with the Baptists has been the subject of many discussions. Why did he stay with them so long since he was not a Baptist? He wrote in May, 1826, "So long as they will hear reproof, suffer exhortation, and allow us to declare our sentiments without restraint: so long as they manifest a willingness to know the whole truth, and any disposition to obey it: so long as they will hear us and cordially have fellowship with us, we will have fellowship with them, we will thus labor for their good, and endeavor to correct what appears to be amiss." (6 pp. 336-337) Apparently, the Redstone Association also saw the differences and excluded the Brush Run church from the Redstone Association in 1824.

At the conclusion of the McCalla debate Campbell became even more favorable to public discussions than ever. Campbell said, "This is ... one of the best means of propagating the truth and exposing error in doctrine or practice... and we are persuaded that a week's debating is worth a year's preaching." (6, p. 109) Campbell's reputation and influence were greatly extended by the debates. Barton W. Stone gave credit to reading this Campbell-McCalla debate with clarifying his thinking on the purpose of baptism being for the remission of sins. It no doubt had a similar influence on many other preachers. In September of 1824, Campbell made an extended trip into Kentucky, which lasted for three months. People in Kentucky were very receptive to the reformation he preached. The Christian Baptist was widely distributed in the state and eagerly read. It was on this trip that Campbell met Barton W. Stone for the first time. Also, it was on this trip that he met a Baptist preacher by the name of Raccoon John Smith (1784-1868).

THE LIVING ORACLES

Alexander Campbell had great respect for the Bible as the inspired Word of God, but he was not happy, however, with the King James Version of the Bible. In the early part of 1826, Campbell announced that he was publishing a new version of the New Testament. For his new version, which came to be known as the Living Oracles, he used the four gospels of George Campbell of Aberdeen, Scotland; Acts and Revelation of Philip Doddridge, London; and the Epistles from James McKnight of Edinburgh. Campbell made various alterations to these and added a preface of some 100 pages. In the preface he told why it was important to bring out a new version. "A living language is continually changing. Like the fashions and customs in apparel, words and phrases at one time current and fashionable, in the lapse of time become awkward and obsolete... Many of them, in a century or two, come to have a signification very different from that which once was attached to them. Nay, some are known to convey ideas not only different from, but contrary to, their first signification." (6, p. 112)

In his version, Campbell resolved to translate every word of the Greek into clear English language. He, therefore, used "immerse" for "baptize"; "John the Immerser" instead of "John the Baptist"; all the pronouns "thee," "thou," "thine," and "thy" were changed to "you" except when applying to prayer. Campbell's Living Oracles appeared in the spring of 1827 in one volume of 550 pages. Richardson says that Campbell was the "first to furnish the English reader a version of the New Testament completely rendered into its own vernacular." (6, p. 112) The Living Oracles went through a number of editions. It was well received by many, while others rejected it as a "Campbellite Bible." Some of the Baptists were so bitterly opposed to it that on a few occasions copies of it were burned publicly.

SEPARATION FROM BAPTISTS

By 1827 the final and complete separation of the Reformers from the Baptists was becoming more and more inevitable. Since 1815 the Restoration Movement had been linked to the Baptist churches because of the Brush Run church being in the Redstone Association. By 1827 it was being recognized as a separate and independent movement. Many within the Restoration were having serious doubts about the scriptural authority of the associations of the Redstone, Mahoning, Beaver, and other such associations in the various states. Those who were searching for the truth began to realize that these associations were inconsistent with the principles they advocated.

In 1827, thirteen churches identified with the Redstone Association formed what they called "The Washington Association," embracing the views preached by Alexander Campbell. The North District Association that had tried Raccoon John Smith for heresy divided in 1830. Those advocating restoration soon dissolved themselves. Within the Bracken Association, the Licking Association, and the Association of Boone's Creek, the story was the same. The regular Baptists would become "corrupted" by the influence of the teachings of Campbell. The association would divide, and the part made up of the advocates of restoration would soon dissolve itself.

THE "BEAVER ANATHEMA"

In 1829 two or three fragments of Baptist churches on the Western Reserve THAT refused to go into the Restoration, had united with a small Baptist association on Beaver Creek, in Pennsylvania. Included were the churches at Youngstown, Palmyra, and the church at Salem. Two preachers, who were violently opposed to Campbell, convinced the association to publish a circular that anathematized the Mahoning Association and "Mr. Campbell of disbelieving and denying many of the doctrines of the Holy Scriptures." The charges of the Beaver Association against the Reformers are listed by Garrison and Degroot as follows: (3, p. 194)

1. They, the Reformers, maintain that there is no promise of salvation without baptism.
2. That baptism should be administered to all without examination.
3. That there is no direct operation of the Holy Spirit on the mind prior to baptism.
4. That baptism procures the remission of sins and the gift of the Holy Spirit.
5. That man's obedience places it in God's power to elect to salvation.
6. That no creed is necessary for the church but the Scriptures as they stand.
7. That all baptized persons have the right to administer the ordinance of Baptism.

The "Beaver Anathema" was scattered widely among the Baptist churches and caused a considerable stir. Other associations were quick to unite in an effort to purge the Baptist fold of "Campbellism."

THE CAMPBELL - OWEN DEBATE

In April of 1829 Campbell had a debate with Robert Owen of Scotland (1771-1858) which made Alexander Campbell an international celebrity. The debate was conducted in Cincinnati, Ohio, and people from many parts of the country attended. Robert Owen was a socialist who traveled across America, preaching a doctrine of godless communism. He insisted that in order for society to survive, private property, religion and marriage would have to be abolished. Wherever Mr. Owen lectured, he challenged the clergy to debate the issues with him. No one, however, had ever accepted the challenge, that is, until Alexander Campbell accepted in a letter to Owen dated April 25, 1828. He said the debate should take place within one year. A few weeks afterward, Mr. Owen made a trip to Bethany to make final arrangements with Mr. Campbell for the debate. A cordial relationship existed between the two men. Campbell later said of Robert Owen, that of all his opponents in debate, "The infidel, Robert Owen, was the most candid, fair, and gentlemanly disputant he had ever met."

One day as they were walking around the farm at Bethany, they came upon the Campbell family burial ground when Mr. Owen stopped and said, "There is one advantage I have over the Christian -- I am not afraid to die. Most Christians have fear in death, but if some few items of my business were settled, I should be perfectly willing to die at any moment."

"Well," answered Mr. Campbell, "you say you have no fear in death; have you any hope in death?" After a solemn pause, he said "No." "Then," Alexander said while pointing to an ox, "you are on the level with that brute. He has fed till he is satisfied, and stands in the shade whisking off the flies, and has neither hope nor fear of death." At this, Mr. Owen smiled and showed some confusion, but was quite unable to deny the justness of Mr. Campbell's inference. (6, p. 114)

The debate came off according to schedule with capacity crowds. Mr. Owen announced with a sense of pride that he had discovered certain fundamental laws of human nature that, if properly applied would abolish such things as marriage, religion, and private property. This, in turn, would provide the good life for mortal man. In his second speech, Mr. Owen read a long manuscript in which he listed his twelve fundamental laws of human nature. He spent all of his time during the debate repeating and emphasizing these twelve laws, much to the amusement of the listeners. J.M. Powell records all of the twelve laws of Mr. Owen. (6, p. 114)

The most notable event of the debate was Mr. Campbell's twelve hour speech on the defense of the Christian religion. By the sixth day of the debate, Robert Owen had really said all that he had to say about the twelve fundamental laws of human nature and society, and so suggested that Campbell take the rest of the time. Campbell started to speak a half hour before lunch intermission on Friday, returned and spoke all Friday afternoon, started speaking again Saturday morning, spoke until evening, and then on Monday he resumed and spoke until 4 p.m. that afternoon. Eva Jean Wrather who wrote a historical account of this debate said that he delivered this twelve hours of lecturing without the use of notes of any kind. Judge Jacob Burnet, a member of the Ohio Supreme Court, served as president moderator of the debate. Even though Burnet's sympathies were not with Mr. Campbell's religion, he made the emphatic remark, "I have been listening to a man who seems as one who had lived in all ages." (6, p. 116)

"At the conclusion of the debate, Campbell called upon all in the audience 'who believe in the Christian religion, or who feel so much interest in it as to wish to see it pervade the world' to stand. Almost everyone rose to his feet. He then asked all those who were 'doubtful of the truth of the Christian religion or who do not believe it, and who are not friendly to its spread and prevalence over the world' to arise. Only three persons stood." (65, p. 80)

THE CONSTITUTIONAL CONVENTION OF VIRGINIA

After the debate with Mr. Owen, Campbell entered politics by successfully running for the Constitutional Convention of Virginia in 1829. Though he was criticized for turning to politics, he justified his actions by saying he wanted to do something to end slavery in Virginia. In this new role Campbell met many of the important political figures of the day and discussed important issues with such noted Americans as James Monroe and James Madison, former presidents, also John Randolph of Roanoke, and John Marshall, Chief Justice of the Supreme Court of the United States. While in Richmond, Campbell preached every Sunday in one of the churches in the city. Many of his fellow delegates were in attendance to hear him. W. K. Pendleton tells of the following incident that took place in 1830:

> Ex-President Madison was returning from the convention, of which he had been a member, and spent the night at my father's house, which was just one day's journey from Richmond. The next morning Mr. Madison rose early and he found my father walking on the portico in the early sunlight, when the latter asked Mr. Madison his opinion of Alexander Campbell. After speaking in very high terms of his abilities as displayed in the convention, he said, "But it is a theologian that Mr. Campbell must be known. It was my pleasure to hear him often as a preacher of the gospel, and I regard him as the ablest and most original and powerful expounder of the Scripture I have ever heard. (6, p. 117)

THE MILLENNIAL HARBINGER

Sometime before his debate with Robert Owen, Campbell had decided to discontinue the Christian Baptist. He felt the name "Christian Baptist" would be associated with the Baptist Church and thus applied as a party name to those advocating restoration. He determined to immediately drop the paper, and put this name out of existence. Also, in the Christian Baptist his approach had often been described as harsh. Many of his friends had encouraged him to be more moderate in his condemnation of evil. He believed it best to cease publication of the Christian Baptist at the close of 1829, and begin another paper.

On January 4, 1830, Campbell became the editor of the Millennial Harbinger. The name of this new periodical was significant. Campbell believed in the millennium. His view was that the millennium was a period of time when "the nations of this world are all to become the kingdoms of our King--they are all to submit to his government, and to feel the benign and blissful influence of his scepter." Campbell believed that eventually Christianity would triumph over the whole world and the influence of Christ would be preeminent. But, Campbell also believed that "the sectarian establishments could not admit of this spread and triumph of Christianity." Therefore, the only way to have the millennium was to restore the ancient order, and to destroy sectarianism in all its forms. (27, p. 71-72)

Campbell announced that each number of the Harbinger was to have forty pages. It was to be published on the first Monday of each month. The cost of a subscription was $2.50 a year. Alexander Campbell believed in the power of the printed word, so he continued his advancement of the restoration through the printed page of the Harbinger. His intention was to be more diplomatic, less harsh and severe in his denouncement of all that was wrong in the religious world. But, he was ready and prepared at anytime to use this new platform to defend and promote his views.

MAHONING ASSOCIATION DISSOLVED

Step by step the advocates of restoration were being separated from the Baptist ranks. There was an awakening to the fact that associations were without scriptural authority. In 1830 the Mahoning Association met in the church building in Austintown on the Western Reserve. The Mahoning Association had given refuge to Campbell and members of the Brush Run church when the Redstone Association was out to get Campbell. Most within the Mahoning Association agreed with the views of Campbell and advocated a return to the New Testament church.

The meeting opened with songs, exhortations, and prayers. John Henry, one of the preachers, stood up and said: "I charge you to look out what you are about to do here; we want nothing here which the word of the Lord will not sanction." He then suggested the resolution that the Association be dissolved, and it was carried. Commenting later, Campbell said of that meeting:

> Such a meeting was not witnessed in the memory of any present, as was the late meeting of churches in Austintown. The first day, Friday, was spent in declaring the wonders which God had wrought in various portions of the Western Reserve by the restoration of the ancient gospel. Songs of praise and tears of joy mingled with these reports, translated us nigher the regions of bliss than we had ever before approached. The next day, finding no business to transact, no inquiries to answer, nothing to do but "to love, and wonder, and adore," it was unanimously agreed that the Mahoning Association as "an advisory council," as "an ecclesiastical tribunal," exercising any supervision or jurisdiction over particular congregations, should never meet again. This Association came to its end as tranquilly as ever did a good old man attenuated thread of life, worn to a hair's breadth, dropped asunder by its own imbecility. "Night dews fall not more gently to the ground, nor weary worn out winds expire more soft" than did this Association give up the ghost. (1, p. 73)

THE CAMPBELL - STONE
UNITY MEETINGS

In chronological order we are at the period when the unity meetings took place between the "Christians" associated with Barton W. Stone and the Disciples or Reformers associated with Alexander Campbell. There was a four day meeting at Great Crossings near Georgetown that took place December 23-26, 1831. They agreed to have another four day meeting which culminated on January 1, 1832 in Lexington, Kentucky. Since we have covered this important event in the section on the life of Barton W. Stone, we briefly mention it here to indicate its place in order of time. Alexander himself was not present for those meetings. However, Raccoon John Smith and others were there to represent the "Reformers." Stone and others associated with him were there to represent the "Christians."

THE CAMPBELL - PURCELL DEBATE

Campbell's next debate was in Cincinnati, Ohio January 13, 1837. His opponent was a Roman Catholic Bishop named John Baptist Purcell. The discussion was the outgrowth of a lecture that Campbell gave on "Moral Culture" at the Teachers' College in Cincinnati. In his speech Campbell connected the rapid march of modern improvement with the spirit of inquiry produced by the Protestant Reformation. Bishop Purcell took exception to this argument and countered by saying, "The Protestant Reformation had been the cause of all the contention and infidelity in the world." (6, p. 119) After an exchange of letters, Bishop Purcell agreed to meet Campbell in public debate. The positions were arranged as follows:

Campbell's position:

1. The Roman Catholic Institution, sometimes called the "Holy, Apostolic, Catholic, Church," is not now, nor was she ever, catholic, apostolic, or holy; but is a sect in the fair import of that word, older than any other sect now existing, not the "Mother and Mistress of all Churches," but an apostasy from the only true, holy, apostolic, and catholic church of Christ.
2. Her notion of apostolic succession is without any foundation in the Bible, in reason, or in fact; an imposition of the most injurious consequences, built upon unscriptural and anti-scriptural traditions, resting wholly upon the opinions of interested and fallible men.

3. She is not uniform in her faith, or united in her members; but mutable and fallible, as any other sect of philosophy or religion - Jewish, Turkish, or Christian - a consideration of sects with a politico-ecclesiastical head.
4. She is the "Babylon" of John, the "Man of Sin" of Paul, and the empire of the "Youngest Horn" of Daniel's sea monster.
5. Her notion of purgatory, indulgences, auricular confession, remission of sins, transubstantiation, supererogation, etc., essential elements of her system, are immoral in their tendency, and injurious to the well-being of society, religious and political.
6. Notwithstanding her pretensions to have given us the Bible, and faith in it, we are perfectly independent of her for our knowledge of that book, its evidences of a divine original.
7. The Roman Catholic religion, if infallible and unsusceptible of reformation, as alleged, is essentially anti-American, being opposed to the genius of all free institutions, and positively subversive of them, opposing the general reading of the scriptures, and the diffusion of useful knowledge among the whole community, so essential to liberty and the permanency of good government. (6, pp. 119-120)

On Friday, January 13, 1837, the debate began. The audiences were large and enthusiastic from the beginning. An unusual incident occurred during the debate that is worthy of special mention. Campbell quoted this passage from the Moral Philosophy of Alphonsus de Ligouri as follows:

> A Bishop, however poor he may be, cannot appropriate to himself pecuniary fines without the license of the

apostolic see. But he ought to apply them to pious uses. Much less can he apply those fines to anything else than religious uses, which the council of Trent has laid upon the non-resident clergymen who keep concubines. (6, p. 120)

The object of this stinging quotation was to show that, among the Roman clergy, marriage was a greater sin than concubinage, because marriage brought excommunication, while concubinage was fined and winked at. In reply to this, the Bishop insisted that no such doctrine was ever taught by the Catholic Church, and no such passage was ever written by St. Ligouri. The Bishop continued by saying, "I have examined these volumes (pointing to 9 volumes of this author on the stand) from cover to cover and in none of them can be found the infamous charges." (6, p. 120)

The Bishop then requested a classical scholar, who was present, to examine the works of St. Ligouri and find, if possible, the statement in question. The next day, the classical scholar announced to the large and excited audience that he had examined the volumes and found no such passage. Things looked bad for Campbell. It appeared that he would be discredited on this point, and this would affect his credibility on all else. The situation was even more tense for Campbell because he had not taken the quotation directly from Ligouri, but rather from an English synopsis, made by a Mr. Smith of New York. Campbell got in touch with Smith, who told him that he could find the passage in question on page 444 of volume eight. Returning to the debate, Campbell, asked the bishop if he could look at Volume eight. Taking the bishop's own volume he turned to page 444 and found every word that he had quoted. Campbell was vindicated and his prestige was enhanced. (6, p. 120

It is noteworthy that after the debate, Campbell conducted a meeting in which there were forty baptisms. Years after the debate, Bishop Purcell had this to say about Alexander Campbell:

Campbell was decidedly the fairest man in debate I

ever saw, as fair as you can possibly conceive. He never fought for victory, like Dr. Johnson. He seemed to be always fighting for the truth, or what he believed to be the truth. In this he differed from other men. He never misrepresented his case nor that of his opponent; never tried to hide a point; never quibbled. He would have made a very poor lawyer, in the ordinary understanding of the term lawyer. Like his great friend, Henry Clay, he excelled in the clear statement of the case of issue, no dodging with him. He came right out fairly and squarely. (6, pp. 120-121)

BETHANY COLLEGE

In 1840 Campbell founded Bethany College in what was then Virginia and is now West Virginia. He was fifty-two years old. Campbell's own formal education had ended with his freshman year at Glasgow University thirty years previously. He donated ten acres of his farm land for the campus of the college, and through the years contributed liberally of his finances and labor. When Bethany was founded, there was only one state institution of higher learning in Virginia, the University of Virginia, founded twenty years earlier by Thomas Jefferson. Bethany College was granted a charter in 1840 and the first classes met on October 21, 1841. Approximately one hundred and fifty students from nine states and Canada enrolled in the twenty classes of the first year. Classes began at 6:30 a.m. and concluded by 4:30 p.m.

On the first Bethany faculty were W. K. Pendleton, professor of natural philosophy; Robert Richardson, professor of chemistry and related sciences; Charles Steward, professor of Algebra and general mathematics; and A. F. Ross, professor of ancient languages and history. Alexander Campbell became the teacher of philosophy and Christian evidences. Campbell's 6:30 class was a survey of the Bible that began the first term of the year with Genesis and concluded with lectures on the New Testament at the end of the school year.

In addition to his teaching duties, Campbell was selected by the Board of Directors to be the first president of Bethany. He held this position for the next twenty-five years.

Bethany College acquired some of the best talent in the brotherhood to make up its faculty. Students flocked to sit at the feet of the illustrious Alexander Campbell, who also helped the college secure financial aid from his many wealthy friends and acquaintances. Most colleges closed during the Civil War, but Bethany's location among the mountains prevented the war from disrupting its classes. Restorationists who went out from Bethany College were numerous and outstanding. Among them was J. M. Barnes, who would later become a noted evangelist in Alabama. Perhaps the best known graduate of Bethany was J. W. McGarvey. He who was not a Christian upon his arrival at Bethany, but in a short time he was baptized by W. K. Pendleton in the Buffalo River. Another well known graduate of Bethany was Moses E. Lard. He graduated with valedictory honors and went on to serve the church mightily in writing, preaching, and teaching the gospel. In addition, there were many other brethren important to the Restoration who passed through Bethany. James A. Garfield, twentieth president of the United States, was never a Bethany student, but he served on the board of trustees. Bethany College today, unfortunately is controlled by the extremely liberal Disciples of Christ. Although it is separated from the call to return to the "old paths," it continues to operate academically, serving a student body of about 1,200. (2, pp. 249-250)

CAMPBELL - RICE DEBATE

Campbell's fifth and final public discussion was with Nathan L. Rice, a Presbyterian minister. The debate occurred in Lexington, Kentucky, November 15 through December 1, 1843. Henry Clay served as the moderator for the debate. Baptism, creeds, and the Holy Spirit were the prime subjects under consideration. Campbell presented a clear-cut explanation of Acts 2:38. He struck hard at the doctrine of Calvinism. This doctrine had driven Barton Stone out of the Presbyterian church, and Raccoon John Smith out of the Baptist fold. Relative to creeds, Campbell commented, "Creeds are the root of bitterness and apples of discord." (2, p. 73)

Feelings ran high at times and some amusing incidents occurred. Two ladies were in the gallery speaking of the merits of their favorite debater. One stated, "you can easily see that Mr. Rice is by far the most learned man, just see how many books he has on his table, while Mr. Campbell hardly has any." The other lady replied, "But you do not appear to know that the books on Mr. Rice's table were written by Mr. Campbell." Since Campbell and Rice were debating, a few puns had to happen. On one occasion, a Mr. Irvin, a warm friend of Campbell, complained of poor health and remarked that he had not eaten for a number of days. Colonel Speed Smith jokingly remarked, "You have been feeding on camel (Campbell)." "Not so," said the Presbyterian preacher, Mr. Brown, "I believe he has been living on rice (Rice) during those days." "If so," rejoined Colonial Smith, "he has been living on extremely light diet." The debate was published in 1844 in a book of 912 pages. (2, p.74)

PREACHING STYLE

Preaching the gospel was the first love of the talented Alexander Campbell. He spoke extemporaneously, without relying heavily on his outline. Campbell rarely made a gesture, and there was no beating of the pulpit, as he relied upon the power of truth as the means of informing and persuading. Campbell's preaching resulted in obeying the gospel, coming back to the Lord, and others seriously challenged to study their Bibles. He usually turned away from sensational themes, and especially enjoyed preaching on the scheme of redemption and the church. The Scriptures were the final authority with him. The concepts of religious unity preached by the Campbells may be summarized as follows:

1. The Bible is the final court of appeals for God's people and is inspired of God.
2. Congregations which follow the New Testament

pattern will have the same organization, work, and worship.
3. It is unnecessary to trace the church back through the centuries in order to have the true church. It is vital to have the New Testament and to obey its contents.
4. When men follow the New Testament, the New Testament church will come into existence.

TRIP TO GREAT BRITAIN

On May 4, 1847, Campbell set sail for Great Britain. This was the fulfillment of a long held desire to visit his native land, and the positive response to invitations from the church in Great Britain and Ireland to visit them. While in Scotland, England, and Ireland, Campbell preached often to large and receptive audiences. He spent about four months in Europe.

It appears that prior to Campbell's arrival, considerable excitement existed among some of the Congregational churches in Edinburgh and its vicinity in reference to Campbell's religious views. Two influential members had recently left the Morrisonian church at Leith, near Edinburgh, under the care of "Reverend" M. Kennedy, and united with the Disciples in the city. Another church in the city, under "Reverend" Kirk, as well as some of the preachers of the denomination, were disturbed upon the subject of the Reformation. Since Campbell was far above their match, they did not choose at this time to debate him, but rather, they sought to find a way to discredit him so the people would turn against him and would not be interested in hearing his message. Since Campbell was known to be from Virginia and the anti-slavery excitement at this time ran high in Scotland, this seemed to be the ideal point on which they could attack him.

ENTRAPMENT

Three men from the Scotch Anti-slavery Society, a "Reverend"

Kennedy, "Reverend" James Robertson, and a Mr. Hunter, visited Campbell, and without informing him of their purpose of their visit, sought to take him off guard in order to obtain some expression of sentiment from him which they could use against him. Campbell regarded them as friendly visitors and made no attempt to conceal his disapproval of the course of action being taken by the abolitionists in Great Britain and America. They were apparently aware that Alexander Campbell had been a slave owner at one time, but were not interested in the details of that ownership. The following will help us understand Campbell's attitude toward slavery.

"In 1819 he had indeed purchased two young Negro brothers to relieve their owner, a Methodist preacher, from the need to take them south when he was transferred to that territory. He kept both boys until they reached the age of twenty-eight and then gave them their freedom, and the two men, Charlie and Jim Poole, remained his good friends for life, Charlie remaining in his employ until Mr. Campbell's death." (67, p. 130)

In 1832 Campbell had written in the Millennial Harbinger in no uncertain terms what he thought about slavery. "Slavery, that largest and blackest blot upon our national escutcheon, that many-headed monster, that Pandora's box, that bitter root, that blighting and blasting curse under which so fair and so large a portion of our beloved country groans, that deadly gas whose breath pollutes and poisons everything within its influence." (67, p. 129)

As Campbell entrained his insincere guests, he was certainly not in favor of slavery. He had made that emphatic disapproval known more than fifteen years earlier. During his term in the Virginia Constitutional Convention in 1829 Campbell had proposed a plan of gradual emancipation for the Negro that might have prevented the Civil War if it had been adopted. It provided for the setting of any agreed upon date, after which no person born would be considered a slave. (67, p. 129) Perhaps this position was what he had in mind when he told his guests that he did not approve of the methods being used to accomplish the removal of that institution. He further said that the people in Great Britain did not understand the subject as well as the Americans, and that their interference would bring no beneficial results. Having some fragments of truth, these men departed and in a few hours had posted, in public places in Edinburgh, placards having printed upon them in immense letters, "Citizens of Edinburgh, Beware! Beware! The Reverend Alexander Campbell of Virginia, United States of America, has been a slaveholder himself and is still a defender of manstealers!"

The charges were false, but the placards followed him wherever he went to speak. Robertson challenged him to debate but Campbell's schedule did not allow for such then, but he offered to have a written debate. After a great deal more persecution as he was hounded from place to place by these placards, he wrote to the Edinburgh Journal and said that he would consent to devote the time from the twenty-fourth to the twenty-seventh of September to an oral discussion on his position in regard to American slavery with any one whom the Anti-slavery Society might appoint. Or, he was willing to engage in a written discussion any time that would be acceptable to his opponent. He said, "I will in either way meet any gentlemen whom you may select, even Mr. Robertson himself, provided only that he be not that Reverend James Robertson who was publicly censured from the Baptist Church for violating the 5th commandment in reference to his mother, of which I have heard something in Dundee." (30, p. 553)

During this same time period, on September the fourth, a tragedy was occurring back at Alexander's home in Bethany. On that Saturday, his second son, Wycliffe, then eleven years old, had drowned. He had, along with two other boys, gone to the creek to swim in a deep pool below the apron of a mill-dam. The boys were enjoying themselves, diving under a small boat and coming up on the other side of it. They had done this same thing safely numerous times before, but at this time Wycliffe failed to appear. The alarm was immediately sounded, but more than half an hour elapsed before the body was discovered in the water under the apron of the mill-dam. Alexander would not know about the death of his son until his return to America October 19, 1847. (30, p. 556)

CAMPBELL JAILED

On September 6, in the afternoon, Campbell was preparing to continue his lectures that evening. He was looking forward to completing his schedule of several appointments in Ireland. To his shock he was presented with a warrant from the sheriff of Lanark to prevent him from leaving Scotland. Robertson's previous efforts had not stopped Campbell from presenting his message to the people, and he was still further exasperated by Campbell's allusion to him in his letter from Dundee to the newspaper. Based upon the letter, a suit for damages was filed in the amount of five thousand pounds. Since Campbell was about to leave the country, he had now succeeded in obtaining a special warrant, rarely used, and designed to prevent the escape of debtors. (30, pp. 557-558)

The case was heard before one of the sheriffs who decided that it was legal. It was appealed to the high sheriff who judged it to be legal but reduced the amount to two hundred pounds. Campbell's counsel then appealed to the Superior Court of Scotland. It would be ten days before this hearing could take place. Campbell was faced with posting a bond or going to jail. The Christians there offered to post his bail, but Campbell felt it was a matter of principle. He felt he was being persecuted for the sake of preaching the truth. He chose jail. He was attended daily by the disciples there. The cell was without heat and Campbell got sick. After ten days Lord Murray heard the case, declared the warrant illegal and ordered his discharge. (30, pp. 559-560)

Robertson immediately appealed to all the lords in the "Court of Sessions" at the November term. In this court the decision of Lord Murray was confirmed, and the prosecutor ordered Robertson to pay the costs of both sides. Robertson then offered to withdraw his suit for damages if Campbell would pay one-half the costs. This was at once refused, as it was evident that Mr. Robertson would be unable to prove his charge of libel. Campbell later wrote:

> I am aware it will be said I was imprisoned for a libel. But who libeled me from Edinburgh to Baniff? I

libeled no man--I spoke the truth. There were three Reverend James Robertsons in Edinburgh, and one was accused of insulting and abusing his mother. His exclusion from a church for that offense is matter of record in Dundee. I did not specify any one of the three Reverend James Robertsons. Why did only one of them accuse himself of professing to be the man? Why did the other two not find cause for libel. The truth is no libel in Scotland." (30, pp. 552-565)

Outside of the tragic business of Campbell being unfairly jailed, the trip to Great Britain was a success. Several were baptized while Campbell was there and his teaching bore fruit after he left. Upon his return home, Campbell's heart was broken as he learned about the tragic death of his beloved son Wycliffe.

PREACHED TO MEMBERS OF CONGRESS

In May of 1850, Alexander Campbell was in Baltimore giving a series of sermons at the recently erected church building. During the course of the meeting, George E. Tingle of Washington City brought Campbell a pressing invitation from members of both houses of Congress to deliver an address before them on Sunday, June 2, 1850. For a number of years it had been the custom to invite prominent ministers "of all denominations" to preach in the Hall of the House of Representatives. An advertisement was placed in the May 30 Washington Daily Globe announcing:

Divine Services

Bishop Alexander Campbell
of Bethany, Brook County, Virginia, will preach in
the Hall of Representatives
at Eleven O'clock a.m.
on Sunday next, the 2nd of June

At the appointed time, Campbell appeared at the House of Representatives and was introduced to those assembled by Congressman John S. Phelps of Missouri. The hall was crowded to overflowing with representatives of the nation, of both branches of the legislature, members of their families, and many others. He used as his text John 3:17. He spoke for an hour and a half to an audience "as attentive, and apparently as interested and absorbed, as any congregation I have had the honor to address." (6, p. 127)

He was again in the company of political figures when he made a fund raising trip in December of 1857 to raise money to rebuild part of Bethany College after a fire. He first visited the eastern cities, including Washington City. It was here that he was invited to preach at the Baptist Church. President Buchanan with some of his Cabinet and several from both Houses were present. Among the prominent men present was Judge Jeremiah Black, Attorney General in Buchanan's Cabinet. Several years before, Judge Black had been baptized by Campbell. After the sermon had been delivered, President Buchanan invited Mr. and Mrs. Campbell to come to the White House for dinner the following Tuesday night. Along with the Campbells were their daughters, Virginia and Decima. (6, p. 128)

LAST YEARS

On this tour to raise money for Bethany College, Campbell arrived in Nashville April 1, 1858, and stayed in the home of the fine evangelist, Philip S. Fall. This was Campbell's sixth and last visit to Nashville. Alexander was rapidly entering the sunset of life. He had accomplished so much for the kingdom. The Restoration for which he had been pleading since he was a young man had experienced amazing growth. However, for one who had always been strong and vigorous, it must have been quite sobering to realize that his own health was now declining. Because the rebuilding of the college and the completion of the endowment still demanding additional funds, Campbell continued to travel and address the public in various parts of the country on behalf of the school. (6, p. 128)

The sudden decrease in the enrollment at Bethany and the departure of some of the faculty members threatened to close the school. Campbell began to rely heavily on W. K. Pendleton and others to do the work that he had previously done. In 1862, owing to a scarcity of paper, the Harbinger was reduced from sixty to forty pages per issue. More and more, Pendleton was assuming the editorial responsibility of the Harbinger. By 1865 W. K. Pendleton had taken complete control of the paper.

For the last two years of Campbell's life, his strength decreased, but he was ever cheerful, ever happy and knew what was approaching. He preached his final sermon at Bethany in 1866. His topic that day was "The Spiritual Blessings in Christ." Those who heard this sermon said that it was vigorously presented. He was an elder in the Bethany congregation at the time of his passing. He passed away on Sunday, March 4, 1866, at seventy-seven years of age. It is believed that Alexander Campbell died of pneumonia after getting wet while out on his farm. (2, p. 50) The funeral service was conducted by Robert Richardson. C. L. Loos led the prayer. The burial took place in the Campbells' family cemetery across the road from the Campbell home. Later, a tombstone was erected on which were carved the following words:

> In Memoriam
> Alexander Campbell
> Defender of the Faith
> Once Delivered to the Saints
> Founder of
> Bethany College
> Who being dead yet speaketh
> By his numerous writings
> And holy example
> Born in the County of Antrim, Ireland
> September 12, 1788
> Died at Bethany, Virginia
> March 4, 1866

TRIBUTES TO CAMPBELL

Many fine tributes to Alexander Campbell could be cited, both from within and without the church, but perhaps J.M. Powell said what was really important about the man when he wrote, "No person ever had more reverence for the Bible as the Word of God and more respect for its authority than Alexander Campbell. No person ever studied this book more and lived daily by its precepts." (6, p. 133)

Lyman Beecher, father of Henry Ward Beecher, was intrigued with Campbell's vast and ready knowledge, and his expert use of it in his speeches. He asked Campbell how he possessed himself of such stores of methodized knowledge. Campbell replied, "by studying sixteen hours per day." These habits he maintained through life. But the secret of his triumphant success was his familiarity with the Bible, not only in the English language but in French, Latin, Greek, and Hebrew. In his early twenties, Campbell could quote from memory most of the Psalms, Ecclesiastes, Proverbs, Song of Solomon, and much of the Law, and Prophetic books. In the New Testament he memorized the four gospels, Matthew, Mark, Luke, and John, not only in English but in Greek as well. The reputation of Alexander Campbell was without spot or blemish. His bitterest enemies failed to find a flaw in his character for truth, integrity and genuine goodness. (6, p. 134)

CHAPTER 11
RACCOON JOHN SMITH

Without a doubt, John Smith was one of the most unique characters of the Restoration Movement. The undignified name of "Raccoon" was no more peculiar than the man who wore it. Although he was quite humorous by nature, his life had more than its share of tragedy. He lacked formal education, and yet he was brilliant. He was noble, and he was certainly courageous.

John Smith was born October 15, 1784 in what later became Sullivan County, East Tennessee. He was four years older than Alexander Campbell. His parents, George and Rebecca, were members of the Baptist Church and were strong believers in Calvinism. This included the Calvinistic view that no one could know that he was saved until a mysterious call came from the Holy Spirit assuring him of his election.

In 1795 the Smith family moved over to Kentucky in search of cheap land, settling in Stockton's Valley. John was eleven years old at the time. He began to reach out to God, but Calvinism in its radical form was the only religion that he could find. The Baptist preacher where John's parents attended gave John the following Calvinistic view of salvation:

The sinner is utterly dead, so that he could not obey

God if he would; and utterly depraved also, so that he would not obey if he could; that he could not please God without faith; nor have faith till it pleased God to give it; that though he might acknowledge it, he could never truly feel his desperate wickedness till the Holy Spirit should show him how vile and wretched a thing he was. (2, p. 108)

Stockton's Valley was thinly populated and did not have nearby stores from which supplies could be purchased. When John was only twelve years old his father sent him to get seed corn for planting his crop. The place where the seed was to be purchased was 100 miles away. He swam swollen streams and faced other difficulties, but he was successful in purchasing the seed and in returning safely back home again. Smith's father worked hard on the farm all week long and sat in the log cabin on Sundays and read aloud to his family from the Bible. It was in the atmosphere of hard work and sincere religious beliefs that young John grew up.

LOOKING FOR A SIGN

When John Smith was fourteen years old, a Baptist preacher by the name of Isaac Denton moved into Stockton's Valley and organized a Baptist Church near the source of Clear Fork Creek. Denton made a strong impression on young Smith. Denton was committed to orthodox Calvinism with full acceptance of its predestination provision, the need for a sign of salvation, as well as other non-biblical peculiarities that John accepted early on, but which would later cause him great anguish. John attended the church services at Clear Fork Baptist Church and spent a considerable amount of time with Isaac Denton, even working with him in his corn field.

Young Smith waited for some special sign or call to let him know that he was saved, but such did not come. He studied the Scriptures and went through depths of despair, agonizing over his lost condition. After praying fervently and experiencing intense emotional struggles, he chose to go before the Baptist Church in

December of 1804 and relate these struggles as his experience. His hope was this would be considered as a sign of salvation by the church. After John related his experience, the moderator made the following request of the assembly: "All who believe that the experience just related is a work of grace, hold up their right hand." (50, p. 65) He was voted into the Baptist Church and the next day he was immersed in Clear Fork by Isaac Denton. Denton encouraged him to preach. John was quite religious but felt no call to preach.

SEEKS AN EDUCATION

It was about 1805 that John Smith purchased two hundred acres in Horse Hollow, in Wayne County, Kentucky. The purchase price was $50.00. His farm was close enough to the thriving frontier village of Parmleysville where necessary purchases could be made without traveling such great distances as he had known as a boy. The only improvement on the land was an unfinished cabin.

Soon after buying his Horse Hollow farm, John's attention was called back to Stockton's Valley because a teacher by the name of Robert Ferrill was there. John became his student at age twenty-one. He walked almost four miles to school each day. Disappointment soon came when the school closed and Ferrill returned to making wagon wheels full time. But Ferrill was so impressed with John Smith's desire to learn that he invited him to come and live with him and engage in independent study in his library. John moved into Ferrill's shop with the understanding that the wheelwright would permit him to earn his support. So, John worked either in the field or in the wheel shop during the day, and at night he studied by the light of a fireplace. (50, pp. 78-79)

Five years after John began studying by the fire light in Robert Ferrill's shop, fifty miles northwest of Stocton's Valley in a cabin much like his own Horse Hollow structure, Abraham Lincoln was born. As a youth, he likewise struggled in the field or split rails during the daylight hours and studied by the light of the fireplace at night. (50, p. 70)

RETURN TO THE LITTLE SOUTH FORK

John felt that remaining too long with Robert Ferrill would be taking advantage of his kindness and hospitality, so he determined to return to the area of the Little South Fork. When John arrived he chose to live for a time with his brother.

John's Baptist neighbors frequently met in one another's cabins for periods of singing and praying. In the absence of an ordained preacher, someone with the ability to speak would usually "exhort" them. John developed his ability to lead in prayer as well as singing, but at first he was reluctant to exhort at these meetings. However, at the encouragement of his friends he eventually agreed to do so. John spent much time in preparation, but his first effort was most embarrassing to him. At the appropriate time John rose to his feet to speak, but he was so frightened that he could not remember a thing that he had prepared to say. On an impulse he rushed out the door into the night and promptly tripped and fell. When he managed to get up, to his delight, his memory had returned to him and he returned to the group and delivered his speech. (50, pp. 80-81)

MARRIES ANNE TOWNSEND

It was at one of these combination social-religious meetings that John's attention was drawn to a young girl named Anne Townsend. It wasn't long before John approached her father and asked if he could offer a proposal of marriage to Anne. The date was December 9, 1806 when the two were married. They moved into John's unfinished cabin that had a dirt floor and no chinking between the logs. Assisted by his bride, John soon made their crude little house to be on a par with the cabins of most of their neighbors who lived along the Little South Fork. (50, p. 82)

ORDAINED AS A BAPTIST PREACHER

By the time of his marriage to Anne Townsend, John had been placed in a position of religious leadership by his neighbors. Even though he was busy with his farm, he was also active in attending the prayer meetings. John knew that his brethren would soon be insisting that he be an ordained preacher. By this time the desire to be a preacher was there, but John was troubled because the "call from above" had not come, and he had no assurance that it ever would. According to the teaching among the Baptists, a special sign was required to indicate that the Lord had called him to preach.

On one occasion John walked very close to a rattlesnake that did not strike him. He wondered if this might possibly be that call. Again, his narrow escape from a vicious bull was interpreted as possibly the extraordinary message from on high for which he sought. John's waiting for the omen to preach was as elusive for him as his conversion experience had been four years earlier in Stockton's Valley.

Even in the absence of John's capacity to relate a clear, identifiable miraculous call to preach, his fellow Baptists continued to insist upon his ordination. John eventually yielded to their wishes. In May of 1808 he took an examination for his ordination to preach. (50, p. 83)

The elders of the Stockton's Valley Baptist Association came to Parmleysville to preside over the ordination. Smith was asked if he were well acquainted with the Philadelphia Confession of Faith. He replied that he was. He was then asked if he adopted the articles set forth therein. He replied that he did. And with that done, John Smith, at twenty-four years of age was ordained as a full-fledged Baptist preacher.

A CALVINIST

As one would expect, John preached the Calvinistic doctrine of the day. All who had been of influence in John's religious life held Calvinistic ideas. The Calvinists taught that all men, without exception, were born in sin, and of themselves, they could do nothing to please God. They insisted that God predestined a definite number to eternal life, even before the world began. The elect would know of their election by the direct call of the Holy Spirit. It was further taught that the elect could never fall from the grace of God. Finally, it was maintained that non-elect infants would be left to perish in their corruption and in their guilt that was passed on to them.

John would later learn that "Whosoever will may come," and that God is no respecter of persons relative to who may be saved. He would learn that a man must make a faith response to the grace of God. (Gal. 5:6) He would learn that a loving obedience to the gospel of Christ resulted in salvation. (Heb. 5:8-9; Matt. 7:21; Acts 2:38) All this would come later in John Smith's life as a preacher, but at this time he was just another Baptist preacher declaring a doctrine that originated in the mind of John Calvin.

BETHEL BAPTIST CHURCH FORMED

Before long John persuaded his brethren in Parmleysville that there was a need for an organized Baptist church in their community. This became a reality in July of 1810. There were nine members who constituted the new Bethel Baptist Church. It is interesting to note that Anne Townsend Smith is not listed among the membership. Four years after her marriage to John, it is likely that she was still unable to relate an experience to the Calvinists as evidence that she was among the elect.

As much as he might have desired to intervene in her religious struggles, the doctrine of Calvinism prohibited John from interfering in such a private matter as the waiting of an apprehensive soul for the Holy Spirit to instill faith within the heart of one of the elect. These were difficult times for the young couple. (50, p. 85)

Approximately two months after the formal organization of the church, twenty-six year old John Smith became its minister. His brother Philip Smith was chosen as deacon and clerk. John was full of desire and zeal as he studied his Bible and preached to many congregations beyond the Little South Fork where the Bethel church was located.

Smith had a great respect for the Bible as well as the creed book of the Baptists, the Philadelphia Confession of Faith. Little did he realize that a decade later he would experience painful conflicts because of their incompatibility. His profound respect for the Bible was what ultimately led him away from this man-made creed and into the movement to restore the church of the New Testament.

MOVE TO ALABAMA

John Smith met Jeremiah Vardeman, a three hundred pound, fiddle playing Baptist preacher on one of his extended preaching efforts away from the Little South Fork. Vardeman was perhaps the most popular Baptist preacher in Kentucky. He took an interest in Smith, realizing his potential. He urged Smith to seek an area where he would be of greater usefulness to the church.

Smith first moved into the Blue Grass region of Kentucky. However, he was not satisfied there and in 1814 chose to move on to Huntsville, Alabama. One of the reasons that Smith moved into this area was to obtain land and prepare for the support of his family.

> Because Baptists in Virginia had been victims of the despised practice of supporting the clergy by taxation, and had observed the consequences of such an ecclesiastical system, they were essentially opposed to monetary support for preachers. In fact, many of the preachers were repulsed at the thought of accepting money for the proclamation of the mercy and grace of God. John Smith conscientiously shared their sentiments. Indeed, such a practice was among the reasons that had encouraged his beloved father and mother to depart the Old Dominion. (50, p. 91)

Before moving his family, John Smith first traveled to Alabama to explore the area where he planned to move. What he had heard about available land was true. In the northeast section of Alabama was land for sale at a reasonable price. This was land that had previously been under the control of the Indians.

He returned home to get his family and make the move. Making the move with John was his wife and four children, Elvira and Eli, who were five and seven years old respectively, two-year old Jennie and four-month old Zerelda. Anne's younger brother and sister also accompanied the Smiths to assist with the move and setting up housekeeping.

With money in his pocket from the sale of his Horse Hollow farm, it was John's intention to purchase land at the price of $1.25 per acre. The Smiths arrived November 2, 1814 at Hickory Flats, approximately one hundred and fifty miles from Parmleysville. (50, pp. 95-96)

TRAGEDY STRIKES

Approximately two months after arriving at Hickory Flats, John was invited to go fifteen or twenty miles away to preach in an area where some friends of the Smith family had relocated. While Smith was away preaching, his wife Anne had left the cabin to care for a sick neighbor not a great distance away. She had taken the baby with her and left the three remaining children in the care of her brother Hiram Townsend and her younger sister. Suddenly, the cabin caught on fire and quickly burned to the ground. Two of the children were burned alive.

When the sad news reached Smith the next day that two of his children had perished in the fire, he returned home as quickly as possible. As he hurried back John worried about how he could console his wife. The Calvinistic doctrine which he held and preached offered him no comfort whatsoever, but only doubt and uncertainty. He reasoned that if he told Anne that their children were saved, the thought that they might not be among the elect would only bring her greater agony. He tried to convince himself that non-elect persons do not die in infancy. After all, he reasoned, they have not had opportunity to receive the revealing experience. Whatever the case, he could not bring himself to believe that his innocent children were suffering the torments of the eternally damned.

Upon arriving home John beheld the reality of the horrible tragedy. Sympathizing neighbors stood silently while others quietly gathered from the ashes what remained of the bodies of Eli and Elvira. Anne, sitting nearby on a log with little Zerelda Ann, caressed the infant to her bosom, while the two-year old Jennie sobbed at her side. At length, John and she walked alone into the woods to share their darkest hour. (50, p. 98)

TRAGEDY UPON TRAGEDY

Anne could not be comforted over the loss of her children. As the days passed she sank lower and lower into depression. She never came out of it. Finally, she died and was buried beside her two children. In such a short time most of what John Smith held dear in this life had been snatched from him. Not only had he lost his wife and two children, but most of the money from the sale of his Horse Hollow farm had also burned in the fire. (50, pp. 99-100)

Shortly after Smith buried his wife, he became seriously ill with what was diagnosed in that day as "the cold plague." From April until July his chances of recovery were not good. However, due to the care of a compassionate neighbor, John was returned to his health. His health had been restored but he now found himself financially destitute.

All that remained of his earthly possessions was his team and wagon that had brought them on their journey, along with one cow. He could not locate the remaining forty-nine cows and the hogs that he had driven from Kentucky. With the help of neighbors he prepared to return to the Little South Fork in Kentucky. He sold the one remaining cow and gave the proceeds to the doctor who had treated him during his illness. Leaving his daughters Jennie and Zerelda in the care of friends, he turned northward and left behind the worst nightmare of his life. (50, p. 100)

THE CRAB ORCHARD MEETING

While John was traveling back to Kentucky his thoughts returned time and again to his innocent children who had perished in the fire. The doctrine of Calvinism, which included the doctrine of infant damnation, became more and more inconsistent with what he knew of the Scriptures. When John Smith arrived in Kentucky he went to Stockton's Valley where he visited his seventy-four year old mother.

He then went on to the region of the Little South Fork and to his brother William's house in Parmleysville. It was here that he found a letter from Jeremiah Vardeman waiting for him. In the letter Vardeman informed him that he was aware of his misfortunes in Alabama and that a contribution had been made for his benefit by the churches of the Elkhorn Association. Vardeman further advised John to attend the annual meeting of the Tate's Creek Baptist Association which was in session during that very month at Crab Orchard, Kentucky. In addition to receiving the contribution, Vardeman said that he would have the good fortune of being in the presence of many well known preachers. The year was 1815.

> The type of meeting at Crab Orchard to which Vardeman had invited Smith was a common occurrence on the Kentucky frontier. From very early in their history, Baptists made it a practice to group into associations their church which were located within certain geographic boundaries. It was the practice of the associations to have one general meeting per year to which each church sent representatives or "messengers." After a moderator and clerk were chosen, any business, which pertained to particular churches or to the association in general was transacted. (50, p. 106)

So, in August of 1815, the Tate's Creek Baptist Association convened for its annual meeting at Crab Orchard, Kentucky. Due to the large crowd, the building was filled and hundreds were outside milling around. When it came time to conduct the business of the association it was impossible to do so because of the crowd. Jacob Creath, Sr., a highly respected Baptist preacher, made a special plea to have someone engage the crowd outside by preaching to them. In this way a smaller number inside could go ahead with the business matters. Large numbers generally attended these meetings. They usually lasted from Saturday through Monday, and it was not uncommon for members of entire families to be in attendance. Many would be camped out on the grounds.

On this particular occasion, Thomas Hansford, the Baptist preacher at Crab Orchard, Kentucky, was assisting with necessary arrangements. Hansford began searching through the crowd in an attempt to find someone to preach to the large number of people who were in the vicinity of the building. A familiar person dressed in a pair of homespun cotton trousers, loose, and far too short, caught his attention. The man wore a cotton coat, which was once checked with blue and white, but was now of indistinguishable colors. On his head was a shapeless hat that was streaked with perspiration and dust. Upon his shoes hung socks that were too large for his shrunken ankles. He wore a shirt that was coarse, dirty and unbuttoned at the neck. He wore no tie because the only one he owned had been placed into the coffin of his wife whom he had buried approximately five months earlier. Hansford immediately recognized the man as being John Smith. Smith was asked by Hansford to preach. Smith was at first reluctant, perhaps sensitive about his appearance. Eventually, he mounted the speakers' stand that had been constructed in a nearby grove.

Preceding John Smith had been two young preachers who had attempted to preach, but they apparently had expected the Lord to give them some miraculous message. Having failed, they commented, "If the Lord will not give it to me, brethren, then I cannot get it." The disappointed crowd began to disperse as Smith arose and timidly approached the speaker's stand. Observing that some special means would be necessary to convince the crowd to reassemble, Smith began by saying, "Stay, friends, and hear what the great Augustine said." Detecting that he had begun to gain the attention of the crowd, he continued. "Augustine wished three things before he died. He wished to see Rome in her glory and purity, Paul on Mar's Hill, and Jesus in the flesh." (2, p. 118)

His novel approach got the attention of a few who chose to be seated, but the majority smiled and continued to walk away. Smith increased his volume and cried, "Will you not stay and hear what the great Cato said?" Many now were curious enough to take their seats, perhaps anticipating being entertained. (2, p. 118)

"Cato repented of three things before his death. First, he repented that he had ever spent an idle day; secondly, that he had ever gone on a voyage by water when he might have made the same journey by land; and thirdly, that he had ever told the secrets of his bosom to a woman." Observing that the original crowd was now reassembling, to gain the attention of groups standing in the distance, with all the strength he could muster, he continued, "Come friends, and hear what the great Thales thanked the gods for." (2, p. 118)

With all seated and listening with much anticipation, he related that "Thales thanked the gods for three things: first, that he was endowed with reason and was not a brute; secondly, that he was a Greek and not a Barbarian; and thirdly, that he was a man and not a woman." (50, p. 108)

Now that he had their attention he said, "And now, friends, I know you are ready to ask: 'And pray, sir, who are you? What have you to say for yourself?' I am John Smith, from Stockton's Valley. In more recent years, I have lived in Wayne County, among the rocks and hills of the Cumberland. Down there, saltpeter caves abound and raccoons make their homes. On that wild frontier we never had good schools, nor many books; consequently, I stand before you today a man without an education." (50, pp. 108) One of the listeners left the audience to tell Jacob Creath, Sr., about this man, begging him to come and hear him preach. He described him as the "fellow with the striped coat on, that was raised among the 'coons. Come and hear him preach. His name is Smith." Since he was raised among the raccoons of Stockton's Valley and in Wayne County, Smith soon acquired the epitaph of "Raccoon." Everett Donaldson suggests that this nickname was not widely used until several years later. (50, p. 256)

Smith's theme on that day was "Redemption." The hearers were thrilled with the strange speaker. His voice was deep and strong, carrying to the most distant listener in the audience. People crowded closer to hear him, some even climbing trees to be able to see him better. When Smith concluded, there was no question but what he had a great impact on his listeners. The crowd gave a loud "Amen" and then rushed forward to thank John Smith for his great lesson. (2, p. 119) The meeting at Crab Orchard together with the encouragement of so many friends gave Smith a renewed interest in carrying on with his preaching.

MARRIES NANCY HURT

About 1821 friends of Smith encouraged him to consider marrying again. They suggested that he was spending so much time preaching that he was failing to care for his children. For some time, John had known a fine religious woman named Nancy Hurt. Before leaving for a preaching tour in Kentucky, John told Nancy that they would discuss marriage when he returned. When he returned they not only discussed it, but they agreed to be married. The ceremony was performed in a simple wedding December 23, 1821.

"I AM IN THE DARK"

Meanwhile, as Smith continued preaching and studying his Bible, serious questions began to be raised in his mind about the Baptist doctrine that he was preaching. There was something wrong somewhere in that teaching that did not match the teachings of the Scriptures, but he did not know where.

In March, 1822, he was preaching at Spencer's Creek, Kentucky, urging sinners to repent and believe the gospel. Suddenly he became confused. He reasoned to himself, "Suppose the elect did not believe, would they be saved? Suppose the non-elect did believe, would they be saved?" He closed his sermon abruptly by saying,

"Brethren, something is wrong--I am in the dark, we are all in the dark; but how to lead you to the light, or to find the way myself, before God, I know not." (1, p. 246)

MEETS ALEXANDER CAMPBELL

While Smith was pondering the subject of salvation and of Calvinism's teaching, Alexander Campbell of Bethany, Virginia, began publishing the Christian Baptist. Smith, though lacking a formal education, had raised himself by his extraordinary natural abilities. He possessed a big heart and a keen mind, along with a quickness and clearness of insight. He had a retentive memory and a sense of humor.

Even though he had adopted the Calvinism held by the Baptists, he had a consuming ambition to know the truth of God. Smith, because of sickness, could not attend the McCalla debate, but at the suggestion of a friend he subscribed to the Christian Baptist. Smith hardly knew what to think about the things discussed in the paper. They were quite different from what he and other Baptists were preaching.

Campbell's reputation had grown widely as a result of the debates with Walker and McCalla. Although many Baptist preachers looked upon him with contempt, Smith withheld judging Campbell with the same harshness. He studied his Bible and continued to consume the articles by Campbell. Meanwhile, news came that Campbell was going to visit Flemingsburg and Mt. Sterling in Smith's part of Kentucky. As an act of courtesy, Smith proposed that a delegation of Baptist preachers meet Campbell and accompany him on his preaching tour. The other preachers turned him down so Smith went alone.

The year was 1824. John Smith rode horseback to Flemingsburg, a distance of twenty miles, to hear Campbell preach. He arrived in Flemingsburg ahead of Campbell and spoke to William Vaughn, a Baptist preacher, about Alexander Campbell. He asked Vaughn if he had heard Campbell preach. Vaughn answered that he had. Smith then asked him if Campbell was a Calvinist, an

Armenian, an Aryan or a Trinitarian. Vaughn replied that Campbell had nothing to do with any of these things. When Smith inquired if Campbell knew anything about Christian experience, Vaughn replied that he knew everything about it.

Raccoon John Smith was introduced to Alexander Campbell prior to Campbell preaching. The meeting house where Campbell was scheduled to speak was too small to accommodate the crowd, so they met outside under the trees. At the proper time, Campbell arose to speak on the subject of the allegory of Sarah and Hagar found in the fourth chapter of Galatians.

When Campbell finished preaching the audience was dismissed. Smith complained to Bill Vaughn, "Is it not hard, Brother Billy, to ride 20 miles, as I have done, just to hear a man preach 30 minutes?" Vaughn replied, "Look at your watch, Brother John, it has surely been longer than that." Smith looked at his watch, and to their surprise, found that Campbell had spoken for 2 hours and 30 minutes. Smith held up his watch and remarked, "I have never been more deceived. Two hours of my life are gone. I know not how, though wide awake." (6, p.110)

After Flemingsburg, Smith escorted Campbell back to Mt. Sterling, Kentucky, where Campbell was scheduled to preach. On the way Smith asked Campbell to relate his religious experience. No doubt Smith was referring to the Calvinistic practice that required all the elect to receive some experience that assured them of their salvation. Campbell said his experience was simply reading the Scriptures, believing what he read, repenting of his sins and being immersed for the remission of sins.

He learned from Campbell the necessity of depending upon the Word of God rather than feelings as a guide in matters of faith and life. For several days Smith accompanied Campbell from place to place, listening intently to every sermon, and earnestly engaging him in conversation as they traveled.

BEGINS TO THROW OFF CALVINISM

During the months that followed, Smith continued to read

articles from the Christian Baptist, comparing them to the Bible. He was sure there was something wrong with his own teachings, but he was not yet completely sure that Campbell was correct. A major step for Smith was when he was finally convinced in his own mind that human creeds were wrong. By 1825 he was asking the churches for whom he preached to reject them.

As Smith thought and studied more about Calvinism, he could see it as a great evil in the doctrine of Kentucky Baptists. He then began to urge people to become Christians by believing upon Christ as the Son of God, and by obeying Him in baptism. In taking this position as the Biblical way to accept Christ, Smith was turning squarely against his early teachings. Smith had to turn his back on the influence and desires of his aged mother, in addition to his old friend, Isaac Denton, and a host of other friends in the Baptist Church. This was very unpleasant for Smith, but he could not preach a thing that he conscientiously believed to be wrong, nor could he refrain from opposing something that he thought was standing in the way of the salvation of numerous souls. He was fully convinced that this was exactly was Calvinism was doing.

At last it became clear to Smith what his course of action must be. He would throw off the shackles of Calvinism completely. He would turn to the gospel in all of its simplicity, and he would preach that gospel to the best of his ability. By 1826 Smith had joined other gospel preachers of Kentucky who were proclaiming a return to the New Testament church.

When the North District Association of Baptists held their annual meeting at Cane Spring on the fourth day of July, 1827, Smith went, expecting the Association to take action against him. A letter was read before the Association, directed at Smith, although not calling him by name. It charged that "certain ones" were guilty of the following "heresies:"

1. That, while it is the custom of Baptists to use as the Word of God the King James translation, he had on two or three occasions in public, and often privately in his family, read from Alexander

Campbell's translation.
2. That while it is the custom in the ceremony of baptism to pronounce, "I baptize you," he, on the contrary, is in the habit of saying, "immerse you."
3. That in administering the Lord's Supper, while it is the custom to break the loaf into bits, small enough to be readily taken into the mouth, yet he leaves the bread in large pieces, teaching that each communicant shall break it for himself. (58, p. 225)

When Smith heard these charges he, without waiting to be identified as the "guilty" party, jumped up and cried, "I plead guilty to them all." After bitter debating and wrangling over the charges, the Association finally voted to delay bringing up any charges against Smith until the meeting in 1828. Smith's replies had gained for him the sympathies of the people while securing the dislike of the Baptist preachers. When the association met in July of 1828, Smith was uncertain what would take place. As it turned out, the messengers to the meeting favored Smith, and therefore the charges were not mentioned on the floor of the Association. The messengers from the five congregations which Smith had established turned the scale in his favor. In 1830 this association divided. Ten churches voluntarily withdrew and formed a new association which was consistent with Baptist doctrine. The North District Association met for the last time as an advisory council in 1831 and was dissolved one year later. (58, p. 225)

Smith left the Baptists, but he found himself with plenty of company. Jacob Creath, Jr., Jacob Creath, Sr., and John T. Johnson also had left the Baptists to plead for a return to the apostolic order. Together with him they received their "anathema" from the Baptists, and like him they counted it a joy to suffer for the name of Christ and the cause of truth. Together with him they planted the seed of the kingdom over the state of Kentucky. They saw hundreds immersed and witnessed the establishment of many congregations throughout the state.

SMITH WAS UNIQUE

Smith was a unique individual. Alexander Campbell said of him, "John Smith is the only man that I ever knew who would have been spoiled by a college education." (49, p. 18) He was one of the greatest and most influential preachers of the Restoration Movement. He devoted himself faithfully to the preaching of the gospel, and his labors were not in vain. He was able to convince entire congregations of the Baptist Church to turn away from their creeds and theories and accept the Bible way of doing things.

Smith had a down-to-earth way of making his points with his audiences. On one occasion he was contrasting the different theories in religion with the gospel. He said that the gospel had this mark that was peculiar to it: "Whosoever does not believe it shall be condemned. This could not be said of any of the theories of man."

On another occasion, after he had shown the absurdities of the mourner's bench theory of getting religion, he was asked "What is the difference between your baptism for the remission of sins and our mourner's bench?" He replied, "One is from heaven and the other is from the saw mill." (6, p. 111)

John Smith was multi-talented. His brain was strong and clear, his common sense was remarkable, and his memory was excellent. He had a keen wit and a sense of humor that probably came from his Irish mother. One time he wrote to his wife and said, "Nancy, I have baptized 600 sinners, and capsized 1500 Baptists." (2, p. 115)

Nancy cared for the children and the farm while John was out preaching the gospel. Once he stopped at the gate of their house in passing and without dismounting, called to her and said as he handed her his saddlebags, "Nancy, I have been immersing all week. Will you take these clothes and bring me some clean ones right away, for I must hurry on." Nancy replied, "Mr. Smith, is it not time you were having your washing done elsewhere? We have attended to your washing for a long time." John answered, "No, Nancy, I am much pleased with your way of doing things, and I don't wish to make a change." And with that John was off. (2, p. 115)

In his ministry, Smith often used witticisms to illustrate a point. He was never without an answer no matter how unexpected the occasion. Once he baptized several members of a certain family. Afterward, he met the father of that family. He had always been a close personal friend of the man. "Good morning, my brother" said Smith to him kindly. But the old man fixed a scornful look upon him and said, "Don't call me brother, sir. I would rather claim kin with the devil himself." "Go then," Smith said, "and honor your father." (2, pp. 122-123)

Then there is the incident when Smith tried to baptize a Methodist preacher. Smith was conducting a meeting at Slate Creek, Kentucky. A Methodist preacher was in a meeting across town. Smith attended a service by the side of the creek when the Methodist preacher sprinkled water on a screaming infant and called it baptism. When "Raccoon" had a baptism in the same creek the next day, the Methodist preacher was standing nearby on the bank. After the baptismal ceremony, Smith got out of the water and approached the Methodist preacher and began to pull him toward the creek. The Methodist demanded to know what he was doing. "I'm going to baptize you, sir," replied Smith. "But, I do not wish to be baptized." Smith asked, "Do you not believe?" "Certainly, I do," the Methodist stated. "Then, come along, sir. Believers must be baptized." "But, I'm not willing to go. It certainly would do me no good to be baptized against my will." John Smith then stated, "Did you not but yesterday baptize a helpless babe against its will? Did you get its consent first, sir? Come along with me, for you must be baptized." But the man protested and Smith released him. Smith then told the preacher to go his way, and he told the audience on the creek bank, "Let me know if he ever again baptizes others without their full consent, for you yourselves have heard him declare that such a baptism cannot do any good." (2, p. 122)

SUCCESS IN PREACHING THE PURE GOSPEL

The success of John Smith's ministry was truly amazing. The "Reformers," as some called those associated with Campbell, were virtually swamped with new converts from the Baptist churches and associations in regions where John Smith and other Restoration preachers with the same message were active. They responded to the new presentation of the "ancient gospel." Smith's three churches, where he preached on a regular basis, Mt. Sterling, Spencer's Creek, and Grassy Lick in the North District Association of Kentucky, had 302 baptisms during the years 1827 to 1828. He had also evangelized in other communities. The twenty-four churches of the association reported 900 baptisms for that year, mostly by Smith "after the ancient practice." He had organized five new congregations "on the Bible alone" which had joined the Restoration.

No wonder that the orthodox Baptists who had filed charges against Smith just the year before in 1827 did not care to bring it to a vote in 1828. There were large numbers in agreement with Smith's desire to restore the preaching of the primitive gospel. It was this same year, 1828, that the Christian Baptist reported that Jeremiah Vardeman of Kentucky had immersed about 550 persons from November 1 to May 1.

Raccoon John Smith from February 1 to April 20, 1828 immersed 300. From 1827 to 1829 Smith is estimated to have baptized 1400 people. The combined efforts of Walter Scott, Sidney Rigdon, and Adamson Bently in Ohio reported 800 baptisms within a six month period.

To get away from the flood of John Smith's "Campbellite" converts, as the Baptists called them, ten churches of the North District Baptist Association withdrew and formed a new purely Baptist association. The remaining majority, now composed wholly of Reformers, met once more and then dissolved, as the Mahoning Association had done previously. Tate's Creek Association in Kentucky followed the example of Redstone Association, in that an orthodox minority excommunicated a reforming majority, when ten churches that remained soundly Baptist excluded sixteen that followed the teachings of Campbell.

THE UNITY MEETING

One of the highlights of Smith's life was his participation in the unity meetings with the Campbell and Stone groups in December of 1831 and January of 1832. It was then that he delivered his famous plea for the unity of the two restoration groups:

> "Let us then, my brethren, be no longer Campbellites or Stoneites, New Lights, or Old Lights, or any other kind of lights, but let us all come to the Bible and to the Bible alone, as the only Book in the world that can give us all the light we need." (6, p. 59)

Smith was further honored by being chosen along with John Rogers to spread the message of unity to the scattered congregations of "Christians" and "Reformers," encouraging them to take part in the merger.

MORE TRAGEDY FOR THE SMITHS

It was 1814 when John Smith lost two of his children in a cabin fire near Huntsville, Alabama. His wife, with a broken heart, died shortly thereafter. John lost another child in a tragic accident in 1843. It was November and John was away from home attending the Alexander Campbell - Nathan Rice debate in Lexington, Kentucky. It was "hog killing" time back home. Part of the process was to prepare a vat of scalding water into which the slain hogs were dipped. Tragically, John's eight year old son fell into the vat. He suffered excruciating pain before he died. The boy passed away before John arrived home. (49, p. 5)

THE NAME "RACCOON"

Distinguishing one John Smith from another has been a challenge for every generation. Thus, it has been suggested that the

"Raccoon" was necessary for this reason. However, "Raccoon" was not commonly used during Smith's lifetime. Rather, "John Smith of Horse Hollow" or "John Smith of Wayne County" was sufficient for the people close to Smith's home. "John Smith of Montgomery" was apparently the most used name to identify Smith, and the one that he most preferred. He was also called "Elder John Smith."

Smith apparently came to accept the tag "Raccoon," but never to appreciate it. The "Raccoon" name originated in 1815 when Smith spoke at the annual meeting of the Tate's Creek Baptist Association at Crab Orchard, Kentucky. An attempt to properly identify himself as being "from where the raccoons make their home" appears to have been the beginning of his name being prefaced by "Raccoon." (50, p. 255)

Smith charged that Jacob Creath, Sr. and John Davis, a Baptist preacher who lived in Crab Orchard, were responsible for the nickname which he did not prefer. Smith held Philip Fall responsible for publicizing what he referred to as his "ugly name." Fall had used the name "Raccoon John Smith" in advertising a Smith meeting in Frankfort, the state capital of Kentucky. Smith related that the legislature was in session at the time and that all but four representatives from across the state had come to hear him preach. He contended that after the legislators were exposed to the "Raccoon" nickname, they went back and spread the name across the state. (50, p. 255)

A GREAT SOLDIER OF CHRIST PASSES AWAY

John's beloved wife, Nancy Hurt Smith passed away in 1861 at age seventy. John lived seven years beyond his wife. Although Smith had palsy for the last twenty years of his life, he was in reasonably good health until a few days prior to his passing. One biographer of John Smith, John Augustus Williams, said of him when he was eighty years old:

He is generally and justly regarded, by those who

have been acquainted with him, as one of the most remarkable men which the religious controversies of the present century have brought before the public, in the state of Tennessee. (50, p. 256)

Oliver Taylor wrote of Smith:

He was tried by the severest tests of time; he was scourged by a living death, but with a masterful courage and unwavering devotion to the call of duty he arose to a rank that made him a power throughout great portions of Kentucky, Tennessee and the Middle West... Along with Shelby, Clay and Boone, Smith has left an imperishable impress upon the State of Kentucky. (50, p. 257)

M. C. Tiers wrote of Smith as he was at age eighty, four years before his death:

The trembling veteran of the Cross exhibits, to a marvelous degree, the active and powerful mentality of his earlier years. A thousand pleasing memories cluster around the name of John Smith in the hearts and homes of the multitudes who have listened with rapture to his words of truth, being made glad in the consciousness of pardoning favor of God. (50, p.257)

At age eighty, in 1865, Smith made his last visit to Montgomery County where he preached at his old congregation at Upper Spencer Creek. (A small congregation of the church of Christ meets in the old building to this date.)

Smith preached his last sermon on February 9, 1868, less than a month before his death at the age of eighty-three. This was in Mexico, Missouri. Afterward, he walked back to his daughter's house in the cold. He became very ill and was in his bed for three weeks before passing away on February 28, 1868. Three days before he died he sent word by W. J. Mason to Elder Wright, editor of the Christian Pioneer saying, "Tell Brother Wright 'I am better, and almost home.'"

Nearing the end, Smith had his loved ones gather around him. He told his daughters that he had only one regret, that his sons-in-law were not Christians. He requested that they sing a song entitled, "Since I can Read My Title Clear to Mansions in the Skies." He told those gathered around him, "My prospects are entirely satisfactory. I have no fears, whatsoever about the future. I am nearly home. What a great failure after all, would my long and checkered life have been, but for this glorious hope of a hereafter."

Approximately at 8:30 p.m., February 28, 1868, he died. His body was sent to Lexington, Kentucky, from Missouri by train and was met by a committee of brethren who carried it to the church building for the funeral. The service was conducted by J. W. McGarvey and brothers Graham and Elley. Smith was buried beside his faithful wife Nancy, among other restoration leaders in the cemetery at Lexington, Kentucky. The grave marker reads:

> In memory of John Smith, an elder of the church of Christ. Born October 15th, 1784. Died February 28, 1868. True, genial, and pious, the good loved, and all respected him. Strong through affliction and wise by the study of the Word, he gave up the creed of his fathers for the sake of the Word. By its power, he turned many form error; in its light he walked, and in its consolations he triumphantly died. In all his sacrifices his companion was precious in his sight. Nancy Smith was born November 15th, 1792. Died November 4, 1861.

CHAPTER 12
WALTER SCOTT
1796 -1861

POSITION AMONG THE LEADERS

J.J. Haley lists the "Big Four of the Reformation" as Thomas Campbell, Alexander Campbell, Barton W. Stone, and Walter Scott. "The last named is fourth in enumeration, but by no means fourth in distinctive importance. In originality, enthusiasm, courage, boldness and eloquence, he comes near heading the list. He was not the initiator  or representative of any organized movement within the church like his three illustrious comrades, but so far as the distinctiveness of his contribution to the New Movement was concerned, he stands first in historical and theological importance." (6,p. 141) Each of the big four did much to formulate the principles of the Restoration Movement, but it was Walter Scott who gave it popular appeal.

Dabney Phillips said that Alexander Campbell provided the intellectual direction of the Restoration, but it was Walter Scott who provided the evangelistic fervor. Scott successfully built on the sturdy foundation laid down by the Campbells. (2, p. 131) Robert Richardson, Campbell's biographer, stated, "Among the helpers and fellow laborers of Alexander Campbell, the first place must be awarded to Walter Scott. Scott made the apostles his model, and went before the world with the same message, in the same order, with the same conditions and promises." (2, p. 131)

Walter Scott, a distant relative of the poet of the same name, was born October 31, 1796 in Moffat, Dumfrieshire, Scotland, about thirty miles from Edinburgh. His parents were John and Mary Scott, strict Presbyterians. Both parents wanted him to be a Presbyterian minister, and it was Walter's desire to fulfill the wishes of his parents. He was the sixth of their ten children. Scott completed his education at Edinburgh University. While at Edinburgh he lived with his aunt. He was a good student and showed great musical talent in learning to play the flute, even giving concerts in Edinburgh.

William Baxter reported that Scott's father died suddenly while he was away in the neighboring town of Annan. The year was 1821. The shock was so great to Scott's mother that on hearing the news, she died immediately. Both of his parents were buried at the same time in the same grave. (32, p. 30)

MOVE TO AMERICA

Scott's uncle, George Innes, had earlier come to America where he was making a successful living. He urged Scott to come to America, offering to help him find employment. In July of 1818, 26 year old Scott arrived in New York from Scotland. He immediately found employment as a teacher of English, Greek, and Latin in a classical academy on Long Island. However, the tug of the West was strong and, at the urging of friends, Scott decided to go West. He was in New York for less than a year. (33, p. 20) He and a friend walked the 300 miles from Long Island, New York to Pittsburgh, Pennsylvania in four weeks, arriving May 7, 1819.

INFLUENCE OF GEORGE FORRESTER

Shortly after arriving in Pittsburgh, Scott became a teacher in a boy's academy. George Forrester, the school's headmaster had been a Presbyterian, but had broken with them and had become the leader of a small independent Haldanean church. The Haldane brothers had established several congregations in Scotland and Ireland, but there were very few such groups in America. Consistent with the teachings of the Haldanes, this group also believed that the Bible should be the only guide in all religious matters. (33, p. 21)

To their credit the Pittsburgh group practiced baptism by immersion. However, they went to the extreme of practicing the "holy kiss" and foot washing. The community called them the "Kissing Baptists." Scott was impressed with Forester's knowledge of the Bible and decided to study the Bible with him. He soon realized that infant baptism was not the baptism of the New Testament. After a study of his Greek New Testament, Scott requested Forester to immerse him. A short time after his baptism Scott was filling the pulpit for Forester. Tragically, George Forrester's life was cut short by a drowning accident in the river. Scott was placed in charge of the academy.

Scott remained in Pittsburgh for several years as head of the academy and as minister of the congregation for which Forrester had preached. This period was used by Scott for intensive study of the Bible as well as the writings of many who were recognized as great religious writers. This study was greatly enhanced by the use of an excellent library left behind by Forrester. In Scott's The Messiahship, or Great Demonstration, he lists many of the books contained in the library:

> He left behind him also an excellent library containing many volumes on Holy Scripture, as Benson on the Epistles, McKnight's Harmony of the Gospels, Catchebull's Notes, Haldane's Works, Campbell on the Four Gospels, Locke's Reasonableness of Christianity, McKnight on the Epistles, Carson's Works with those of Wardlaw, Glass, Sandeman, Letters published by Eld. Errett, New York, and many other valuable treatises, which with Bishop Newcome's Harmony of the Gospels, Towers, Warburton and Newton, made the author acquainted with the advance steps of the modern reformers -- Carson, Warlaw, Haldane, Glass, and Sandeman, all

of whose efforts were merely ecclesiastical. (33, p. 21, 22)

BAPTISM FOR THE REMISSION OF SINS

In 1821, Scott read a pamphlet "On Baptism" which taught that baptism was for the remission of sin. It had been written by Henry Errett of New York. (The son of Henry Errett would later establish and edit the "Christian Standard," a journal that was very influential in espousing the liberal views of the brethren who digressed and accepted the innovations such as American Christian Missionary Society and instrumental music in worship.)

Walter Scott desired to visit Henry Errett and the "Scotch Baptists" in New York. This was a group associated with the Sandemanians. He sold his Pittsburgh academy and returned to New York. He spent three months there, then made brief visits to Baltimore and Washington, and finally walked back to Pittsburgh. Upon his return to Pittsburgh, Scott was taken in by Nathaniel Richardson, who hired Scott to teach his son Robert. Richardson provided space for Scott to begin an academy which eventually grew to an enrollment of 140 boys. Robert Richardson was Scott's most famous pupil.

MARRIED THREE TIMES

Walter Scott was married three times. He first married Sarah Witsett on January 3, 1823. They had five children and their home life was characterized by spiritual values and family devotions. The Walter Scott home was poor in this world's goods, and it was often made poorer by Scott's generosity. On one occasion they owned two cows but seeing that his neighbor had none, Scott gave him the best one. The children complained only because he gave away the cow with the bell. On another occasion, Alexander Campbell gave Scott a five dollar gold piece after hearing him preach. Afterward, as they rode together they passed a beggar. Scott promptly gave the beggar his five dollar gold piece. Campbell said, "Are you aware of the denomination of that piece of money you gave the beggar?" "No, no, was it the coin you gave me in church?" "Yes," said Campbell, "and it was a five dollar gold piece."

Sarah died in 1849. The next year Scott married Annie B. Allen of Mayslick, Kentucky, who met an untimely death in 1854. They had one child. Scott then married a rich widow, Eliza Sandige, of Mason County, Kentucky. This was an unhappy union, as Scott knew little about money and often gave away what money he had. Eliza, who was difficult to get along with, frequently would drive Scott out of the house. Unhappily, he spent more than one night sitting on a neighbor's porch.

MEETS ALEXANDER CAMPBELL

It was in the winter of 1821-1822 that Walter Scott met Alexander Campbell. It was in the home of Nathaniel Richardson. Scott was twenty-six and Alexander was thirty-four. A friendship was formed that lasted through life. J. M. Powell said that they were made for each other. Each complimented the life of the other. He said that without Scott, Campbell would never have become the great man that history knows. Without Campbell, Scott would never have accomplished the great things that are so well known to students of the Restoration Movement. In many ways they were alike, both of Scottish decent, both intellectual giants, and both were very spiritual. They were also alike in their belief that first century Christianity could be reproduced in any generation by using the New Testament as a blueprint. They were not alike in personality. Campbell was always cheerful, but Scott was given to periods of depression. When Campbell spoke, he was always great, but Scott's efforts were not always consistent. When he was in one of his depressed moods and tried to preach he disappointed his audience. Campbell was fearless, self-reliant and firm, but Scott was at times timid and yielding. While Campbell was calm and steady, Scott was excitable.

CONTRIBUTIONS TO THE RESTORATION

In appreciating Walter Scott, one needs only to look at the contributions he made to the Restoration. Scott was the first to popularize the expression "Gospel Plan of Salvation." In his evangelistic meetings on the Western Reserve, Scott introduced the custom of extending the gospel invitation at the conclusion of each sermon--inviting and admonishing people to come to Christ upon the terms set forth in the New Testament. It was Scott who emphasized the fact that the creed of the first century church was "Christ." The word creed is derived from the Latin word "credo" which means "I believe." The creed of the early church was Christ himself. Belief in Him as the Son of the living God and as a personal Savior was the one and only item of faith essential to baptism.

In the exercise of his analytical mind, Walter Scott soon discovered that the testimonies of Matthew, Mark, Luke, and John were written for one great specific purpose, and that was to prove the proposition that "Jesus is the Christ, the Son of God," and that this constituted the central truth and the great essential element of Christianity. It was Scott's idea that Christianity could be summarized in four words: "Jesus Christ, God's Son." This he referred to as the "golden oracle." This became the subject of countless sermons by Scott. Probably as a result of this, Scott himself was called by many admirers as "The Golden Oracle."

Scott emphasized in his preaching that baptism was for the remission of sins. The idea came to him with great force in 1821 after he read Henry Errett's pamphlet on baptism. In the same year, Alexander Campbell also had access to this information. It was some time later, however, before either Scott or Campbell publicly proclaimed this Biblical doctrine. Campbell gave brief mention of it in his debate with William McCalla in 1823, but his position was firmly stated for all to see in an "Extra" of the Millennial Harbinger of July 5, 1830. This issue was centered around an article on baptism titled "Remission of Sins." Scott articulated the plan of salvation clearly and simply so that all could understand. He was, as far as we know, the first to point out that the Gospel has facts to be believed, commands to be obeyed, and promises to be enjoyed. He referred to the primary facts of the gospel as the death, burial, and resurrection of Christ.

MAHONING ASSOCIATION EVANGELIST

In 1826 Scott moved to Steubenville, Ohio. Shortly after that, on August 25, 1826 he attended the annual meeting of the Mahoning Association as a guest and was invited to preach. This was done even though Scott was not a Baptist. However, at this time the Mahoning Association was moving in the direction of restoring the New Testament church. The next year Alexander Campbell urged Scott to go with him to the annual meeting of the Mahoning Association. Scott was reluctant to go because he was not a regular Baptist and he did not want to impose on their hospitality.

The Mahoning Association in 1827 listed seventeen churches. There were fourteen represented at the meeting. The reports for the year were not encouraging. There had been a total of thirty-four baptisms and thirteen additions. Thirteen had been excommunicated. The net gain was sixteen, and this at a time when the population was doubling and redoubling. Wellsburg and Hiram, the two churches that had gone farthest in "reform" had done better than average. Between them they had twenty of the thirty-four baptisms and only one of the thirteen excommunications. The Association decided that it needed an evangelist to labor among the churches. It appointed a committee to find the man. The committee nominated Walter Scott, and the Association elected him. He was to work for whatever the churches pleased to contribute to his support. Scott accepted the appointment even though he was not a member of the Mahoning Baptist Association, not a Baptist, not a member of any church in the town where they lived, not a resident of the district in which the Mahoning churches were located. In fact, he was not even an ordained minister. Nevertheless, this proved to be an excellent appointment, not for the Baptists, but for the advancement

201

of the Restoration.

Alexander Campbell had heard in advance form Jacob Osborne that the Association would probably appoint an evangelist at the meeting. Campbell knew the views of Scott were similar to those that he held. Without a doubt he wanted Scott to be appointed to that position. Campbell said that the "Mahoning Association at that time was almost to the man, on the side of going forward to the ancient and primitive order of things." (2, p. 83) Scott could work within the Association in preaching the ancient gospel to those congregations and at the same time establish new congregations dedicated to the pattern of the New Testament Church. With the appointment of Walter Scott, the Restoration Movement was at last underway in the sense of presenting the gospel plan of salvation to large numbers of people.

EVANGELISTIC WORK IN WESTERN RESERVE

Scott's assigned area was the Western Reserve. He began his work on November 18, 1827, in New Lisbon, Western Reserve, Ohio. He found that the Baptist meeting house where he was to preach was filled to capacity. He mounted the pulpit and took as his theme the confession of Peter as recorded in Matthew 16:16. In his sermon he proceeded to show that the foundation truth of Christianity was the divine nature of Jesus, and that belief was designed to produce love in the hearts of those who believed it. This would then lead them to true obedience to Christ. In this connection Scott quoted the great commission, and called attention to the fact that Jesus had taught his apostles "that repentance and remission of sins should be preached in his name among all nations, beginning at Jerusalem" (Luke 24:47). He then verbally led his hearers back to Jerusalem, back to the day of Pentecost. He called upon them to listen to an authoritative announcement of the Law of Christ, now to be made known for the first time, by the Apostle Peter.

After a graphic view of Peter's sermon, Scott pointed out its effects on those who heard him, showing that they, being cut to their hearts, cried out in agony, "men and brethren, what shall we do?" The inspired answer came in these words, "Repent and be baptized, every one of you, in the name of Jesus Christ, for the remission of your sins, and ye shall receive the gift of the Holy Spirit." Then in his matchless style, Scott made the application. He insisted that the conditions were unchanged and that the Word of God meant what it said. He declared that to receive and obey it was to obey God and to imitate the example of those who, under the preaching of the apostles, gladly accepted the gospel message.

WILLIAM AMEND RESPONDS

When Scott was drawing to the conclusion of his sermon, he noticed a stranger enter the door. As it turned out this man was a highly respected citizen and a devout elder in the Presbyterian church. He was a diligent student of the Scriptures, and had long been convinced that the Savior's command to convert the world was not now obeyed as it was preached by the apostles. He often spoke to his wife about the matter saying, "When I find any person preaching, as did the apostle Peter in the second chapter of Acts, I shall offer myself for obedience and go with him." (6, p. 154) The name of this Presbyterian elder was William Amend, and just as he entered the building, Scott was pleading with the people to "Repent and be baptized every one of you in the name of Jesus Christ for the remission of our sins, and you shall receive the gift of the Holy Spirit." Amend kept on walking until he got to where Scott was standing. He made the good confession and, along with others, was baptized for the remission of his sins.

Several years after this incident, Scott wrote a letter to Amend in regard to his conversion. In a few days Scott received this reply:

> Now, my brother, I will answer your questions. I was baptized on the 18th of November, 1827, and I will relate to you the circumstances which occurred a few days before that date. I had read the second Chapter of Acts when I expressed myself to my wife

as follows: "Oh, this is the gospel: This is the thing we wish, the remission of our sins. Oh, that I could hear the gospel in those same words as Peter preached it. I hope I shall someday hear, and the first man I meet who will preach the gospel thus, with him I will go." So, my brother, on the day you saw me come into the meeting house, my heart was open to receive the Word of God, and when you cried, "The Scripture shall not longer be a sealed Book, God means what he says. Is there any man present, who will take God at his word and be baptized for the remission of sins?"--at that moment my feelings were such that I would have cried out "Glory to God!" I have found the man whom I have long sought for. So, I entered the kingdom, when I readily laid hold of the hope set before me. (signed William Amend) (6, pp. 154-155)

Scott wrote back to Amend and in it we see the importance which Scott placed on that day and that beginning:

The above letter is a very simple document, but on the occasion to which it relates, there certainly was resolved, not by words merely, but deeds also, questions the most interesting and important. The Rubicon was passed, and the Church of God on that day, had restored to it, publicly and practically, the ancient gospel, and a manner of handling it, which ought never to have been lost by the servants of Jesus Christ. (6, p. 155)

Scott continued by saying:

Permit me through this medium to acknowledge, publicly, my obligations to our beloved and justly esteemed brother Alexander Campbell, who, being the first to move for my appointment, which resulted in the restoration of the ancient gospel. May Almighty God bless him through Jesus. (6, p. 155)

FIVE FINGER METHOD OF PREACHING

The movement to restore the church of the New Testament did not take hold with any marked degree of success until the thirty year old Walter Scott began his simple method of preaching on the Western Reserve. The five-finger method of preaching the gospel plan of salvation took hold at once. The results were staggering. It was the common practice of Scott to illustrate the five items -- faith, repentance, baptism, remission of sins, and the gift of the Holy Spirit -- by holding up his left hand and using his thumb for Faith, and so on. He then would contrast it with the five points of Calvinism. This made the gospel plan of salvation so plain that little boys could carry it home. There was great excitement wherever he went. Such a change as took place on the Western Reserve, the northeast section of Ohio, under the preaching of Scott has seldom, if ever, been equaled. The Bible was read with new interest as the living Word of God and not a dead letter. The Mahoning became a second Jordan, and Scott another John the Baptist, calling on the people to repent and be baptized for the remission of their sins.

Scott liked to ride into a village near the close of the day and speak to the children returning home from school. As the children gathered around him, he would say, "Children, hold up your left hands." As they held up their left hand he would say, "Now, beginning with your thumb repeat after me: faith, repentance, baptism, remission of sins, gift of the Holy Spirit -- that takes up all your fingers. Now again, faith, repentance, baptism, remission of sins, Gift of the Holy Spirit. Now again, faster altogether." He would go over the five items rapidly and in unison. He then would say, "Children, now run home -- don't forget what is on your fingers, and tell your parents that a man will present the gospel tonight at the school house, as you have it on your hand." Away went the children repeating as they went. Soon the story would be repeated in every house of the village, and long before the hour of meeting, the house would be filled, the children sitting on the front seats. When Scott arose to preach he would hold up his left hand and the children would follow him eagerly as he presented his sermon. People were invited and urged to become Christians upon the terms of the gospel. Ordinarily, there were many responses with baptisms every day. (6, p. 156)

SIX EVILS AND SIX CURES

The plan of salvation as set forth by Scott had wide acceptance among the people. According to this plan, God and man cooperate in the process of salvation. Scott liked to preach that before God can do anything for man, man must first recognize six existing evils and their cures.

The six evils are: 1. Love of sin; 2. Practice of sin; 3. State of sin; 4. Guilt of sin; 5. Power of sin; and 6. Eternal consequences of sin. The six corresponding cures are: 1. Faith, which cures the love of sin; 2. Repentance, which cures the practice of sin; 3. Baptism, which cures the state of sin; 4. Forgiveness, which cures the guilt of sin; 5. The Gift of the Holy Spirit, which destroys the power of sin; and 6. Everlasting Life, which is the escape from the eternal consequence of sin. (6, p. 156)

Walter Scott was not admired by all. He, in fact, was considered by many as the enemy of their particular sect.

> It is no wonder the avowed purpose of what was now recognized as a new 'Movement' led by Walter Scott, soon became suspect. His innocent-sounding plea for all Christians to unite on his simple plan of salvation, had within it the seeds of heresy. He was out to expose the errors of the denominations, to eliminate their creeds, to make an onslaught on every established church. A skeptical observer of the period writes: 'A shrewd follower of Campbell comes to a certain village where these errors are unknown. He

at first calls himself a Baptist, and no one suspects the contrary. He professes great liberality of sentiment toward other denominations, preaches to please all, and appears full of zest. After a while he announces that on such a day he will preach a sermon on Christian Union. At the appointed time he portrays in glaring colors the evils of sectarianism, and traces it all to creeds and confessions. He then purposes a plan in which all can unite. (67, p. 41)

GREAT SUCCESS

It was not long before the "Plan of Salvation" was being preached with phenomenal success, not only on the Western Reserve, but throughout Ohio, Pennsylvania, Indiana, and Kentucky. In one year, Scott baptized more than 1,000 people. Talented men such as John Secrest, John Henry, A.S. Hayden, Adamson Bentley, William Hayden, and many others were baptizing hundreds of people. In Kentucky, "Raccoon" John Smith baptized 1,400 during the years 1827-1829. In six months Jeremiah Vardeman baptized 550. This is just a sample of what was going on in the Restoration Movement in those great years.

In 1828 the Mahoning Association came together in Warren, Ohio, and excitement was in the air. New converts had been numerous, and prospects were indeed bright. J. M. Powell points out, "This time the Association came together purely and simply as an assembly of Christians. Though under the form and name of a Baptist Association, the creed system was abandoned, and neither that denominational name, nor any other, was on its standards." (6, p. 157) It was unanimously agreed by the Mahoning Association to re-appoint Walter Scott as the Association evangelist for the following year.

HAYDEN ACCOMPANIED SCOTT

Scott chose William Hayden as his fellow evangelist. Hayden

developed into one of the most effective preachers in the Restoration Movement. His ministry of thirty-five years saw him traveling 90,000 miles in preaching the gospel. A full 60,000 of those miles was on horseback, a distance of more than twice around the world. The baptisms by his own hands were 1,207. He preached over 9,000 sermons, averaging more than 261 per year during his public life. The year 1829 was very fruitful for Scott and Hayden. Wherever they went large audiences assembled and hundreds obeyed the gospel and were baptized into Christ.

MAHONING ASSOCIATION DISSOLVED

In 1830 the Mahoning Association met for the last time as an authoritative body. This took place in Austintown, Ohio. John Henry who had entered into the ranks of the Restoration stood up and moved "that Mahoning Association, as an advisory council, or an ecclesiastical tribunal, should cease to exist." This was in accordance with the general feeling, but Alexander was at the point of rising to oppose the motion when Scott, sitting nearby, placed his hand on the shoulder of Campbell and asked him not to oppose the motion. The motion passed unanimously. This action at Austintown may be regarded as the formal separation of the Reformers from the Baptists.

EDITOR, WRITER, ADMINISTRATOR, EVANGELIST

In December of 1831, Walter Scott moved his family to Cincinnati, Ohio. He began editing and publishing a periodical called The Evangelist which continued for a number of years. In a short time he moved to Carthage, eight miles from Cincinnati, where he lived and labored for thirteen years. Here he started a congregation which had a membership of 104 by 1835.

In 1836, Scott wrote The Gospel Restored, a systematic view of Christianity. Moses Lard later told Scott that it was this book that first taught him the gospel. In 1857 Scott completed his greatest work, the three hundred and eighty-four page book, The Messiahship or the Demonstration. Campbell styled the book as "interesting, edifying, cheering, and a fascinating volume." Isaac Errett said, "Immense labor has been bestowed upon it by one of the best minds God has given us. It sparks and shines all over the peculiar genius of the author." Dr. Robert Richardson, Campbell's biographer, thought it was a highlight of Restoration literature.

Scott's talents were recognized in several areas. He served as the first president of Bacon College in Georgetown, Kentucky, which was the first Restoration college in Kentucky. The governor of Ohio appointed him to the Board of Trustees of Miami University in Oxford, Ohio. But, it is as a preacher that Scott is best remembered. He had a very analytical way. In one series that lasted for twenty-one months he preached twice a week on the gospel of Matthew alone.

Scott could be extremely effective when he was at his best. It was in 1830 that Scott was preaching in Virginia. "He was on his favorite theme before a great audience in a grove near Wheeling, Virginia, and Mr. Campbell was among the hearers. His distinguished hearer, usually calm and self-composed, on this occasion was aroused; his eyes flashed, his face glowed, and his emotions became so intense that he shouted, 'Glory to God in the highest!'" (54, p. 29) Thomas Campbell said of Scott, "We have learned how to fish, but Scott catches the fish." His preaching touched off an epidemic of Bible reading. Converts carried New Testaments with them everywhere, reading and memorizing them constantly. Those who were outside the Movement began to call them "walking Bibles." (34, p. 7)

William Girrard said of Scott,

> In his life and thought, Walter Scott reflected the central concerns of the Reformation of the nineteenth century. One could well look upon him as the mirror of a movement and of the times in which he lived. But at the same time he left his mark on the movement as a pivotal figure. Walter Scott's writings were read by preachers in his own generation and in succeeding ones. His theology was influential in

helping shape the style and content of preaching for future generations of Restoration ministers. This is especially true of his method of evangelism and the five-finger exercise... Scott was much sought after as a preacher and evangelist by the congregations of the movement and he was in a remarkable way able to communicate both with preachers and lay persons. (33, pp. 208-209)

A MAN OF INTENSITY

With Scott, there was always a sense of urgency. He rode everywhere at a gallop, holding meetings day and night. "When he spoke his whole face throbbed with earnestness and life. He wasn't kidding around. He shot for the heart and expected results." (34, p. 8) The real secret behind Scott's power lay in the truthfulness and power of his message. He centered his messages around the divinity of Christ and the stories of the Gospels. He felt that the Messiahship of Christ was the greatest truth of all time. He called it the "Golden Oracle." Scott was nicknamed "the voice of the Golden Oracle." (34, p 8) Scott preached to people where they lived. He spoke in schoolhouses, courthouses and barns. He spoke on flatboats and steamboats. In good weather he spoke outdoors in groves or at crossroads, sometimes using a wagon for a pulpit and God's creation to illustrate his message. The creek bank was a powerful pulpit too. Baptismal scenes by moonlight or torch light were not uncommon. During a time of illness and depression, Scott utilized the written word as his pulpit. (34, p. 9)

Scott could be very dramatic in his preaching. One time, when his audience was sleepy, he began to tell a story of how he used to torture frogs as a boy. Soon the entire audience was weeping with sympathy for the frogs. Then he turned on them and said something like, "You weep over a few dead frogs but sleep when I tell you about the crucified Christ." (34, p. 9) Another time he arrived late and sat in the back pew with his hat down over his head. In the candlelight no one noticed him. He listened to the people discuss what kind of preacher this "Scott" fellow could be. Finally he rose up in his seat and quoted Jesus' words, "What went you out into the wilderness to see?" and he preached from the back pew. When Scott could not get people to respond to the invitation, he would sometimes call for his preaching partner, William Hayden to sing to them. He would say, "He will sing you out." If that did not work he might confess his failure and play on their sympathies. (34, p. 10)

Frontier audiences would be very hard on the preachers. They learned to expect trouble and Restoration preachers got more than their share of it. Slander was common. Restoration preachers were called names such as "water salvationists, heretics, 'Scotties,' and 'Campbellites.'" (34, p. 10) One man threatened to shoot Scott if Scott baptized the man's mother. Scott went ahead with it anyhow and later baptized the man who had made the threat. It was not uncommon for members of the audience to stand up during the sermon and challenge the preacher or even threaten his life. Many preachers carried guns or knives to defend themselves. Troublemakers even did their mischief during baptisms. Once a man heckled Scott with a large stick during a baptism. Another time he was threatened with a sword-cane. On another occasion, someone cut off his mare's tail and set the animal lose. Scott bore all this calmly, believing it to be a sure sign that the gospel was performing its intended function. (34, p. 11)

DIES AS CIVIL WAR NEARS

When rumblings of civil war shook the nation, Scott pleaded for preservation of the Union. He was so upset over thoughts of civil war that he could not take Communion for a period. About a week before Walter Scott died he wrote to his son in Pittsburgh:

> The fate of Fort Sumter, which you had not heard of when you wrote--which, indeed, occurred subsequently to the date of your letter--will not have reached you. Alas, for my country! Civil war is now

most certainly inaugurated, and its termination who can foresee? Who can predict? Twice has the state of things filled my eyes with tears this day. Oh, my country! my country! How I love thee! How I deplore thy present misfortunes! (32, p. 445)

In the above letter, no mention was made of Scott being ill. On Monday, April 15, 1861, he was able to visit with friends and was apparently in normal health, although depressed by the war conditions. However, on Tuesday, April 16, he came down with typhoid pneumonia. His illness grew more severe over the next few days. By the following Sunday it was determined to inform his children by telegraph that his condition was critical. The pioneer preacher, John Rogers, happened to be in Mayslick and called upon Scott. Although Scott was very ill, Rogers was able to talk freely with him. (32, p. 445)

John Rogers thought that the end for Scott was near. He asked him, "Brother Scott, is this death?" He replied, "It is very like it." The next question from Rogers was, "Do you fear death?" Scott answered, "Oh! no. I know in whom I have trusted." L. P. Streator visited him several times during his illness, and spoke openly with him in regard to his approaching death. He asked him if he was aware that he was dying. Scott answered, "Yes, and many a true soldier has gone before me over Jordan." On Sunday April 21, 1861, Streator called on Scott and found him much worse, and taking his hand at parting, said, "Brother Scott, you will soon pass over Jordan." (32 p. 446)

Walter Scott then had a period in which he spoke of the joys of the redeemed when they would be ushered into heaven to be in the presence of the patriarchs, prophets, apostles, and martyrs, and the hosts who had been washed in the blood of the Lamb. He then fell into a quiet sleep. He then awakened, recounted the names of a number of the great and good men with whom he had labored. Among them he mentioned Thomas and Alexander Campbell, John T. Johnson, Barton W. Stone, and "Raccoon" John Smith. (32, pp. 446-447)

By Sunday evening Walter was too weak to speak. On Tuesday evening, April 23, 1861, he peacefully fell asleep in Jesus. He was sixty-five years of age. Although his children did not waste time leaving Pittsburgh, once they were notified of their father's condition, they did not arrive until the day following his death. The funeral services were conducted by John Rogers and L. P. Streator. He was buried in Mayslick, Kentucky. (32, p. 447)

CHAPTER 13
GROWTH OF THE CHURCH

CENSUS OF 1860

It is thrilling to see the tremendous growth of the church by the time Walter Scott died in 1861. The U.S. Government took a census in 1860 which listed the size of churches based upon the number of "seatings" in each building. The number of seatings had been determined to be three times the number of members. The census takers did not always have accurate figures on the number of congregations in the brotherhood. Figures had to be updated where there was direct evidence of additional congregations. For example, the correct number of known churches in Kansas was more than three times the number originally found by the census taker.

The following figures come from Garrison & DeGroot. (3, pp. 328-329) They estimate that the total number of disciples in 1860 was 192,323. This figure is probably conservative. The following list is based on the number of New Testament Christians estimated to be in the top twenty-five states:

1. Kentucky   45,000
2. Indiana   25,000
3. Ohio   25,000
4. Missouri   20,000
5. Illinois   15,000
6. Tennessee   12,285

7.	Iowa	10,000
8.	Virginia	8,430
9.	Pennsylvania	4,500
10.	New York	5,000
11.	Texas	2,500
12.	No. Carolina	2,500
13.	Alabama	2,458
14.	Mississippi	2,450
15.	Arkansas	2,257

While we are looking at figures we can also consult the Search for the Ancient Order by Earl West. Brother West picked up estimates from those who wrote to the various brotherhood periodicals of the time. While there were several congregations of Christians associated with Barton W. Stone, very few congregations had been started by those associated with the Campbells down to the year 1827. This would include Brush Run and Wellsburg. The formative years for the "Reformers" were from 1809 to 1827. During this period the Campbells were thinking and re-thinking many issues. In 1823 Campbell started the Christian Baptist and pointed his literary guns toward the denominational clergy and let loose with an unrelenting barrage that shook the denominations as they had never been shaken. Such teaching had a tremendous effect, but it was not strongly evangelistic. Campbell was planting the seed but up to 1827 he saw little evidence of a harvest.

It was the year of 1827 that dramatic changes would take place. Walter Scott went out into the Western Reserve as an evangelist and kept the baptismal waters stirring. Other evangelists caught the fever and began preaching with renewed vigor and the results were amazing. By 1836 D.S. Burnet wrote in the Christian Preacher periodical that the disciples numbered over 100,000. In 1850, fourteen years later, a writer in the Ecclesiastical Reformer reported that the total number of Disciples was over 200,000. (1, p. 129)

In 1851 Alexander Campbell wrote an article in the Harbinger that gave us a good idea of the extent geographically that the gospel had been spread:

> The territory over which the doctrine of the reformation has more or less been diffused, within one quarter of a century, is unprecedented in any age known in history and to me. It is preached or read in books, not only in all the United States, and in all the British provinces of North America, from St. Johns to San Francisco, and from Oregon to the Neuces: it has also been preached or read in England, Scotland, Ireland, Wales, and the Isle of Man. It has crossed the Pacific to Australia and New Zealand, and visited Liberia, on the coast of Africa. At some of these points it has, indeed touched but slightly, but even there, like a little leaven hid in a large measure of meal, it must work, as the Messiah said, until the mass be leavened. (1, p. 129)

Some years after the fact, Isaac Errett reported in the Christian Standard of 1873 that, based on the rate of increase, the disciples were "first in the decade from 1850-1860." Errett said by 1870 it was the fifth largest religious body in the U.S. (1, p. 130)

DIFFICULTY IN DETERMINING EXACT NUMBERS

Determining the exact number of Disciples for this period was difficult. If we take the state of Kentucky we can appreciate the difficulty. In 1844 the Christian Journal reported that there were 50,000 in the state. However, S. M. Scott, who was sent to visit all the congregations in the state in 1845, reported 380 congregations with a membership of 33,830. This figure seems more likely than the 50,000 reported the year before. Based on the U.S. Census five years later, Garrison and DeGroot estimated 45,000. The U.S. Census listed 304 buildings with seating for 104,980. Many Christians were not meeting in church buildings. Scott reported that there

217

were 195 preachers in the state. He also reported that in 1844, 136 congregations had been established in the state. Earl West feels that the figure of 50,000 by 1858 is probably fairly accurate.

NEED FOR MORE TEACHING

The amazing growth of the church, combined with the fact that the emphasis of the early preaching was primarily on first principles, naturally left the church in need of teaching that it was not getting. The lack of qualified preachers and the lack of elders to oversee the congregations was at the heart of the problem. The congregations needed to be taught on many subjects, including the questions, "What is the nature of the church?" "How should the church be organized?" "What are the qualifications for elders and deacons?" Because there was a lack of the proper conception of the church, Tolbert Fanning in his Christian Review undertook to write many articles on "Church Organization." As early as 1845, Fanning wrote of the glorious progress of the cause, yet he paints a darker picture, citing examples to show that in many cases the church was degenerating into a sect. In 1846 Benjamin Franklin came out in the Reformer with the warning that the cause of the Restoration was suffering. He wrote: "Let us, then, brethren make one mighty effort to save the church from corruption, lukewarmness, speculation, and sin of every kind, that it finally may be presented to the Lord, a glorious church, without spot, or wrinkle, or any such thing…" (1, p. 131)

CHAPTER 14
THE AMERICAN CHRISTIAN MISSIONARY SOCIETY

DIVISION COMES

There was a marvelous unity and amazing growth in the Restoration Movement for the first few decades, but this was not to last forever. The seeds of controversy were being sown, and a heartbreaking harvest would soon be reaped. Two opposing attitudes developed toward the Scriptures. One view was that the organization, worship and work of the church was revealed in the New Testament. This position insisted that there must be a positive command or approved example in all these areas. The opposing view maintained that the Scriptures presented a loose framework for activities, and that no specific pattern was required in the worship, organization and work of the church.

These two positions were severely tested in the matter of church societies and instrumental music in the worship. Although there were other areas of tension, the conflict in these two areas raged with intensity.

The early leaders in Virginia and North Carolina, James O'Kelly and Elias Smith, taught that each congregation was autonomous. They believed that societies and associations were contrary to the New Testament. The Springfield Presbytery under the leadership of Barton W. Stone stated that there was "neither precept nor example in the New Testament for such confederacies as modern church sessions, Presbyteries, Synods, General Assemblies, etc." In their Last Will and Testament it was stated, "We will, that our power of making laws for the government of the church and executing them by delegated authority, forever cease." (2, pp. 153-154)

The Brush Run church in 1815 was accepted into the Redstone Baptist Association as an independent congregation. In 1823, the church switched to the Mahoning Baptist Association because the Redstone Association intended to excommunicate Campbell for his teaching. By 1830, Walter Scott had influenced the Mahoning Baptist Association to disband because there was no scriptural authority for it.

CAMPBELL'S EARLY POSITION

In 1823 Alexander Campbell, in the initial copy of the Christian Baptist, launched an attack against organized missionary societies of his day. He did this on the basis that institutions rob the church of glory. Campbell apparently changed his mind later in life about the missionary society, but some of the proponents of the Society such as W.K. Pendleton argued that Campbell did not change. Pendleton said that in the early years Campbell was not condemning societies, but the abuse of them.

Please observe a portion of an article that Campbell wrote which appeared in 1823 in the Christian Baptist. It should be very difficult or even impossible for a reader without bias to reach any other conclusion but that Alexander Campbell opposed societies at the time of that writing. Reflecting on the first century congregations Campbell wrote:

> Their churches were not fractured into missionary societies, bible societies, educational societies: nor did they dream of organizing such in the world. The head of a believing household was not in those days president or manager of a board of foreign missions, his wife, the president of some female educational society: his eldest daughter the corresponding secretary of a mite society: his servant or maid,

the vice-president of a rag society... They knew nothing of the hobbies of modern times, as in the church capacity did they alone move. They neither transformed themselves into any kind of association, nor did they fracture and sever themselves into divers societies... They dare not transfer to a missionary society, or bible society, or educational society, a cent or a prayer, lest in so doing they should rob the church of its glory, and exalt the inventions of men above the wisdom of God...(2, pp. 154-155)

Campbell was not opposed to members of congregations coming together for mutual fellowship and encouragement, but when the assembly assumed the form of an organization for the formation of policies of the congregations composing it, he felt they were inexcusably imitating the Roman Catholic Church. His attitude was made clear in a later article that he wrote and published in the Christian Baptist:

"I have no objection to congregations meeting in hundreds, at stated times, to sing God's praises, and to unite their prayers and exhortations for the social good. However, when a forum is called for the business of the churches, they are a popish calf, or muley, or a hornless stag, or something akin to the grand beast of seven heads and ten horns." (2, p. 155)

CAMPBELL'S POSITION SOFTENED

Even to the casual student of Restoration history, it is very obvious that Campbell opposed the societies in his earlier years. However, in the 1840's the winds of change began to blow. Even the sharp pen of Alexander Campbell softened on the society issue. In the beginning he encouraged cooperative meetings, which were the forerunner of the organizations and societies. Cooperation looked innocent since they left the congregations independent and their resolutions were only recommendations, not laws. The term "cooperation" obviously indicates a working together for some specific purpose.

"The great question among the pioneers was, how and in what manner can the various congregations work together to convert the world? The scope of this question at first limited itself to districts, then to states, and then to the entire brotherhood. Consequently, district cooperation meetings were among the earliest held, but one soon reads of state meetings and then finally of brotherhood attempts at cooperation which were realized in the formation of the American Christian Bible Society and the American Christian Missionary Society, the latter being the greater of the two." (1, p. 151)

A NATIONAL ORGANIZATION ADVOCATED

In 1841 Campbell wrote a series of sixteen articles in the Millennial Harbinger pertaining to Christian organization. He began to insist upon a national organization to expedite gospel preaching. It was Campbell's belief that the educational, benevolent and missionary interest of the Restoration would be taken care of by a national organization. In 1842 Campbell began a series of essays on "Church Organization" which lasted up through 1848. In his first article on this subject he sets forth six arguments for church organization:

1. We can do comparatively nothing in distributing the Bible abroad without cooperation.
2. We can do comparatively but little in the great missionary field of the world either at home or abroad without cooperation.
3. We can do little or nothing to improve and elevate the Christian ministry without cooperation.
4. We can do but little to check, restrain and remove the flood of imposture and fraud committed upon the benevolence of the brethren by

irresponsible, plausible, and deceptious persons, without cooperation.
5. We cannot concentrate the action of the tens of thousands of Israel, in any great Christian effort, but by cooperation.
6. We can have no thorough cooperation without a more ample, extensive, and thorough church organization. (1, pp. 159-160)

THE ISSUE DISCUSSED

In 1843 the matter of cooperation received further attention in the Millennial Harbinger and other church papers. In November of 1843 at the Campbell-Rice debate in Lexington, Kentucky, the subject of cooperation was being now considered so much that few brethren could get together for long without it being discussed. In between sessions several brethren got together and discussed cooperation along with the possibility of forming a missionary society. Earl West notes that Jacob Creath, Sr. "by his tears, his prayers and his arguments" got the brethren to abandon their plan temporarily. (1, p. 161) In October of 1844 a meeting was held at Steubenville, Ohio to exchange views on cooperation. At the conclusion a committee of five was appointed to draft some propositions for a more general meeting at Wellsburg on December 26, 1844. At the Wellsburg meeting the propositions were discussed, but only a few congregations were represented. Another meeting was held at Wellsburg on April 1, 1845.

Campbell made it plain that these meetings were only for the purpose of discussion. "No individual or set of individuals has any authority to dictate to their brethren or enforce upon them any views of rules of action on any subject connected with their spiritual relations to the Lord and to one another." In 1845 Campbell wrote: "Much has been written, and a great deal said, and little done, on the whole subject of Christian organization. But there is a growing interest in the subject manifested, and there is a growing need for a more scriptural and efficient organization and cooperation." (1, p.

162)

The very fact that the cause for greater cooperation, and for organized institutions outside the church, had Alexander Campbell behind it was enough to put it over. Yet, there was some scattered opposition. One of these was T. M. Henley who had in 1836 written in the Millennial Harbinger critical of the trend toward organizations.

The church in Nashville, Tennessee, very early had its own misgivings about these cooperative organizations. A number of brethren met in the church house in January 1842 to discuss cooperation. They studied the Bible as though they had never seen it before. At the end they reached the following conclusions:

1. That there is a positive scriptural authority for every religious work that is well pleasing to God;
2. That the church of Christ is the only divinely consecrated organization on earth for Christian labor; and
3. All other organizations through which men propose to perform spiritual labor tend but to obscure, discredit, and subvert the reign of the Messiah. (1, p. 163)

"Now, as the call for a general convention rang over the land, came a chorus echoing Tolbert Fanning's warning, 'Where is the scriptural authority for such a gathering'? Alexander Campbell had a reply... 'In all things pertaining to public interest, not of Christian faith, piety or morality, the church of Jesus Christ in its aggregate character is left free and unshackled by any apostolic authority.'" (66, p. 121) The position that Campbell advocated with those words was a great disappointment for many who believed that he had greatly softened his once firm stand on the need for authority for the work and organization of the church.

STATE ORGANIZATIONS FORMED

Nevertheless, the way for the American Christian Missionary

Society had its way paved for it by district and state organizations springing up over the nation: (1, pp. 163-164)

1. In 1836 the Illinois State Meeting was held for the first time.
2. In 1839 a Cooperation Meeting was held in Richmond, Virginia, representing twenty-five congregations.
3. In 1839 the churches in Indiana had their first state meeting.
4. In 1842 a convention of South Kentucky churches was organized.
5. In 1842 a convention in Northern Missouri was organized.
6. In 1842 a convention was formed at Warrensville, Ohio.
7. In 1844 one reads of the General Cooperation of Disciples in Virginia.
8. By 1850 the Kentucky State Missionary Society was organized with John T. Johnson as president.

AMERICAN CHRISTIAN MISSIONARY SOCIETY FORMED

Finally, after all the writing and discussing the time arrived. The American Christian Missionary Society was formed in Cincinnati, Ohio in October of 1849. Campbell's frequent essays on church organization between 1841 and 1848 produced their results. The magic name of Campbell behind any idea usually was enough to discourage any opposition from becoming too effective. On the other hand, his name frequently caused some to accept things too quickly without proper consideration. There was opposition to his articles, but he proceeded slowly and knew that he had the bulk of the brotherhood behind him.

So, at the beginning of the year 1849 Campbell was confident that the proper groundwork had been laid for a general organization for cooperation. Campbell felt that the church in the universal sense had the duty of converting the world, and that since Christ had given no divine plan for the church, in this sense, the church was left free to devise its own plan. Critics of the Society saw several weaknesses in Campbell's plan:

1. The Lord did have a plan, and it was through the organization of the local congregation that the gospel would be carried as in the New Testament times.
2. The church universal had but one set of officers - the apostles, and these were the personal ambassadors of Christ sent on a special mission to supervise the work of the church during the infancy of the church.
3. Through the apostles the divine Word was spoken by Christ, and through the apostles Christ established and confirmed his Messiahship.
4. At the close of the apostolic age, when the last apostle had died, the church was known only by the individual congregations scattered over the world.
5. The work of Christ through the church to evangelize the world was carried on through the influence of the local church in its community.
6. Even in apostolic times the churches felt no need for an organization, devised by human planning, through which the church could cooperate to evangelize the world.

THE CONSTITUTION OF THE SOCIETY

When the American Christian Missionary Society met in October of 1849, there were ten states represented by 156 people.

Alexander Campbell was not present, but his views were presented by his son-in-law, W. K. Pendleton. Even though he was absent, he was elected president. In the absence of Campbell, D. S. Burnet presided and helped to draft the constitution of the Society. The convention lasted four days. The constitution contained thirteen articles. Article three, rightly so, soon became a source of controversy immediately:

> The Society shall be composed of annual delegates, Life Members and Life Directors. Any church may appoint a delegate for an annual contribution of $10. Twenty dollars paid at one time shall be requisite to constitute a member for life, and one hundred dollars paid at one time, or a sum which in addition to any previous contribution shall amount to one hundred dollars, shall be required to constitute a director for life. (1, p. 176-177)

Article 4 stated that the officers would consist of a president, twenty vice-presidents, a treasurer, a corresponding secretary, and a recording secretary who would be elected by the members at the annual meeting.

Article 5 also stated that twenty-five managers would be added to the officers and the life directors to form the executive board. It took only seven to make a quorum to do business.

Article 7 gave them wide power and completely took control of the mission work out of the hands of the local congregation. It states that the Society "...shall establish such agencies as the interest of the Society may require, appoint agents and missionaries, fix their compensation, direct and instruct them concerning their particular fields and labors, make all appropriations to be paid out of the Treasury, and present to the Society at each annual meeting a full report of their proceedings during the past year." (1, p. 177)

A WEDGE OF DIVISION

This was a sad time for the Lord's Church. Those who set

out to free themselves of man-made creeds and organizations, who had operated so wonderfully for many years in a spirit of unity, characterized by unprecedented growth, now found themselves a body divided. A wedge had been driven into the church which would ultimately contribute heavily to a complete split in the brotherhood. The American Christian Missionary Society was to become a hotly debated item for many years after its establishment.

FURTHER LOOK AT CAMPBELL'S POSITION

Those who study the Restoration Movement, and the American Christian Missionary Society in particular, are left with questions about the attitude of Alexander Campbell toward the Society. At the time the Society was originally being promoted, it is likely that many failed to speak out on the issue because of their great respect and admiration for Campbell. Had they been able to remove the man from the issue, more open discussions would likely have taken place, perhaps even to the failure of the Society to become a reality. Far too often we ascribe to a man a greatness that should not be his when we should be giving honor to truth and right. Earl West points out this important observation:

> Indeed, it is the danger of the study of the whole restoration movement, for with many there seems to be a fundamental interest in restoring the restoration rather than the New Testament Church. In the restoration movement no authority of any kind is to be found. No man is qualified to intelligently approach the study unless he recognizes that those who played the important roles were just men, and liable to errors. We lose nothing in admitting that at times they were wrong, for there is only one authority -- the New Testament scriptures. (1, p. 181)

The study of the Restoration Movement must be approached, not with the idea of attempting to fit any pioneer leader into a mold, but to study as objectively as possible what he taught. "Where they were wrong, we shall frankly state it; where they were right, we shall gladly uphold it." 1, p. 181 But, those on both sides of the Society issue held Campbell in the highest esteem. It was only natural that each should want to feel that Campbell favored his position.

While it is admitted that Campbell, in the period immediately preceding and following the establishment of the Society, favored this organization, yet, those who opposed the Society felt that Campbell was then in old age and was under the influence of younger men who swayed him in favor of the Society. It was only natural that these younger men should deny this charge, and should stoutly defend Campbell as being in favor of Society.

SEGAR'S STATEMENT

Perhaps the leading champion of the view that Campbell changed his position on the Society was David Lipscomb. For many years, following 1866, Lipscomb was the influential editor of the Gospel Advocate. Lipscomb built this conviction upon two or three facts, the first of which was a statement made by Charles V. Segar. Segar was not a member of the church, but was assigned by W. T. Moore to write the introduction to a book of Campbell's Lectures on the Pentateuch which had been delivered by Campbell at Bethany College in 1859. To get the necessary information, Segar paid a visit to Mrs. Alexander Campbell. After this meeting Segar wrote about the trip Campbell made to Great Britain and the terrible ordeal he had which confined him to jail for a period of 10 days. Segar had the following to say about Campbell:

> The labors and events of this tour, added to the burden of the college, seemed to have materially affected his mind and general health; but the deadliest portion mingled in his cup of baleful care and sorrow was the sad news which awaited his touching the shores of his adopted country. The son of his old age, the child of his prayers and hopes, was no more! Wycliffe Campbell had been drowned at his father's mill. It

is said by those who were near him, that Alexander Campbell never was equal to himself after this stroke; but it was long before the admiring world perceived any change." (1, pp. 182-183)

The closing statement, "It is said by those that were near him, that Alexander Campbell was never equal to himself after this stroke," especially impressed Lipscomb and was often used by him. (1, p. 183)

FANNING'S STATEMENT

Still another fact that helped Lipscomb form the conviction that Campbell had changed was a statement made by Tolbert Fanning a few years after the Society was formed. Lipscomb was then a young man, an admirer of Fanning who had tutored him. Fanning grew distressed at the course Campbell was taking in favor of the Society and made a visit to him at Bethany. Speaking of Fanning's return, Lipscomb years later wrote:

> "I remember him well, on his return he stated that he was shocked to find his (Campbell's) mind so shaken that he could, with difficulty, keep it on one subject; that he could converse in general terms on things he had studied in the past, but that all of close, connected reasoning was gone; that he had to be continually prompted to keep up on an ordinary conversation." (1, p. 183)

In responding to a proponent of the Missionary Society who quoted Campbell's support of it, David Lipscomb replied with a number of quotations from the Christian Baptist to show his early opposition to it and had this to say:

> "...that he afterward worked in Societies we have no disposition to conceal, that in doing it, he violated his

own principles, built again the society he destroyed and destroyed that supreme and undivided respect for the Word of God, and his appointments which he had vindicated is beyond doubt, true. It represents another case, so pregnant in the history of the church, opposing oaths, substituting the appointments of the institution of God, yet doing them himself." (1, p. 183)

Lipscomb goes on to point out that in later years Campbell's mind and will power lost much of their force and that his friends convinced him that these organizations were harmless, so he submitted. Earl West and Dabney Philips both concluded that Campbell had changed.

LEFT NO MONEY TO THE SOCIETY

Although Alexander Campbell was president of the society for more than sixteen years, he never presided over any of its sessions. It is most interesting that in his will of 1862, Campbell did not leave any money to the Missionary Society. He did leave Bethany College $10,000 and his personal library. He left $5,000 in the hands of the Bethany church elders to "send out evangelists to preach the gospel," but he did not leave one cent for the American Christian Missionary Society.

SUMMARY OF ARGUMENTS AGAINST THE SOCIETY

There were four general arguments against the Missionary Society which were presented in earlier years. They remain as arguments against it today:

1. The Missionary Society was a substitute for the church. This argument was strongly made by Tolbert Fanning, Jacob Creath, Jr., Ben Franklin,

and David Lipscomb. .
2. The Society caused division. The Restoration Movement had grown earlier without the society, so why bring in a disturbing element to divide God's people
3. It was felt that the society would, and in fact did, dictate to the congregations. Preachers who were not enthusiastic regarding the organization were frequently snubbed.
4. The Society was actually a poor investment financially. It was alleged that forty percent of the money contributed was funneled off to pay salaries for clerks, secretaries, staff members, and other business matters pertaining to running the organization. This left only sixty percent to be used for the purpose for which the money was contributed.

CREATH AND FANNING SPEAK AGAINST SOCIETY

Jacob Creath, Jr. wrote to Campbell and said, "If you were right in the Christian Baptist, you are wrong now. If you are right now, you were wrong then." Campbell was gracious to give Creath space in the Harbinger to disagree with him. In an 1850 edition, Creath wrote, "You say our Savior and the apostles did not denounce conventions, as such. Did they denounce infant baptism, creed making or auricular confessions, as such? It is for you to show where they authorized conventions." (1, p. 158)

Tolbert Fanning, the leading southern preacher at this time, wrote in the Gospel Advocate, "The church of God is the only divinely authorized missionary, Bible, Sunday School, and temperance society; the only institution in which the Heavenly Father will be honored... and through no other agency can man glorify his Maker. It was wrong for Christians to do the work of the church through human agencies." (1, p. 206) Fanning urged the congregations to cooperate in mission work, rather than give through a human agency.

LIPSCOMB SPEAKS OUT

In the February 7, 1867, issue of the Gospel Advocate, David Lipscomb wrote, "To operate through an institution of man's devising in preference to the church of God, is in our esteem, to exalt man of superior wisdom and power to God. To call in question the efficiency of God's appointments, as the best (we had like to say the only) that can be ordained for the accomplishment of God's designs, is to call in question the power of God." (1, p. 159)

BEN FRANKLIN OPPOSED SOCIETY

Ben Franklin, the editor of the American Christian Review, wrote:

> "The circumstance that they had no missionary societies in the first age of the church, of itself does not prove that we may not have them. But, the fact that the Lord ordained the congregations with their officers, and made it their work to convert the world with the additional fact that we have their example in the sending out preachers, with the circumstances that they had no missionary societies, but the churches, proves that it was wrong for individuals to create missionary societies, separate from the churches, as substitutes to do the work which the Lord appointed for the churches..." (1, p. 160)

None of the pioneer preachers ever opposed true missionary work, but they did oppose unscriptural schemes. The church of the living God is the pillar and support of the truth, and should support it (I Tim. 3:15). A missionary society is not the support of the truth, and has no business trying to support the truth.

OTHER SOCIETIES FOLLOW

After the American Christian Missionary Society was established, numerous other organizations and societies as well as national conventions made their appearance. Among these, but not limited to these, were the following:

1. The Foreign Christian Mission Society, with headquarters in Cincinnati, Ohio.
2. The Benevolent Association of the Christian Church, St. Louis, Missouri.
3. Christian Women's' Board of Missions, Indianapolis, Indiana.
4. Board of Ministerial Relief of the Church of Christ.
5. Board of Church Extensions of the American Christian Missionary Society, Kansas City, Missouri.
6. In 1919 the United Christian Missionary Society was created by the National Convention in Cincinnati which joined all of the above-mentioned into one organization. The United Christian Missionary Society continued until July 1, 1956, when the work was reorganized into three administrative divisions with an executive chairman giving full time to each: (a). Division of World Mission, (b). Division of Home Missions, (c). Christian Education, and Division of General Departments.

DISCIPLES OF CHRIST AND CHRISTIAN CHURCH

On May 18, 1992 by telephone this writer interviewed James Seale of the Disciples Historical Society, Nashville, Tennessee, regarding the Missionary Society. The information in the remainder of this section was based primarily on that interview. Mr. Seale stated that the United Missionary Society is now divided into two major divisions, the Homeland Missionary Society and the Overland Missionary Society. In 1901 the American Christian Education Society was formed but lasted only a few years. In 1910 the Association of Colleges of the Disciples of Christ was formed. In 1914 the Board of Education of Disciples of Christ was formed with twenty-six institutions affiliated with their presidents constituting the board. In 1907 the National Convention voted to have a brotherhood publishing house to be the official paper for the Disciples of Christ. This was the Christian-Evangelist operated by a thirteen man Board of Directors.

In 1927 at the National Convention in Memphis, Tennessee, a more conservative group than the Disciples of Christ walked out of the convention and went across the street and met on their own. They called themselves the North American Convention. The reasons they pulled away in 1927 included the unacceptable organization of mission work, and the acceptance of the liberal wing of the pious un-immersed into the church. Some missionaries in foreign fields were following the same practice and accepting un-baptized individuals. This was apparently acceptable to the United Missionary Society. Mr. Seale observed that the division was over the organization to do mission work, but today the Independent Christian Church has organized a society to handle the mission work. However, he said, they do not call it a society, but a "Missionary Alliance." This is a voluntary organization.

The fellowship between the two groups was determined by individual congregations for several decades following 1927 with no clear cut lines drawn, but eventually a full blown division was to occur. In 1967-68 the Disciples of Christ was "re-structured." It was at this point that the Disciples took the stand that they were no longer a part of the Restoration. They wanted to be recognized as a denomination.

A liberal attitude toward the Scriptures on the part of the Disciples of Christ is seen in the open discussions at the turn of the century and for decades after regarding "higher criticism" of the Scriptures such as the verbal and plenary inspiration of the Scriptures. J. W. McGarvey was recognized as the early leader for the conservative view and Dr. H. L. Willett for the liberal view. The Disciples of liberal leaning favored the acceptance of the un-immersed pious. In 1992, the minister of the Independent Christian Church in San Clemente, California informed me that this was the primary reason for the Independent Christian Church pulling away from the Disciples. The focal point was the Society structure, but the underlying cause was the position that one could be accepted into the church without being baptized. Two of the elders of that particular Christian Church congregation left the Disciples because they could no longer take the ultra-liberal views of the Disciples of Christ.

In the Disciples of Christ today, congregations give whatever amount they choose to mission work on a voluntary basis. They may give in one of two ways: First, they may give to the Basic Mission Finance. This is controlled by a fifteen person board with a specified number on the board being women. The board will direct the money and the work as they choose. Secondly, congregations may elect to direct their funds to a specific mission work.

In 1967 when the decision was made by the Disciples of Christ to restructure the church, the Independent Christian Church sent out letters to all their congregations as well as the Disciples of Christ congregations stating, in effect, if you do not agree with the position of the Disciples of Christ you can get out and become a part of the Independent Christian Churches. Those who wanted to be officially removed from the Disciples of Christ needed to request that their names be removed from the "Yearbook," the official membership roll of the Disciples of Christ. In 1971 the Independent Christian Church asked to be recognized separately from the Disciples in the U.S. Census. The membership today of the Independent Christian Church is a little over one million.

CHAPTER 15
INSTRUMENTAL MUSIC IN WORSHIP

MORE DIVISION COMES TO THE RESTORATION

After the merger of the groups associated with Barton Stone and Alexander Campbell, the church experienced phenomenal growth for the first two or three decades. The Gospel was preached in its simplicity and purity. Thousands were being baptized for the remission of sins. Churches were springing up all over the land. Men of prominence, including James A. Garfield, who would become the twentieth president of the United States, were active in this movement to restore first century Christianity. Even though things ran smoothly and successfully in the movement that was sweeping the country like a prairie fire, it was not long before some became dissatisfied with simply preaching and practicing the New Testament pattern.

A wave of innovations began to disturb the peace in the brotherhood. We have already discussed one of those, which was the American Christian Missionary Society, but an even greater wedge was driven into the heart of the brotherhood by the introduction of instrumental music in worship. As we notice the history of the introduction of the instrument into worship, we see it quietly began to make its place but ultimately it robbed faithful Christians of their meeting houses and put a wedge into the church that has not been removed in the 138 years since.

J. B. HENSHALL SPEAKS OUT

The origin over the controversy over instrumental music perhaps begins with a brief flare up in Kentucky. On February 22, 1851, a man who signed his name "W" wrote to J. B. Henshall, associate editor of the Ecclesiastical Reformer, asking him what he thought of using the instruments such as organs or bass viols. He asked, "Would not such instruments add greatly to the solemnity of worship, and cause the hearts of the saints to be raised to a higher state of devotion?" He said, "We are far in the rear of Protestants on the subject of the church music." (One is reminded of Israel's desire for a king in order to be like the other nations around them.)

Henshall replied by saying that, in proportion to men becoming worldly minded, so they begin to require helps to their devotion. He argued that to those who live in the light of the gospel privileges and enjoy God's mercies and providence over us, is to say that we have no gratitude in our hearts, and that we are in every way unworthy of these benefits. (1, p. 309) There were other articles in the Reformer, but these give the drift. On the one side, there were those who felt that the denominations were using instruments, and that the brethren were allowing the denominations to advance ahead of them. Others felt that instruments in worship belonged only to those destitute of real spirituality.

CAMPBELL REACTS

The pioneer preacher, John Rogers, read the articles in the Reformer which advocated the use of the instrument in worship. Rogers was a preacher of the old paths. He was baptized by Barton W. Stone at the age of 18 in Wilmington, Ohio in 1818. His preaching career was spent around Carlisle, Kentucky. He baptized over a thousand people in the years between 1823 to 1848. When Rogers read of the use of instruments in the churches of Kentucky, he wrote to Alexander Campbell, "But my brother, would you believe it? A popular preacher has come out in two numbers in the 'E. Reformer' in favor of instrumental music in churches." (1, p. 309) Rogers begged

Campbell to make a statement on the subject at this early date. After some delay, Campbell wrote a short essay on the subject. In referring to instruments being used by the denominations, Campbell said:

> I wonder not, then that an organ, a fiddle, or a Jews-harp, should be requisite to stir up their carnal hearts, and work into ecstasy their animal souls, else "hosannas languish on their tongues and their devotions die." And that all persons who have no spiritual discernment, taste or relish for their spiritual meditations, consolations and sympathies of renewed hearts, should call for such aid, is but natural.... So to those who have no real devotion or spirituality in the church, and whose animal nature flags under the oppression of church service, I think with Mr. G. that instrumental music would be not only a desideratum, but an essential prerequisite to fire up their souls to even animal devotion. But I presume, to all spiritually-minded Christians such aids would be as a cow bell in a concert. (1, p. 310)

RAINS AND FRANKLIN SPEAK OUT

Aylette Rains, in 1851, was preaching at Millersburg, Kentucky. Rains was in the habit of keeping a diary, and on April 27, 1851, he made the following entry: "Brother S (Saunders) wishes to introduce the melodeon into the church." (1, p. 310) Rains was bitterly opposed to using the instrument in worship, and it did not get in at Millersburg at this early date.

The subject of instrumental music did not come up again before the brotherhood until 1860. At this time a letter was sent to Ben Franklin, asking him to express his views on the use of the instrument. Franklin's reply is framed in irony. He said there might be occasions when the instrument would be permissible, such as the following:

1. Where a church never had, or has lost the Spirit of Christ…
2. If a church has a preacher who never had or has lost the Spirit of Christ, who has become a dry, prosing and lifeless speaker, so as to be entirely incapable of commanding and interesting an audience, it is thought that instrumental music would draw out and interest the people.
3. If a church only intends being a fashionable society, a mere place of amusement and secular entertainment, and abandoning all idea of religion and worship, instrumental music would be a very pleasant and agreeable part of such entertainment. (1 p. 311)

L. L. PINKERTON AND THE CHURCH IN MIDWAY, KENTUCKY

After the appearance of the above article, Ben Franklin heard from L. L. Pinkerton, a preacher at Midway, Kentucky. His letter was published in Franklin's American Christian Review in February of 1860. Pinkerton wrote:

> So far as known to me, or, I presume, to you, I am the only preacher in Kentucky of our brotherhood who has publicly advocated the propriety of employing instrumental music in some churches, and that the Church of God in Midway is the only church that has yet made a decided effort to introduce it. The calls for our opinion, it is probable, came from these regions. (1, p. 311)

The church in Midway, Kentucky is given the dubious credit of being the first on record to use the instrument of music in worship. The year was 1860. The introduction of the instrument owed its introduction into the worship of the Midway congregation to the terrible singing that characterized the group. This singing was reported to have degenerated into screeching and brawling that would, as Pinkerton said, "scare even the rats from worship." At first it was suggested that a meeting be held on Saturday night to practice the songs. Shortly afterward, someone brought in a melodeon to be used in getting the right pitch. Before long, one of the sisters was accompanying the singing with her playing on the melodeon during these practice sessions. The group observed that the effect of the use of the melodeon was good on the singing, and so it was decided to try to use the instrument in the Lord's day worship. Thompson Parrish played the instrument at the worship.

While the church at Midway was the first congregation on record to use the instrument in worship, it is not entirely accurate to say that this was the first congregation among the pioneers to do so. It is likely that the instrument was used very sparingly as early as 1851, which would explain the flare up in the brotherhood papers already mentioned. After 1860 the subject of the instrument died down for the next four years. The occurrence of the Civil War immediately turned the attention of the brotherhood to other more immediate problems.

PENDLETON PLACES INSTRUMENT IN AREA OF EXPEDIENCY

In 1864 the question was again renewed as a brother who signed his name "Ancient Order" wrote to W. K. Pendleton at the Millennial Harbinger to ask, "Is it in accordance with the Scriptures to use in the churches organs or other instrumental music connected with the worship?" In Pendleton's reply, he stated that it was not used by the primitive church. He stated that the best authorities agreed that the organ was first introduced in church worship after the time of Thomas Aquinas, for he declared in a A.D. 1250: "Our church does not use musical instruments as harps and psalteries, in the praise of God, lest she should seem to Judiaze." (1, p. 313)

Pendleton said that he had no personal objection to using the instrument in worship, but he likened this to Paul's conclusion about meats, that he would rather never hear one again than have it interfere with heartfelt congregational singing. He also defended the instrument by saying that many things in the practical affairs of the church of the present age which are right, were not a part of the church of the apostolic days, such as the church owning church buildings.

This was to be the substance of the argument that advocates would make in favor of the use of the instrument in years to follow. Pendleton admitted that the early church did not use the instrument. As we have already seen in the case of the missionary society, those who advocated such made no claim that such existed in New Testament times. Pendleton did not consider the silence of the Scripture on these points a sufficient reason not to use them. In both cases the silence is admitted but promptly ignored.

J. W. MCGARVEY SPEAKS OUT

In 1864 the controversy over the instrument gained momentum when J. W. McGarvey entered the battle. In an article published in the Millennial Harbinger, November 1864, McGarvey stated:

> In the earlier years of the Reformation, there was entire unanimity in the rejection of instrumental music from our public worship. It was declared unscriptural, inharmonious with the Christian institution, and a source of corruption. In the course of time, individuals here and there called in question the correctness of this decision, and attempt was occasionally made to introduce instruments in some churches. (1, pp. 313-314)

McGarvey went on to say that at first the newness of the thing caused the brethren to shrink from it, so men would refrain from pushing it on the ground that it was offensive. Next, brethren got to the point where they did not care. McGarvey pleaded that the brethren lay aside all feelings either for or against the instrument and start fresh in responding to the question, "Ought we to make use of musical instruments in public worship?" He asked brethren to come out with their views on it, concluding, "Let us, then, have the question fully discussed and finally settled." (1, p. 314)

McGarvey himself began this discussion by stating that if instrumental music were authorized in the New Testament, and if God, by his written word, approved this use, then, the advocates of the instrument should produce those Scriptures. He then proceeded to discuss the question by examining the Scriptures commonly used by those who maintained that the Word of God approved their use. Advocates of the instrument frequently, when and if they affirmed that the written Word upheld the instrument, usually relied on the Old Testament Scriptures. McGarvey, as well as many other pioneer preachers, saw that the very fact that the church, when established, rejected the use of the Jewish worship of the Old Testament, was proof enough that the instrument was not to be a part of the New Testament church worship.

The worship of the Jews was appointed for the time in which they lived. Their worship consisted of offering sacrifices, ceremonial washings, burning of incense, and the use of instruments of music, among other things. The church, on the other hand, is a part of those old ordinances and practices, but fully spiritual in scope. Here God chose a worship where the worshipper, directly from the heart, worshipped the Lord without the aid of incense, animal sacrifice, or mechanical instruments.

McGarvey, then, after the reasoning upon the differences in the two dispensations and of musical instruments being out of place under the Christian dispensation, closed by saying, "Now, Brother _____, if this argument is valid, I again repeat, that every man who bows to the authority of God's word, must oppose the use of instrumental music in the church. If it contains any fallacy, please point it out, for I declare to you, I am unable to see it." (1, p. 315)

Z. F. SMITH ARGUED AGAINST THE INSTRUMENT

The same argument that McGarvey had presented was also made in the American Christian Review by a Z. F. Smith:

> It is very clear that musical instruments were used by the Jews in their praises to God. It is equally clear, to every one familiar to the New Testament, that not one evidence, either in precept or example, of such practice, is found in the appointed orders of Christian worship. This omission must be esteemed a consideration of great importance in solving the question of its right; and especially when viewed in the light of those circumstances which marked the change from one dispensation to another. Whatever was peculiar to the genius and character of both, was preserved; what was peculiar to the former alone was omitted... The religion of Jesus Christ is purely spiritual; as such, its genius and character forbade the introduction of a carnal element. (1, p. 315)

Early in 1865, S. Salisbury of Mumford, New York, wrote advocating the use of the instrument. He pointed to the fact that instrumental music was used not only in the Old Testament, but, according to the book of Revelation, were also to be found in heaven. McGarvey seems to have paid little attention to these arguments, as the answers should have been self-evident. Much of the written discussions in 1865 took place between McGarvey and A. S. Hayden.

MOSES LARD ENTERS THE DISCUSSION

Moses Lard got into the discussion in March of 1864 by writing in the Lard's Quarterly, "What defense can be urged for the introduction into some of our congregations of instrumental music?

The answer which thunders into my ear from every page of the New Testament, is NONE." In the same issue of the Lard's Quarterly, Lard raises and answers the question, "What should be done with the pro-instrument churches?"

> What shall be done with such churches? Of course, nothing. If they see fit to mortify the feelings of their brethren, to forsake the example of the primitive churches, to condemn the authority of Christ by resorting to will worship, to excite dissension, and give rise to general scandal, they must do it. As a body we can do nothing. Still, we have three partial remedies left us to which we should at once resort." (1, p. 316)

Lard said every preacher should resolve never to enter a meeting house where the instrument is used, and that no brother who is moving his membership from one congregation to another ever unite with a congregation using the instrument. He also stated:

Let those brethren who oppose the introduction of an organ first remonstrate in gentle, kind and decided terms. If their remonstrance is unheeded, and the organ is brought in, then let them at once, and without even the formality of asking for a letter, abandon the church so acting; and let all such members unite elsewhere. Thus these organ grinding churches will in the lapse of time be broken down, or wholly apostatize, and the sooner they are in fragments the better for the cause of Christ. (1, p. 316)

Of course, both McGarvey and Lard were beginning to be looked upon by some brethren as extremists, but they were men of firm and deep conviction in respect to this issue.

MRS. CAMPBELL CONDEMNS THE INSTRUMENT IN WORSHIP

After the War, the instrument began to be used more and more and the issue became more hotly discussed. The Civil War concluded in 1865. Alexander Campbell died a short time later on March 4, 1866. Mrs. Campbell wrote, after the death of her husband:

> As there has been so much controversy amongst the brethren about the organ, I feel it to be a duty to refer to it. That it has, by its introduction into some of the churches, been the cause of sorrow and discord no one can deny... I believe it to be a grievous innovation in the Christian church that our heavenly Father does not approve of -- I think will be discovered by the more reflecting brethren themselves -- and that only a return of apostolic worship in our churches can be acceptable to the great head of the church, who has not left on record his sanction to add or to take from his institutions, ordinances and forms of worship. (6, p. 169)

USE OF INSTRUMENT GROWS

One might get the idea that by the end of the Civil War, the majority of the congregations were using the instrument. However, this would not be correct. In 1868, Ben Franklin estimated that only 50 congregations out of 10,000 employed an instrument. (2, p. 166) Nevertheless, informed brethren could see that the use of the instrument was growing and would continue to do so unless something was done to stop it. When John Rogers, the great pioneer preacher of Kentucky, died in 1867, he expressed great concern over the ever increasing use of the instrument. (38, p. 81)

In 1867 the Olive Street church in St. Louis, Missouri

purchased a building from the Episcopalians. It had a $3,000 organ, and the church did not know what to do with it. Dr. Hiram Christopher, brother-in-law of J. W. McGarvey fought it off for two years but those who wanted the instrument were determined to have their way and use it in their worship. A committee composed of Robert Graham, Isaac Errett, Alexander Proctor, and I. N. Rogers went to St. Louis and achieved additional time in which the instrument was kept out. However, a few years later the advocates of the instrument won and the instrument was used in their worship. Those who opposed it had to leave and start another congregation. (38, p. 81)

In Akron, Ohio in 1868, Ben Franklin went to hold a meeting. The instrument was being used. Franklin thought that ninety percent did not want it, but the ten percent was very influential. In Chicago, Illinois a church building was purchased from a denomination. When the church met January 17, 1869, the organ was used over the protest of the preacher, D. P. Henderson. Nevertheless, the preacher stayed. In 1870 the church in Memphis, Tennessee put in the instrument. David Walk, the preacher, chiefly instigated it, and put on a drive to raise the necessary funds.

In the 1870's several large city congregations began to use the instrument. In 1872 the Central church in Cincinnati brought an $8,000 organ into their new $100,000 building. Ben Franklin was appalled and wrote in his paper, "The organ is the accompaniment of lifeless, formal, and fashionable churches, in cities, where pride, aristocracy and selfishness prevail; where the poor have no sympathy, comfort or peace." It should be noted that those who wanted the instrument were the innovators who caused the division.

With the gradual increase in the number of instruments being added to congregations, it was clear that the Restoration Movement was taking on a new color, one of which for the most part, the earlier pioneers had never dreamed. J. W. McGarvey wrote in the Apostolic Times in 1869, "Once we had no men among us who were known to tolerate instrumental music in worship. After that, there arose some that contended that whether we use it or not is a mere matter of expediency. More recently, a few churches have actually used it, and their preachers have approved, but have not often ventured publicly to defend it." (38, p. 83)

Some argued that worship without an instrument was all right in a society that was accustomed only to the backwoods, but new standards of respectability were not set up, and the church to be progressive must meet these standards. To this McGarvey responded in the Millennial Harbinger, April, 1868, "...the cry of the progress and conformity, it is making its way over the heads and hearts of our best brethren and sisters..." (38, p. 84)

N. A. WALKER PREACHES SELLS ORGANS

In the years following the Civil War, N. A. Walker was a preacher who also sold musical instruments. He was busy most of the time holding evangelistic meetings, and usually managed to sell an organ to the church while he was there. In 1869 he reported that he baptized 300 people and used the organ in every meeting he conducted except one. J. B. Briney thought he detected in Walker's statement that he was saying that the instrument helped him accomplish this many conversions. Briney wrote in the American Christian Review, February 15, 1870: "I suppose he has an improved edition of the commission to this effect: 'Go preach the gospel and play an instrument to every creature.' What a mistake the Savior made in leaving the instrument out of the commission. When N. A. Walker can convert three hundred persons per annum by the use of the instrument, while he might fail altogether with the simple gospel." (38, p. 84)

THE ARGUMENT OF EXPEDIENCY

Those who favored the use of the instrument in worship planted their primary argument for its use squarely upon the matter of expediency. This argument had previously been used in the case for the American Christian Missionary Society. The outspoken advocate of this position was Isaac Errett through the Christian Standard. In the spring of 1870 Errett came out in the Christian Standard using the position that he would counsel against congregations using the instrument for the sake of harmony, but he said that it was just a matter of opinion, and that its use by a congregation should not be a test of fellowship. Ben Franklin disagreed in the June, 1870 issue of the American Christian Review:

We put it on no ground of opinion or expediency. The acts of worship are all prescribed in the law of God. If it is an act of worship, or an element in worship, it may not be added to it. If it is not an act of worship, or an element in worship, it is most wicked and sinful to impose it on the worshippers. It is useless to tell us, "It is not to be made a test." If you impose it on the conscience of brethren and, by a majority vote, force it onto the worship, are they bound to stifle their consciences? Have you a right to compel them to submit and worship with the instrument?... If you press the instrument into the worship, we care not whether you call it an element in the worship or an aid, and drive them away, because they cannot conscientiously worship with the instrument, YOU cause the division -- YOU are the AGGRESSOR -- the INNOVATOR -- you do this, too, for the accompaniment of corruption and apostasy, admitting at the same time that you have no conscience in the matter. (38, pp. 88-89)

Clearly, Franklin felt strongly that the use of instrumental music was not merely a matter of opinion. Man had no right to add an element of human origin to the divine worship. Such was an unacceptable innovation. These two views, championed by Errett on one side and Franklin on the other, were miles apart. Down to the present day this has been the fundamental reason why fellowship between the churches of Christ on one side, and the Christian Church on the other is not achievable. If the use of the instrument is purely a matter of opinion, then, admittedly, any dispute about it borders on being ridiculous. If, however, the instrument is a human innovation, an addition without divine authority, then it is sinful to use it. If one accepts the latter view, there is no possible consistent ground for compromise with the former.

RICHARDSON ARGUED AGAINST EXPEDIENCY

Robert Richardson, the biographer of Alexander Campbell wrote in response to those who argued that using the instrument was just a matter of expediency. "As it regards the use of musical instruments in church worship, the case is wholly different. This can never be a question of expediency; for the simple reason that there is no law prescribing or authorizing it. If it were anywhere said in the New Testament that Christians should use instruments, then it would become a question of expediency what kind of instruments was to be used, whether an organ or melodeon..." (38, p. 91) Another example Richardson used to show that instrumental music would not come under the heading of expediency was that nothing is expedient which is not first of all lawful. He pointed out that it is a command of God to pray, but it is left to expediency to decide the place, time and circumstances.

But the use of instrumental music in the worship of many congregations was not to be stopped. Many would at first reject it, but once they were lulled into complacency, they would be unwilling in the future to listen to any argument against it. Richardson stated it well when he said, "The introduction of a musical instrument into a church is a triumph of the sensual over the spiritual." (38, p. 92)

CONGREGATIONS DIVIDE OVER INSTRUMENT

In the 1870's and 1880's, many congregations split as the organ was introduced. Following are a few examples:

- 1868 Akron, Ohio
- 1869 Chicago, Illinois
- 1870 Memphis, Tennessee
- 1872 Central in Cincinnati, Ohio
- 1872 Frankfort, Kentucky
- 1877 Bloomington, Indiana: The church had four years of weak, non-doctrinal preaching with

sermons that could have been preached in any denomination in town. At the end of that time the congregation had no will to resist, and the instrument was brought into worship.

1879　Bowling Green, Kentucky

1880　Bedford, Indiana: Steven Young had contributed $1,000 to the new building. When it was completed, an organ was brought in and Young and fifty others had to leave or take part in that which violated their consciences.

1881　East Cleveland, Ohio: The church here dedicated a new $2,000 organ on June 26, 1881. They invited the "pastors" of several denominational churches to join with them. They even hired a professional organist from the Methodist church to play for them.

1881　Louisville, Kentucky: The Fourth and Walnut Street church put in the instrument, causing several conscientious people to leave and worship elsewhere.

1882　Anderson, Indiana: George P. Slade was the preacher there. Four years earlier he had participated in a written discussion with J.W. McGarvey on instrumental music. By April of 1882 he had succeeded in bringing in the instrument.

1884　Huntsville, Texas: John T. Poe wrote that "The old church at Hunstville has put the organ in and some of its best members out."

1884　Wellington, Kansas: The congregation split over the instrument.

1884　Santa Ana, California: Carroll Kendrick who had just moved from Texas to California wrote that the church in Santa Ana had just included the instrument in their worship. Those who would not accept the instrument were forced to leave and start over. It is tragic that a little over one hundred years later, in 1996, the Northside Church of Christ in Santa Ana introduced the instrument into worship and in 1997 merged with the Christian Church.

MRS. CAMPBELL AGAIN SPEAKS OUT

Mrs. Alexander Campbell returned to Bethany from a trip and found the organ in the vestibule of the church building. She used her influence and had it removed. Her views were recorded in the American Christian Review in July, 1884: "I must say, however, I could not endure to worship in the church at Bethany if the instrument which had introduced so many discordant notes amongst dear brethren and sisters was made part of the worship..." (38, p. 229) Unfortunately, the removal of the instrument from the Bethany congregation was only temporary.

In 1870 a brother by the name of Enos Campbell wrote an article for the Millennial Harbinger in which he expressed his views favoring the use of the organ. By this time Alexander Campbell had been dead four years. Campbell's widow wrote to Enos Campbell concerning his article. Her response was dated March 28, 1870. A portion of the letter is as follows:

> ... You know full well, too, that as sure as the morning and evening sacrifice was attended to, that the songs of Zion resounded in this old mansion. But never was instrumental music tolerated or called in to aid the worship in the family. No, the revered patriarch (Alexander Campbell) advocated the "melody of the heart" in unison with the "human voice divine" in the worship of the family and in the church; and if he were upon earth now, he would do the same. He wrote about it and spoke about it. That you are well aware of, and he never yielded to the teaching of men in regard to the matter. He never approved nor recognized "expediency" as a doctrine to introduce it

into worship of the living God. (38, p. 92)

THE QUESTION OF FELLOWSHIP

The question of fellowship was discussed in the brotherhood papers. Since the instrument was viewed as an innovation and a sin, fellowship with the instrumental congregations was destined to dwindle as time went on. The Apostolic Times and the American Christian Review advised brethren to withdraw from and refuse to worship with any church which adopted the instrument. J. W. McGarvey in 1881 wrote a series of articles on instrumental music in the Apostolic Times, insisting that its use was a positive sin. A year later the rumor was spread that McGarvey had changed his position, and was then favoring the instrument. This misrepresentation of his views disturbed McGarvey. To make his position perfectly clear, he wrote in a letter dated May 10, 1883, the following: "I have not withdrawn my opposition to the organ. I would not hold membership with, nor contract to preach for a church using one. Its introduction against the conscientious protest of a minority is high-handed wickedness, and can be prompted by no spirit but that of the world and the flesh." (38, p. 233)

David Lipscomb used the Gospel Advocate to point out the inconsistency of some brethren in rejecting the instrument and accepting the Missionary Society. Lipscomb vigorously rejected both the use of the instrument and the Society. James A. Harding also wrote strong articles in the Gospel Advocate in which he objected to the use of the instrument by the churches. Following is an example:

> There are many whom we are told to "mark" and "avoid;" men from whom we are to "withdraw" ourselves; men who trouble the churches of God by forcing upon them untaught questions; who gratify their own tastes by forcing organs and other such things into the worship, thereby driving numbers of the oldest and best members out. From such let us turn away. It is worthy to remark that the things

that are troubling the churches are the inventions of men; the organ, the human missionary society, the suppers and festivals for raising money, etc. are the bones of contention. Did not the apostles get along without the organ? Yes! Are not these things divisive? Yes! They have rent more churches, alienated more brethren, and caused more heartaches among the children of God than any other things that have troubled the Zion of our King in this century. (38, pp. 238-239)

Harding's articles, as well as the writings of other sound brethren, helped to mold an attitude among the readers of the religious papers. The use of the instrument, being sinful, would not be tolerated, and brethren who considered them sinful were now ready to draw lines of fellowship against the innovators.

TWO ATTITUDES

So, there were two attitudes toward the organ. One insisted that its use was a matter of expediency; the other insisted that it was a human innovation into a divine worship and, therefore, sinful. Between these two positions it was evident that there was no compromising or midway point, a fact that has always permanently stood in the way of a reunion between the Churches of Christ and the Christian Church. Here then was the point of the departure; the parting of the ways, the instrument giving the impetus to a division which neither the Civil War, slavery, or even the Missionary Society had done.

Recapping the positions, those who favored the instrument argued that it was an expedient, a simple aid to the singing that violated no specific command. It was argued that when not forbidden by the New Testament, they were free to adopt their program to changing needs. The opposition to instrumental music in worship did not argue that there must be explicit authority for every accessory of worship such as pulpits, pews, meeting houses, hymn books, but only that every element of worship must be scripturally authorized. There is precedent for sermon, song, prayer, Lord's Supper, and contribution, but none for instrumental music.

Opponents of the instrument asked three basic questions on the issue:

    1. Did Jesus Christ ever appoint it?
    2. Did the apostles ever sanction it?
    3. Did the primitive church use it?

To all three of these questions the answer must be a resounding "No!" The use of the instrument was an innovation, without express command or approved example. The use or non-use was symptomatic of an attitude toward the authority of the Scriptures.

POSITION OF PROMINENT RESTORATION LEADERS

It is interesting to observe the positions that various Restoration leaders took on the question of instrumental music in worship:

1. Alexander Campbell stood against it. As early as 1851 he had stated that to the spiritually minded, the instrument would be as a "cowbell in a concert."
2. Jacob Creath, Jr. stood firmly against it. To him it was a divisive thing without authority from the Word.
3. W. K. Pendleton, the son-in-law of Campbell, believed the instrument was a mere expedient.
4. Isaac Errett, editor of the Christian Standard, alleged that the instrument was an unnecessary expedient, but failed to oppose it on scriptural basis.
5. Robert Richardson was against it. He said, "It

can't be expedient since we have no law to use it."
6. J. W. McGarvey disagreed with Pendleton and Errett and stated that instrumental music was "unscriptural, inharmonious with the Christian institution and a source of corruption." (38, p. 441)
7. Moses Lard stood solidly against instrumental music in worship and wrote defiantly against its use. He insisted that the instrument was an "impious innovation on the simplicity and purity of the ancient worship." Lard felt strongly that a preacher should not enter one of the instrumental churches and that no Christian should ever unite with one.
8. Ben Franklin spoke out strongly against the use of the instrument. He said the "organ is the accompaniment of lifeless, formal and fashionable churches in cities, where pride, aristocracy and selfishness prevail."
9. David Lipscomb was solidly against the use of instrumental music in worship. He used the Gospel Advocate to denounce the practice.

MUSIC IN THE NEW TESTAMENT

The history of the New Testament worship clearly shows that only acapella music was used. The word "acapella" literally means "as is done in the church." A careful study of these passages pertaining to singing in the New Testament will reveal that there is no authorization or justification for using mechanical instruments of music. In Ephesians 5:19 the instrument there on which melody is to be made to the Lord is identified as the heart.

1. Matthew 26:30: "And when they had sung a hymn, they went out to the Mount of Olives."
2. Acts 16:25: "But at midnight Paul and Silas were

praying and singing hymns to God..."
3. Romans 15:9: "For this reason I will confess to You among the Gentiles, and sing to Your name."
4. I Corinthians 14:15: "What is the conclusion then? I will pray with the spirit, and I will also pray with the understanding. I will sing with the spirit, and I will also sing with the understanding."
5. Ephesians 5:19: "Speaking to one another in psalms and hymns, and spiritual songs, singing and making melody in your heart to the Lord."
6. Colossians 3:16: "Let the word of Christ dwell in you richly in all wisdom, teaching and admonishing one another in psalms and hymns and spiritual songs, singing with grace in your hearts to God."
7. Hebrews 2:12: "In the midst of the assembly I will sing praise to You."

Secular historians such as Thomas Aquinas, Joseph Bingham and Edwin Dickinson verify that vocal singing was the music of the early church. With rare exceptions, there is no mention of instrumental music in Christian worship until after the middle ages. While our decision to refuse to use the instrument in our praise to God is based solely upon the Word, it is interesting to learn that many of the "church fathers" were so opposed to instruments in worship that they would not allow them in any form. There are numerous quotations from religious leaders such as Huldreich Zwingli, John Calvin, Adam Clark, John Wesley, and Martin Luther that are most interesting. The famous Charles Spurgeon did not use the instrument in his 10,000 seat tabernacle in London. (2, p. 68)

THREE SPIRITUAL LAWS ARE BROKEN

The use of instrumental music in worship violates three spiritual laws:

1. It violates the law of faith: Romans 10:17, "So then, faith comes by hearing, and hearing by the word of God." 2 Corinthians 5:7, "For we walk by faith, not by sight." Those who use the instrument in worship go beyond the Word and are not operating by faith. They go beyond the authority of the Lord.
2. It violates the law of worship: The nature of worship is spiritual and personal. John 4:24, "God is spirit; and those who worship him must worship in spirit and truth." It is not a spiritual worship when mechanical instruments are included.
3. It violates The law of unity: I Corinthians 1:10, "Now I plead with you, brethren, by the name of our Lord Jesus Christ, that you all speak the same thing, and there be no divisions among you, but that you be perfectly joined together in the same mind and in the same judgment." Those who added the instrument into worship divided the body Christ and split the church in such a way that it can never be united.

USED IN THE OLD TESTAMENT

Some have tried to justify the use of instrumental music in the worship of the New Testament church because it was used in the Mosaic dispensation. This cannot be a valid argument since the entire ritual of the Old Testament has been abolished. No part of it can rightly be perpetuated except that which is newly authorized in the New Testament. Hebrews 7:12 states, "For the priesthood being changed, of necessity there is also a change of the law." Colossians 2:14 tells us that the old Law has been abolished. "And He has taken it out of the way, having nailed it to the cross." If one goes to the Old Testament for authorization for the use of instrumental music in worship, consistency would demand that animal sacrifices, the offering of incense, as well as all aspects of the Old Law should also be practiced under the New Covenant.

INSTRUMENTS IN HEAVEN?

Others have drawn an inference in favor of the instrument from the fact that in the visions of Revelation, John saw the redeemed harping upon harps. This conclusion is false on three counts:

1. John's visions were symbols, not realities.
2. Some things may be proper in heaven that would not be suited to our conditions on earth. For example, incense was seen in some of the visions, as well as pavements of gold upon the streets. But, it would be wrong to burn incense in the worship of the church, and it would be wickedly wasteful to pave our streets with gold. Obviously, heaven and earth are two different places.
3. Heaven is a spiritual realm with no place for the physical things that accompany this existence.

WHO IS RESPONSIBLE?

It is a serious matter to divide the people of God. The Lord continues to frown upon those who sow discord among the brethren (Proverbs 6:16). Found in the Millennial Harbinger in 1867 is the following statement from Jacob Creath, Jr., a man who had seen the tragedy God's people being divided as a result of innovations being brought into the church: "The tendency of all such things (modern music in churches, prizes, fairs, etc.) is to promote two parties among us and then ultimately to throw the blame of the split upon those who have strictly adhered to our rule." (2, p. 169)

In our modern times we must continue to teach and to indoctrinate our people on this fundamental issue. It is obvious that new generations have arisen in the church who have little or no conviction on the subject of instrumental music in worship. Why has this happened? To whom should the finger of blame be pointed?

Some elders must bear responsibility. Too many shepherds have abandoned their work of guarding and nourishing the flock. Instead, they have assumed the role of corporate officers and administrators. Too often their concern is concentrated on balancing the budget, keeping the people happy, and meeting in a beautiful building. As a result, they have failed to keep the church pure in work, worship and doctrine. They have failed to demand from the preacher sermons that will fortify the congregation against false teaching.

Some preachers must also bear the responsibility. There are too many preachers who are more concerned with their position and image before the church and the community than they are about preaching sound doctrine. They have long ceased preaching about such things as instrumental music. Few members who have come into the church in the last several years have developed any convictions on the subject, and in fact know little about it. They have not heard the preacher preach on the subject or teachers teach about it. Yes, preachers are to blame.

Some deacons also are responsible. Too often men are placed as deacons in the congregations who are not grounded in sound doctrine. When innovations such as instrumental music are discussed these men can be found using their influence for the acceptance of such.

Some college professors have contributed to the problem. Too many young people have gone to Christian colleges to sit at the feet of Christian teachers only to have their faith weakened rather than strengthened. Apparently some college professors have become overly impressed with their own importance and their own image, perhaps feeling that it is beneath them to teach the old truths. Instead of defending the truth, they may be found ridiculing the things for which faithful brethren have stood since the early days of the Restoration. Some appear to be more concerned with the search for some new teaching that will set them apart as special in the eyes of the brethren or the world than they are in teaching sound doctrine to their students.

The scriptural position about instrumental music has been vindicated over and over again in the past in sermons and debates. The arguments advanced against the use of instrumental music in worship are scriptural and sound and will continue to stand the test of time and controversy. However, as the leaders of the church fail to do their job in teaching on this subject, so we will have a corresponding abandonment of opposition to it. The next step is the embracing of the instrument in worship and after that any other digression that seems desirable at the time.

PART III
OTHER PIONEERS OF THE RESTORATION MOVEMENT

A tremendous debt is owed to those pioneer preachers who went before us and gave themselves sacrificially to proclaim the gospel and build up the kingdom. Some, like Barton Stone, Thomas Campbell, Alexander Campbell, Walter Scott, and "Raccoon" John Smith are well known for their contributions to the Cause. However, we must not forget that there were numerous others who fought the good fight of faith as well, and who deserve to be remembered. Sadly, some of those brethren will never be given credit in this world for the work they did. While the number of such silent heroes of the faith is great, as well as those whose names are remembered, each shared in the noble work of restoring and presenting the ancient gospel. We will mention only a few more of these brethren who played an influential role in this great work. They will appear in chronological order, with no attempt being made to list them in their importance to the church. Further, this list does not include any of the men born after 1850 who played a tremendous role in preaching the gospel and in keeping the church from going off into error with innovations.

As one reads about the lives of these men and their accomplishments, he is made to remember that the church was placed into our hands through the hard work and sacrifice of such men. Rarely is such sacrifice seen today in the lives of those who preach the gospel. So many of those pioneer gospel preachers actually did without in order to proclaim the soul-saving gospel of Jesus Christ. These men inspire us. We honor their memory.

CHAPTER 16
JACOB CREATH, SR.
1777 - 1857

Jacob Creath, Sr. was born in Nova Scotia, Canada, February 7, 1777. At the age of ten he and his parents moved to Virginia. He joined the Baptist church at the age of twelve and was preaching for that group by the time he was eighteen. He was ordained as a Baptist preacher in Louisa County, Virginia in 1798 at the age of twenty-one. Five years later Creath moved to Kentucky and settled in Fayette County.

Jacob had an older brother named William. In 1799 when William's second son was born, he left the naming of the infant to his younger brother, Jacob. Jacob chose to give the baby his own name. In the years that followed, the older Jacob would be called Jacob Creath, Sr., and the younger was called Jacob Creath, Jr. Both were destined to be powerful and influential leaders in the Restoration Movement.

Jacob Creath, Sr. was a very effective speaker. This was in spite of the lack a formal education, never having attended school. "However, his language was clear and accurate for one untrained in literary education. He was oratorical and had a vivid imagination. The statesman, Henry Clay, pronounced him to be the finest natural orator he had ever heard. Very few men possessed more of the simple elements necessary to a popular orator than Jacob Creath." (36, p. 34)

Being a leader in the Baptist Church, Creath defended its

doctrines zealously. Although he saw several of his preaching brethren leave the Baptist Church to plead for a restoration of primitive Christianity, he did not leave the Baptists easily. Before making this dramatic change, Creath carefully examined the teachings of the Baptists with the New Testament and found many man-made doctrines that lacked Bible authority. His sermons began to reflect more Bible and less of the doctrines of the Baptist that he had formerly preached. This was not an easy transition for Creath. He had many good friends among the Baptists. He also knew that they would turn on him when he turned his back on the Baptist Church. Nevertheless, the time came when he fully saw the truth and knew that he could no longer preach the errors of Baptist doctrine.

When the Elkhorn Baptist Association convened in 1829 in Lexington, Kentucky, an effort was made to adopt a resolution to exclude all of those from the Baptist Church who believed in taking the "Bible alone." This number included Jacob Creath, Sr. It was through the efforts of John T. Johnson that the action against these men was postponed for another year. In 1830 the Elkhorn Association met with Raccoon John Smith, Jacob Creath, Sr. and Jacob Creath, Jr. Charges were made against these men and passed without allowing any of the three to speak in his own defense. In this way, these three men were expelled from the Baptist fellowship in Kentucky. Philosophically, they had already separated from Baptist views much earlier.

Like Raccoon John Smith, when Jacob Creath, Sr. left the Baptist Church he took many from the Baptist faith with him. As a preacher of the truth, he would move from county to county, establishing congregations where he went. It is said that when he would move, many of the members of the congregation would move with him, making it easier to start a new work. He preached the gospel with such power and simplicity that hundreds were converted and whole Baptist churches turned to the truth. "As an exhorter, he possessed rare and valuable talent, and his power has affected his entire audience upon many an occasion. Upon one occasion he delivered a sermon to the Baptist Association in which he set forth with such clearness and effectiveness the individual rights of the local churches that Thomas Campbell and other competent judges who were present regarded it as unequaled in eloquence and power." (936, p. 35)

In 1850 Alexander Campbell was in Kentucky and heard Jacob Creath, Sr. preach. He described him in the following language:

> "Though his once brilliant eye is quenched in darkness, and his subduing voice is broken into weak tones, he rises in his soul while nature sinks in years; and with a majesty of thought which naught but heaven and hope can inspire, he spoke to us a few last words, which so enraptured my soul, that in the ecstasy of feeling produced by them, when he closed there was silence in my heart for half an hour; and when I recovered myself, every word had so passed away that nothing remained but a melancholy reflection that I should never again hear that most eloquent tongue, which had echoed for half a century through Northern Kentucky with such resistless sway as to have quelled the maddening strife of sectarian tongues and propitiated myriads of ears and hearts to the divine eloquence of Almighty love. Peace to his soul; and may his sun grow larger at its setting, as his soul expands in the high hope of seeing as he is seen, and of loving as he has been loved." (30, p. 404)

For the last seven years of his life he was totally blind. Creath was on his way to Mississippi, but while in Memphis, Tennessee he suffered an attack of jaundice that left him blind. This brought to a close his remarkable ministry. He was not bitter or complaining, but remained cheerful. He spent his last seven years encouraging his fellow Christians to remain faithful. He died on March 14, 1857 at the age of eighty.

CHAPTER 17
JOHN T. JOHNSON
1788 - 1856

John T. Johnson was born in October 5, 1788 at a place called Great Crossings, Kentucky. This was in Scott County about three miles from Georgetown. The name "Great Crossings" appears prominently in Restoration history, especially about the time of the merger between the Campbell and Stone movements. "This place got its name from the fact that in the early days a main buffalo path had here intersected North Elkhorn Creek." (54, p. 32)

Johnson was born at a time of unrest and danger. He was part of a large family. "I was ... the eighth of eleven children, nine males and two females. Indians committed depredations and murder in the vicinity of the Great-Crossings, after my birth; and I distinctly recollect the stockading around my father's yard." (57, p. 12)

"In appearance, Johnson was slightly under six feet tall. He was erect and slender. Early in his life his hair was the color of Walter Scott's -- black as a raven's wing, but later it became very thin and sprinkled here and there with silver. He had a bilious temperament although he was never discouraged and even buoyant under the most adverse of circumstances. He had little time for clownishness. In his conversation, he was easy and somewhat familiar although always chaste, dignified and almost exclusively he dealt with things concerning the kingdom of God. In his speaking, whether public or private, he was always in earnest." (1, p. 231)

Johnson's father, Robert Johnson, was a colonel in the Army. His brother, Richard Mentor Johnson, was a colonel in the Army in the War of 1812. He later turned to politics and was very successful. He was a U.S. senator, and then rose to be the ninth vice president of the United States under Martin Van Buren.

John T. Johnson also served his duty in the military. During the War of 1812, he served under General William Henry Harrison. On May 5, 1813 Indians attacked Fort Meigs where Johnson was stationed. He was not hurt in the fierce battle, but his horse was shot out from under him. After the battle, Harrison sent Johnson to join the forces of his brother, Richard, but on the way he came down with a fever and barely was able to get home alive. He was very ill for some time but recovered.

EDUCATION

John T. Johnson was well educated for a man in those days. He studied at an academy near his home that was run by Malcomb Worley. Although Worley was originally a devout Presbyterian, he later followed Barton W. Stone out of that religion and became a part of the Restoration. Unfortunately, when Shakerism attacked the Stone movement, Worley left the Restoration to become a part of their group. After finishing his schooling with Worley, he entered Transylvania University where he studied law. Upon graduation, before he was twenty-one years old, he applied for and received his license to practice law. On October 9, 1811, Johnson married Sophia Lewis. Sophia was the fifteen-year old daughter of the family with whom he boarded during the last six months of his time at Transylvania University.

With his new wife, Johnson settled on a farm of one hundred and fifty acres of superior land on the South Elkhorn near Georgetown, Kentucky. He and Joel, his younger brother, built a mill in partnership and managed it successfully for several years. Johnson went into politics in 1815, being elected to the state legislature. He was re-elected for the next four years. Earning an income from his farm, the mill, and politics, John was quite successful financially. However, in 1819 a severe financial panic struck the country and dealt a heavy blow to Johnson. Johnson had been generous and sympathetic with his friends and neighbors, and had signed guarantees for promissory notes for several of them. When the panic hit, they couldn't pay, so the obligation fell on Johnson. In order to cover these notes Johnson gave up about $50,000.00 worth of his real estate.

POLITICS AND RELIGION

In 1820 Johnson was elected to the United States House of Representatives. He was re-elected in 1822, 1824, 1826, and 1828. After his re-election of 1828, Johnson announced that he would retire from politics after he completed his term. Even though Johnson was busy with his politics, he never stopped thinking about religious matters. He was only a boy of thirteen when the great revival of Cane Ridge led by Barton W. Stone took place in 1801. Young Johnson was present for the Cane Ridge meeting and was greatly impressed with what he saw. He was also impressed with his own personal need to become a Christian. "Yet, being raised amidst the fogs and mists of Calvinism, no one could teach him the simple gospel plan of salvation. Instead of being directed to repent and be baptized for the remission of sins, he says, 'I was told that if it was the Lord's work, he would most certainly complete it.' Thus he was left to wait for, and expect some mystic, nondescript influence, which God has never promised, and waiting for which his good impressions gradually wore off, and he became careless upon the subject of religion." (57, p. 13)

In 1821, just prior to going to Congress, Johnson joined the Baptist Church at Great Crossings. He gave credit to this act by saying "It preserved me from a thousand temptations, and kept me a pure man." (57, p. 21) In 1823 when Alexander Campbell began publishing the Christian Baptist, Johnson was too busy to investigate what Campbell was writing. During the years of 1829 and 1830, Johnson began to give serious attention to the paper. At the time the whole community was aroused over what some called "Campbellism."

He determined in his own mind that he would examine this teaching in light of the scriptures. Of this he later stated, "I was won over, and contended for it with all my might in the private circle. I was astonished at the ignorance and perversity of learned men, who were reputed pious, and otherwise esteemed honorable. My eyes were opened, and I was made perfectly free by the truth. And the debt of gratitude I owe to that man of God, A. Campbell, no language can tell." (57, p.21)

Johnson fully embraced the principles of the Restoration and began to preach this message. Having been raised a Baptist, and being a member of the congregation of Baptists at the Great Crossings, he fervently attempted to enlighten the church of which he was a member and bring them into the truth. His efforts were scorned. He resolved to start a congregation based on the scriptures. In February of 1831, B.S. Chambers, W. Johnson, and John T. Johnson formed a congregation of the Lord's church at Great Crossings. At that meeting he baptized his wife, his brother Joel, and his brother's wife. He determined from that day on to work for the cause. He surrendered a lucrative law practice and made many sacrifices the remainder of his life in order to keep that commitment.

"It would seem almost superfluous to say that, in all this, he showed himself to be the true moral hero. He gave up the honors and emoluments of the world, and all the advantages of connection with a very large congregation, and the most numerous and popular religious party in the state, to associate with a mere handful of what were regarded the most desperate religious adventurers. But the die was cast--the Rubicon was passed--he had counted the cost, and, live or die, sink or swim, he was determined to devote his life, his fortune, and his sacred honor to the best of all causes--the cause of uniting God's people and saving the world." (57 pp. 25,26)

THE CHRISTIAN MESSENGER

After leaving the Baptist Church, Johnson became good friends with Barton W. Stone as both lived in the vicinity of Georgetown and both contended for a restoration of the New

Testament church. Stone had for many years published the Christian Messenger. Johnson admired and respected Stone and referred to him as "deservedly the most eminent preacher in the Christian connection in the west." Stone strongly encouraged Johnson to become the co-editor of the Messenger. He began as co-editor in January of 1832 and continued until the paper closed at the end of 1834.

THE UNION OF 1832

Johnson was among the strongest promoters among the Campbell movement who favored a union of those associated with Stone. Not long before Barton W. Stone passed away, he spoke highly of John T. Johnson in the following way: "Among other Baptists who received and advocated the teaching of A. Campbell, was J. T. Johnson, than whom there is not a better man. We lived together in Georgetown, and labored and worshipped. We plainly saw that we were on the same foundation, in the same spirit, and preached the same gospel. We agreed to untie our energies to effect a union between our different societies." (57, p. 27)

A MAN OF COURAGE

John Rogers, contemporary of Johnson, praised him highly for the courage that he manifested during the merger. "Having been actively engaged as a preacher some twelve years before the union was consummated, and knowing as I did the state of religious parties during that period, I hesitate not to say that J.T. Johnson, in taking the very prominent part he did in advocating and consummating the union, and ever after vindicating it, has given one of the most conclusive proofs of his moral courage and conscientiousness." (57, p. 28) Verbal abuse was hurled unmercifully at those who preached the Restoration message. "They were denounced by the self-styled orthodox parties as unworthy of the Christian name--as Arians, Socinians, Atheists, Deists, Pelagians--disorganizers, agents of hell. We were represented as denying the Lord that bought us, and bringing in damnable heresies. And the people were, therefore, warned by their spiritual guides not to receive us into their houses! Their private houses, many of them, were thus shut against us; and their meeting-houses, as some of their leaders said, must not be polluted by our unhallowed breath." (57, pp. 28-29) John T. Johnson, former state legislator, United States congressman, lawyer, and a man of popularity, had left it all to preach and stand with those who were unfairly and unkindly persecuted by the denominations.

A TRIBUTE TO JOHN T. JOHNSON

H. Leo Boles had high praise for this good man and his work:

It has been said that of all the pioneers of the Restoration, John T. Johnson was the most devoted, zealous, self-sacrificing. He could well say, like Paul, to his fellow apostles, that he had labored more abundantly than they all. There were few states in the Union at that time in which he did not preach the gospel and establish churches. Most of the large cities at that time were visited by him. He was a man of marked individuality. He was apparently a delicate man. His bearing was gentle, refined, and dignified. His address was pleasing, his enunciation clear and distinct, and his reasoning convincing. He spoke rapidly. He was calm, self-possessed, and his deep, earnest manner of tone, gesture, and expression of countenance aroused the human souls to action. The audience always listened with rapt attention to him. He labored incessantly as an evangelist for seventeen years and became known as "The Evangelist of Kentucky." (36, p. 45)

DEATH COMES TOO SOON

The death of John T. Johnson came as a great shock to the brotherhood. His health had apparently been good, and there had not been the slightest indication that death was even close. He had attended the annual convention of the Missionary Society in October of 1856 but had stayed only two days. He left Cincinnati early in order to take a tour into Missouri. There he preached at Columbia, Fayette, and Rocheport. He then went on to Lexington, Missouri, arriving November 23. Arriving on the steamer Sunday morning he immediately went to services and found Allen Wright already preaching. Wright stopped his sermon and insisted that Johnson address the congregation. This began a protracted meeting in which he spoke twice a day. This would be his last gospel meeting. On Sunday morning Johnson preached his last sermon. He was staying in the home of Thomas C. Bledsoe. He quickly developed pneumonia and suffered greatly for the next several days. Bledsoe informed him that he would not recover from his illness. Johnson's reply was, "I did not think that death was so near, but let it come." Asked if he had any fears in dying, Johnson replied, "None, none whatever; I have lived upon Christianity, and can die upon it." A few hours before his death he asked Allen Wright and a Brother Duval to sing, "O Land of Rest For Thee I Sigh," a favorite song. Johnson also tried to sing along. Only a few minutes after sunset on the evening of December 18, 1856, John T. Johnson closed his eyes in death. (38, pp. 235-236)

Upon hearing of the death of Johnson, Alexander Campbell wrote: "I presume no laborer in word and doctrine in the valley of the Mississippi has labored more ardently, more perseveringly, or more successfully than has Elder John T. Johnson, during the whole period of his public ministry. How many hundred, if not thousands, of souls he has awakened from the stupor and deathlike sleep of sin and inducted into the kingdom of Jesus, the King eternal, immortal, and invisible, the living know not." (36, p. 45)

When the news of Johnson's death reached Walter Scott, Scott wrote that the sadness of his death "carries to the bosoms of the brethren and relatives of the deceased so great a burden of grief, of woe, of wailing, and tears, that any effort on our part to increase or intensify it by words would be equally indiscreet, unfeeling, and unavailing. The stroke has fallen on our hearts with the unexpectedness of a jet of lighting from a cloudless sky." (36, pp. 45-46)

CHAPTER 18
AYLETTE RAINS
1788 - 1881

Aylette Rains was born in Spotsylvania County, Virginia, January 22, 1788. Because of the time in which he lived, his opportunity for a formal education was limited. His parents were poor and Aylette was raised knowing poverty first hand. His parents, being members of the Episcopal Church, had Aylette sprinkled when he was four years old.

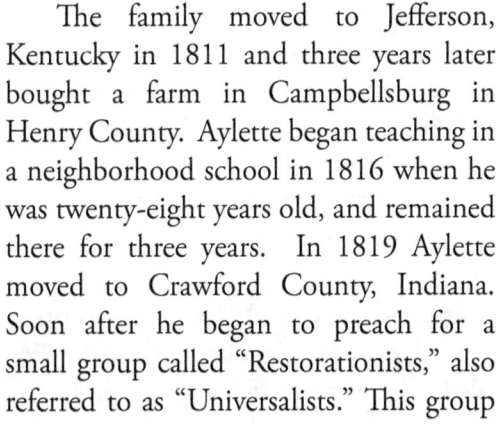

The family moved to Jefferson, Kentucky in 1811 and three years later bought a farm in Campbellsburg in Henry County. Aylette began teaching in a neighborhood school in 1816 when he was twenty-eight years old, and remained there for three years. In 1819 Aylette moved to Crawford County, Indiana. Soon after he began to preach for a small group called "Restorationists," also referred to as "Universalists." This group is not to be confused with the Restoration Movement. After about five years he became disillusioned about the Universalist doctrine he was preaching, as well as the group with which he had associated himself.

About this time Rains heard Walter Scott preach. "The first sermon that Rains heard Scott preach was 'styled the six points of the gospel'. The next day he heard him again; this subject being the 'Resurrection of Christ.' The text was the fifteenth chapter of I Corinthians. Rains was 'exceedingly amazed. Germs of truth, and beauties and glories sprang from the bosom of that chapter' under the skillful handling by Scott. The next day, Rains heard Scott preach on 'The Two Covenants;' and 'here again I was amazed.' In a few days Rains heard Scott again, the subject being Hebrews, chapter eleven. Rains said 'Scott convinced me that I ought to lay my philosophy aside and preach the gospel as the apostles preached." (6, p. 179-180) After leaving Scott, Rains went to Warren, Ohio and met with Ebenezer Williams, a staunch Universalist preacher and friend. Rains told Williams about Walter Scott and what he preached. They spent many hours, day and night, in examining the positions presented by Scott, measuring them against the Bible. "After an impartial and thorough investigation, they both mutually determined that they must submit to the ordinance of Christian baptism. They both went alone to a beautiful pool of water near by. Rains baptized Williams on a profession of his faith in Christ, and for the remission of his sins. Williams then taking the confession of Rains, baptized him for the remission of sins, and then they went their way rejoicing." (63, p. 35)

There was great rejoicing over the conversion of these two Universalist preachers. There was also concern among some of the disciples that these two might not have abandoned all of their previously accepted doctrines. J. M. Powell stated that Rains did not deny the doctrine of future punishment, but he believed it would be limited in duration and that, in time, the wicked would be made happy and holy. (6, p. 180) At the Mahoning Association meeting in Warren, Ohio in 1828, both the Campbells and Walter Scott pleaded with the others for tolerance for the views of Rains. In turn, Rains pledged that he would not preach those views nor contend for them, but he would preach the whole gospel to the best of his ability. In 1830 Rains wrote, "I wish to inform you that my 'Restorationist' sentiments have been slowly and imperceptibly erased from my mind, by the ministry of Paul and Peter, and some other illustrious preachers." (63, p. 37)

In 1868 Rains wrote of this period in his life by saying how kindly the Campbells had treated him. "Had they brow-beat me, I might have been ruined forever. But treating me kindly convinced me that my opinion, whether true or false, dwindled into nothingness in comparison with the faith of the gospels... the opinions faded, and in ten months was numbered with all my former errors."

In 1834 Rains and his wife moved to Paris, Kentucky where they bought a home. They lived there until 1862. Brother Rains is a good example of what might be called a "monthly" preacher. He preached once each month for several congregations that grew under his preaching. W. G. Rogers recorded that he preached for the church in Paris, Kentucky for twenty-eight years; for the church in Winchester twenty-eight years, and for the church in North Middletown twenty-six years.

Rains has been justly called "one of the truly great preachers in the nineteenth century." In his latter years Rains was concerned with various innovations that were beginning to plague the church. He wrote several articles in the American Christian Review, warning the church to remain faithful.

Aylette Rains died suddenly on September 7, 1881 at the age of ninety-four. He was sitting in his chair listening to his granddaughter read when his head fell to his breast. She called for help and Brother Rains was moved to a couch, but he never revived to speak another word. He had been a gospel preacher for more than fifty years. He died as he had lived, strong in the faith.

CHAPTER 19
THOMAS MILLER ALLEN
1797 - 1881

In the early days of the Restoration Movement many took up the cause who were in the depths of poverty. These men considered that preaching the primitive gospel was the most important thing in life. It seemed not to matter much to them that they lived without much of this world's goods. However, there were also men of wealth who took up the cause of the Restoration and willingly used their wealth in an effort to spread the kingdom on earth. Thomas M. Allen is numbered among the latter group.

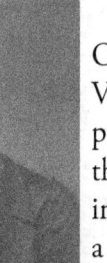

Thomas Miller Allen was born October 21, 1797 in Shenandoah County, Virginia on the Shenandoah River. His parents were Presbyterian and he took up the cause of the Presbyterian Church early in his life. When Allen was a young man a tragic accident happened to him that would handicap him for life. On May 10, 1816 he was returning to Virginia from a visit to Kentucky. He was six miles west of Washington, Pennsylvania when a sudden storm came up. He was riding on horseback with a young woman. The two took refuge under a tree. Lightening struck a nearby tree and shattered it. A large section of the tree fell on the young woman and killed her instantly. The horse on which Thomas was riding was also killed. Although the accident did not kill Thomas, it did leave him with a crippled

283

arm and hand for the remainder of his life. Allen did not allow this handicap to cause him to shrink back from an active life. On the contrary, he was very active in the secular world as well as the realm of religion. He liberally gave of himself and his talents in the cause of the Lord. (36, p. 82)

On May 24, 1818 Allen was married to Rebecca W. Russell. Barton W. Stone performed the ceremony. He settled on a farm near Lexington, Kentucky and studied law at Transylvania University. After the university he moved to Bloomington, Indiana in 1822 and opened a law office there. His partner was James Whitcomb, who would later become governor of Indiana, and then still later a U.S. Senator from Indiana. Soon after that, Allen moved back to Kentucky where he again became more interested in religion. After he had served in the War of 1812 his interest in religion had declined. In Kentucky he heard Barton W. Stone preach about a restoration of primitive Christianity, and he became interested at once. He was baptized in May of 1823 when he was twenty-six years old. He became a member of the "Old Union" congregation in Fayette County. Stone had established this congregation with six members. In the spring of 1825 Allen began to preach publicly. At that time those who left the Presbyterian Church and were preaching independently were called "New Lights." (38, pp. 193-194)

Allen preached the gospel in his own county and adjoining counties. He preached often in Bourbon County, Kentucky and established many congregations in that county. In his early days as a preacher he often associated with Barton W. Stone, F. R. Palmer, and Joel H. Haden. Like Allen, these men had emerged from the confusion of denominational error and had come into the light of truth.

At the close of 1827 Allen wrote the following: "During the year 1827 I married eight couples; baptized fifty-one, planted two churches, one at ... Bourbon County, and the other at ... Harrison County, both having increased considerably and at this time are in a very flourishing condition." (36, p. 83) In 1830 he wrote: "I attended the Baptist Association at Silas on the fifteenth of August and saw the association exert their lawless and unauthorized power over all usage, constitution, precedent, or rule in the exclusion of Brethren J.

Creath, Sr., J. Creath, Jr., and the churches to which they respectfully belong, simply because of their opposition to all human creeds and their view on gospel liberty. The conduct of the orthodox part of this association convinced me that they were actuated by the same spirit that in former days planted the stake and lighted the fagot." (36, p. 83) It was in 1830 that Thomas Allen heard Alexander Campbell preach for the first time. Allen was thirty-three and Campbell was forty-two. Since Allen had already obeyed the gospel and was a Christian before he met Campbell, he could hardly be called a "Campbellite" as some unfairly called him. Allen had great success in preaching the primitive gospel in Kentucky. He established congregations at Paris, Clintonville, and Bryant Station.

> Although Allen was seeing many responses to his gospel preaching in Kentucky, he made the decision to move to Boone County, Missouri. He settled on what was called the "Two-Mile Prairie." He began traveling and preaching immediately. "Perhaps no other man in the State of Missouri ever did as much traveling on horseback and preaching the gospel as did Thomas M. Allen. In private houses, in barns, in open groves, in courthouses, in the Hall of Representatives at Jefferson City, and in nearly all the meeting houses of his section of the State, was the voice of Thomas M. Allen heard pleading for the truth and the union of God's people by returning to the apostolic doctrine and practice. No man did more to spread the cause of Christ in the State of Missouri than did Thomas M. Allen." (36, p. 83)

Even after moving to Missouri, he returned time and again to Kentucky to visit the congregations that he had established as well as to establish new ones. He also preached in other states as well. It was through the influence of Thomas Allen that Alexander Campbell visited the congregations in Missouri and strengthened them. Allen wrote frequently to the Millennial Harbinger in which he reported the progress of his gospel meetings as well as that of other preachers.

Allen was about six feet tall and weighed about one hundred and eighty pounds. In spite of his handicap, he was a man of great strength and endurance, which served him well as he preached the gospel. He had a commanding personality and a clear, strong voice.

POLITICS

Allen never aspired to any office. He was frequently urged by his political friends in the old Whig party to become a candidate for governor of the State of Missouri, but he lacked the interest to do so. Once he declined an appointment to Congress to fill an unexpired term on the ground that it might impair his influence as a minister of the gospel and it would set a bad example to the young preachers. Allen was a successful businessman and was quite wealthy. He contributed generously to Bethany College, which was established by Alexander Campbell. He served on the Board of Directors for Missouri University and was honored several times by being elected president of the Board. (36, p. 84)

DEATH COMES

Brother Allen continued actively as a preacher of the gospel until the fall of 1871, having served in the pulpit for over fifty years. He died on October 10, 1871 in Columbia, Missouri. The funeral services were conducted by Joseph K. Rogers, president of Missouri University. His funeral was attended by one of the largest crowds ever seen in Columbia. A great tribute was paid to the memory of Thomas M. Allen when the doors of the businesses in town were closed during his funeral. He was a man who influenced those around him with his religious convictions and godly life.

CHAPTER 20
PHILIP S. FALL
1798 - 1890

Philip Sydney Fall was born in Keloedon, England in September of 1798. He was the eldest of twelve children. Philip was educated religiously as an Episcopalian and remained with that belief until he came to America. The trip to America with his parents occurred in 1817 when Philip was nineteen. They settled near Russellville, Kentucky. After only one year in their new home, both of his parents died, leaving Philip to become the head of this large family. (36, p. 86)

Fall had received a good education in England. It seemed a natural thing for him to turn to teaching as a means of making a living. In 1818 he established an academy near Louisville, Kentucky. He conducted this institution of learning successfully for some time.

ORDAINED BAPTIST MINISTER

In the same year of 1818 Fall united with the Baptist Church. In December of 1819 he was ordained as a preacher in the Baptist Church. He married Annie Bacon in 1821. In that same year he received an invitation to preach monthly to a newly organized small congregation of Baptists meeting in the courthouse in Louisville. In

1823 he moved to the city of Louisville and established a school, continuing to preach for the same Baptist congregation.

INTRODUCED TO RESTORATION PRINCIPLES

In 1822 Fall read Alexander Campbell's "Sermon on the Law." The next winter he openly preached these ideas himself and received considerable criticism. "He was led by the writings of Alexander Campbell to study prayerfully the New Testament Scriptures. He soon became convinced that the New Testament was a sufficient guide in all matters of religion. He led his congregation to adopt the New Testament as the guide and to follow the principles revealed therein, and the entire congregation put away the Baptist creed." (36, p. 87)

P.S. Fall became the first resident Baptist preacher in the state of Kentucky to accept the plea to return to the New Testament church. It did not take long for him to be held in disfavor by the Baptists of the area. He was the secretary of the Long Run Baptist Association, and in 1824 was invited to write the circular letter to the churches. Fall did so, explaining that the New Testament was the only rule of faith and practice. Unfortunately, the letter was rejected.

MOVED TO NASHVILLE

Fall moved to Nashville, Tennessee in 1825. This was the result of an invitation from the Nashville Female Academy. In addition to his teaching, he began preaching for the Baptist Church. Prior to accepting the preaching position with the Baptist Church, Fall explained his conviction that he must be free to preach only the Bible, and furthermore, that he would reject all human creeds. The congregation agreed. This Baptist Church was a member of the Concord Baptist Association. "Fall's insistence that the church take only the New Testament for its rule of faith and practice soon put it into disfavor with the Baptist Association. The minutes of the Concord Baptist Association for 1827 refer to P. S. Fall as 'a thorough dyed Campbellite under a Baptist cloak.'" (38, p. 238). With but few exceptions, the congregation accepted Fall's plea for a restoration of the New Testament way of doing things. This marked the beginning of the Lord's church in Nashville.

FALL AND CAMPBELL

P. S. Fall and Alexander Campbell became close friends. When Campbell visited Louisville for the first time, he stayed with Fall. The two had corresponded but had never met. Campbell was invited to speak at the regular Friday night meeting. Fall recalls the event: "My schoolroom was well filled, and five Presbyterian ministers were present. Brother Campbell read a portion of the Epistle to the Hebrews and spoke nearly two hours, with each person present giving him the utmost attention. His method of reading the Scriptures, of investigating their truths and of exhibiting their statements, was so entirely new and so perfectly clear as to command the respect, if not the approval, of all that listened." (36, p. 88) Campbell returned to Nashville several times to visit Fall and the church in the years that followed.

Due to ill health, Fall left Nashville in 1831 and returned to Kentucky, locating near Frankfort. When Fall left Nashville, he left a congregation that had pulled away from the Baptists and was standing on the Bible alone. In Frankfort he established the Female Eclectic Institute, which he directed for twenty-six years. During this time Fall preached around the state, bringing on the displeasure of the Baptists.

TROUBLE IN NASHVILLE

In 1852 the church in Nashville began having serious trouble because of false and divisive teachings of a man named J.B. Ferguson. Ferguson did not believe in punishment after death. He argued that heaven and hell were not places but states. Ferguson went off into spiritualism, teaching that men could communicate with the spirit world. Ferguson had a large following and the church was badly divided. When Fall left the congregation in 1831 there were 250 members. After the Ferguson division, only about twenty-five members remained. Fall was called back to Nashville in 1858 and began the task of rebuilding the congregation. By 1860 the church numbered 200 members and they once again enjoyed peace. He remained in Nashville until 1877, at which time he resigned, recommending that a younger man take over. Fall returned to the Frankfort area where he spent the remainder of his life. He spent his last years in peaceful retirement, preaching occasionally as his strength would permit and writing frequently for the brotherhood papers. (36, p. 90)

Any history of the churches of Christ in Nashville must include Philip S. Fall. He was a pioneer preacher, pleading for a return to the New Testament order in that city. He had no sympathy for error and hated sin in every form. He passed from this life December 3, 1890 at the age of ninety-two. He lived a long, useful life, and remained mentally alert to the end. He was buried in Frankfort, Kentucky.

CHAPTER 21
JACOB CREATH, JR.
1799 - 1883

One of the most colorful characters of the entire Restoration Movement was Jacob Creath, Jr. He was fearlessly independent in his thinking and he marched to his own drummer in most areas of life. Typical of his idiosyncrasies were the events surrounding his death. Two years before he died, he wrote out his own obituary. Since Jesus and the apostles all died without a funeral sermon being preached for them, Creath determined that there would be none for him either. He requested that he be buried in a plain, cheap coffin, with his pocket Bible placed under his head and a copy of Campbell's Living Oracles under that. He had lived and waged many a spiritual battle with his Bible in one hand and the Living Oracles in the other. Nothing would suit him better than that they should be the pillow for his head in death. (1, p. 115)

John F. Rowe called him the "Iron Duke of the Restoration." Earl West says of Creath, "Men like Jacob Creath are what make the Restoration Movement breathe the atmosphere of romance. Not often has the world known such men, and less often has it appreciated those few it has known." Rowe further says of him, "In the person of Jacob Creath we have stalwart Christian manhood, solidity of character, sternness of purpose, invincible willpower, a disposition that tolerates no wrong, a sense of justice that knows no relenting." (1, p. 115)

BAPTIST BACKGROUND

William Creath, Jacob's father, married Lucretia Brame, a young lady of English descent. She gave birth to sixteen children. Since William was away most of the time preaching, the care of the family fell almost entirely upon his wife. She was very devout and required her children to read the Bible and commit large portions of it to memory. Five of her nine sons became ministers. The home of William Creath was the home of Baptist preachers from Maine to Georgia. When William's second son was born January 17, 1779, he left the naming of the child to his younger brother, Jacob. Jacob chose his own name for the child. So, Jacob, Sr. was the uncle of Jacob, Jr.

Since his father was a Baptist preacher it was only natural for the son, Jacob, Jr., to be concerned about his soul's salvation from the viewpoint of Baptist teaching. Baptists, true to the doctrine of Calvinism, believed and taught that a man could do nothing to be saved, that something had to happen to him before he could know that he was among "the elect." Creath tried to get an experience, and at times, thought he had one, but emotion subsided, and he was left destitute of any hope. Discouraged, he tried at one time to be an infidel, but he could not honestly accept that. In April of 1817, at a Baptist meeting of the Meherrin Association in Virginia, Creath responded to the invitation to come to the altar for salvation. This he did and they prayed over him and declared him saved. Then, in May of 1817 Creath was immersed by his father. He said that he had a measure of peace when he came up from the water. (1, p. 118)

ORDAINED BAPTIST PREACHER

With financial help from the Charleston Baptist Association, he attended the University of North Carolina at Chapel Hill and remained there from 1819 to 1820. He moved to Caswell County, and it was during this time that he became an ordained minister in the Baptist Church. The ordination took place on September 23-24, 1820 at the Mill Creek Meeting House in Caswell County. In

November, 1821 Creath entered Columbia College in Washington, D.C. and, while going to school, worshipped with the First Baptist Church in that city.

Creath's preaching took him to various congregations of the Baptist Church in Louisville, Lexington, and Great Crossings, Kentucky; Natchez, Mississippi; New Orleans, Louisiana; and Nashville, Tennessee. While he was in Tennessee, he visited the Hermitage, the home of President Andrew Jackson, with letters of introduction from Richard M. Johnson, brother of John T. Johnson. He also visited with Robert Foster, lieutenant governor of Tennessee. In the fall of 1827 he almost died of yellow fever, and as a result went to Bethany, Virginia. Before long he was back in Kentucky and preached at Versailles, Cane Run, and South Elkorn. (1, p. 120)

TRIED BY BAPTISTS FOR HERESY

One of the most trying circumstances of his life came when the Great Crossings Baptist Church tried him for heresy. From reading the Christian Baptist, Creath had become acquainted with the restoration principles. He denounced creeds and taught that the word of God was the instrument through which conversion took place and that to be converted a person simply had to obey the word of God. The church sent Creath a letter dated May 17, 1829, demanding that he give an account of himself. At the trial by the Great Crossings Baptist Church, Creath read Paul's defense before Agrippa and Festus. John T. Johnson, then a Baptist, was present for the trial. After the trial Johnson said, "Absolutely, if they don't let that man alone the stones of the street will cry out against them." (1, p. 120)

Later, Johnson told Creath that he would never have been connected with the Restoration Movement except for Creath. When the Elkhorn Baptist Association convened in August, 1829, an effort was made to adopt a resolution to exclude all of those from the Baptist Church who believed in taking the "Bible alone." Through the efforts of Johnson, the resolution was defeated and for another year, the preachers remained free to preach.

EXPELLED FROM THE BAPTISTS

In 1830 action was taken against Jacob Creath, Jr., Jacob Creath, Sr., and Raccoon John Smith. The Franklin Baptist Association which met a month earlier at Frankfort, Kentucky had prepared charges against the Elkhorn Baptist Association for not taking action against those in their number who had taken positions contrary to the accepted Baptist view on conversion. The Elkhorn Association was under pressure to do something or face criticism from other Baptist Associations. At the meeting of the Elkhorn Association Raccoon John Smith, Jacob Creath, Sr., and Jacob Creath, Jr. were present to hear charges made against them and passed, but not one of the three was allowed to speak in his own defense. All three men were expelled from the Baptist Church at this association meeting in 1830. Doctrinally and philosophically, they had left the Baptists long before this. (1, p. 121)

MARRIED SUSAN BEDFORD

In September of 1831, Creath married Mrs. Susan Bedford, widow of Sidney Bedford of Bourbon County, Kentucky. For the next few years Creath farmed through the week, and then preached on Saturday and Sundays. In 1834 he held a debate with Lewis Green, professor of Ancient Languages at Danville College. The debate was held in July in Lincoln County. For the next three years Creath entered more extensively into preaching. He and John T. Johnson were almost continual companions. In 1835 Johnson and Creath held a meeting together in Fayette County, Kentucky. The same year they preached at Versailles and baptized one hundred and forty. For the next three years they preached continuously until the denominations became alarmed for fear the whole country was going to the "Campbellites." (1, p. 121)

Susan Bedford Creath died on July 16, 1841. She left behind a son from her previous marriage to Sidney Bedford. Bedford had owned considerable property that was left to the boy, the stepson of Jacob Creath, Jr. Creath had been appointed his guardian. Meanwhile, the brothers and sisters of Bedford wanted the property. They lured the boy away from Creath and secured the guardianship. The boy died under age and the elder Bedford's relatives got the possessions. Jacob Creath was ruined financially in the whole transaction.

Creath moved to Palmyra, Missouri in 1841 and married another widow, Mrs. Prudence Rogers of Bowling Green. Using Palmyra as his base, Creath traveled continuously, preaching the gospel and establishing congregations. His work took him through Illinois, Missouri, Louisiana, Kentucky, Indiana, and Tennessee.

A MAN OF PRAYER

Creath was a man who fervently believed in prayer. J. B. Wilkes wrote in the American Christian Review in 1884:

> In 1854 J. B. Wilkes went to Lagrange, Missouri to preach. We went to the home of a Brother Gill and found Jacob Creath, Jr. there. The next morning after breakfast Brother Creath asked J. B. Wilkes to take a walk. After they had walked about 1/4 mile in silence they came to a fallen log. They both bowed down while Creath prayed. As Brother Creath prayed, Brother Wilkes said, "My soul trembled with excitement. Brother Creath talked so to God that I voluntarily felt for the moment that if I should open my eyes I should certainly see him upon whom no one can look and live. I never heard such a prayer before, and now 30 years have passed since that remarkable experience, and yet I have heard no such prayer since..." (1, p. 124)

On one occasion, during the Civil War, a company of troops was encamped near Palmyra, intending to capture the city. Creath went out to the grove to pray and the leader of the troops happened to be near. He edged closer to the grove and listened as Creath prayed for his neighbors, his town and for peace. The next day the troops withdrew with no attempt to capture the town.

A TYPICAL DAY

On December 9, 1862, Jacob Creath made an entry in his diary that gives us a picture of his daily routine:

> For the sake of others, when I am dead, I will here state the order of my family. I rise at four o'clock in the morning in the summer season, and at five in the wintertime. I make a fire, and wash my face, head and feet in cold water, to prevent colds, fevers, catarrh in my head, and other diseases, and to preserve my hearing. My wife then rises and dresses herself, and we read a chapter in the Bible, I one in the morning and she one in the evening. We then unite in prayer to God for his blessing and direction. We have breakfast between six and seven o'clock, and we eat supper about six in the evening. After breakfast, I walk about one mile west of my house, to a woods, and there I spend from fifteen to twenty minutes in private prayer, where I have more real happiness in close communion with God than all this world can afford me. I would not be deprived of this source of enjoyment for this world and all its vanities. Vanity of vanities, all is vanity, saith the Preacher. It will soon perish in our hands. I then return home, and spend the time in reading and writing until twelve or one o'clock, when we dine. I then go to the post-office, and spend the afternoon in visiting the families of the city, and in reading the papers. Every Christian man should have a family altar in his house, and bring his family morning and evening, and in times of affliction three times a day, as I have done. There is no other way to train our families in the instruction and discipline of the Lord." (11, pp. 189-190)

CONCERN FOR THE CHURCH

As the years slowly came upon Creath, his physical frame began to fail him, but his mind remained active. In 1884 John F. Rowe was on a trip and stopped by to see Creath, who was 84 years old. Creath was just going to bed, but upon seeing Rowe stayed up and talked for three hours. Creath did almost all of the talking. The cause of the church was heavy on his heart. Rowe said of their conversation, "He fully comprehends the present crisis of the churches, many of which he was instrumental in bringing into life; and though cheered by the prospect of a home in heaven, he mourned over the desolation of Jerusalem. We assured him that all was not lost, but that the heart of the great brotherhood, when not misdirected by the 'kingdom of the clergy' rising up in our midst, still beats responsive to the loud call of the gospel." (1, p. 123)

Jacob Creath had good reason to be upset about the condition of the church. One of the causes of concern was the acceptance by many congregations of the American Christian Missionary Society that had been formed in Cincinnati in October of 1849. No one more bitterly opposed the Society than did Creath. He was the first great opponent of human organizations. He boldly challenged Alexander Campbell, and told him that he had changed his position from his earlier years when he had condemned societies in the Christian Baptist.

Campbell had argued that societies such as the American Christian Missionary Society had not been condemned by Jesus and his apostles. To this Creath responded strongly:

> You say our Savior and the apostles did not denounce conventions, as such. Did they denounce popery or corrupt Protestantism, as such? Did they denounce infant baptism, or creed making, or auricular confessions, as such? It is for you to show where they authorized conventions... (11, p. 11)

Creath also answered the position that Campbell advanced, that the Society had been accepted by many brethren:

> It will be seen, in this discussion, the advocates of conventions have totally abandoned the rule... They have not produced one passage of scripture, to countenance those assembles from the New Testament... As to the argument offered to sustain these associations, that they are acceptable to our brethren--we would say, that they have been unacceptable to them until recently. What has produced this change in them? What new light is this which has sprung up so recently upon this subject? I confess I have no more light now, upon the subject of associations, than I had twenty-five years ago. Will these brethren, who have been so recently and suddenly converted from their former faith upon this subject, furnish us with a small portion of this new light, that we may be converted too? I suppose the golden calf was acceptable to all the Jews, except Moses. I believe the calves set up at Dan and Bethel were popular with Jeroboam and the ten tribes. The report of the spies was acceptable to all the Jews, except Caleb and Joshua. The pope is very acceptable to the Catholics; so are creeds and clerical conventions to all the Protestant parties. But does all of this prove that they are acceptable to God? (11, pp. 12)

In addition to the harm and division that was caused by the Missionary Society, Creath was also grieved by the innovation of instrumental music being adopted by many congregations. In 1860 L. L. Pinkerton of Midway, Kentucky had announced in a church periodical that the church in Midway was using the instrument in worship, and to the best of his knowledge, they were the first. Through the years more and more of the congregations accepted this innovation. Creath was an opponent of the use of instrumental music in worship. By nature he could not refrain from speaking out against practices that he felt were wrong. This did not make him popular among the liberal brethren.

Earl West points out that Creath was of the firm conviction that around 1849 a great change came over the Restoration Movement, and over Alexander Campbell personally. The Millennial Harbinger of these years was not the same paper that it was before. He believed that Campbell was easing out of the picture, and that his corps of younger teachers and friends were influencing him in the wrong direction. In 1857 Dr. Robert Richardson published in the Harbinger some articles on "German Theology and French Philosophy." Neither Jacob Creath or Tolbert Fanning liked it. Both wrote Campbell in protest. Creath wrote that if what Richardson was printing was the gospel, 99 out of 100 readers of the Harbinger did not know what the gospel was, and he added, "I am one of that number." (1, p. 125)

THE END COMES

Jacob Creath, Jr. passed from this life January 9, 1886 in Palmyra, Missouri. Palmyra had been his home since 1846. His wife honored the requests that he had made concerning his burial. No funeral service was held. He was laid to rest in a plain, simple coffin in which was placed his Bible and a copy of the Living Oracles. John F. Rowe, editor of the American Christian Review said of Creath, "... he was made of such stuff as martyrs. (64, p. 219)

"In his later years, he had written of his mother and his last visit with her. 'The Lord bless you, my son, Jacob,' she said as she held him in her arms and kissed him for the last time. 'You have been a good son to me! If I never meet you on this earth again, I hope to meet you in the resurrection of the just.'" (64, p. 219)

CHAPTER 22
JOHN ALLEN GANO
1805 - 1887

When B. A. Abbott listed the eight most prominent men who gave temper, direction, and pace to the early Restoration Movement, he included among them an associate of Barton W. Stone by the name of John Allen Gano. He referred to Gano as "the indefatigable evangelist." (69, p. 20) Gano deserves to be included among the most successful of the pioneer preachers of the Restoration. He is reported to have baptized more than ten thousand people and established a great number of congregations. (70, p. 222)

John Allen's ancestry is quite interesting. His great, great, great grandfather left Roman Catholicism about the middle of the seventeenth century and became a leader in the Protestant Hugenot Movement. When the government began efforts to exterminate French Protestantism, he and his family barely escaped certain death. The Ganeau family migrated to America in 1661 and anglicized the name from Ganeau to Gano. John Allen's grandfather, a Baptist minister, was a chaplain under George Washington during the Revolutionary War. Even though he was part of a denomination, he had a great desire to allow the Word of God to be his only rule of faith and practice. This principle in time passed on to his children and led several members of the family into the Movement to restore New Testament Christianity.

This number included his grandson, John Allen Gano. (70, p. 222)

John Allen Gano was born in Georgetown, Kentucky to Richard M. Gano and Elizabeth Ewing Gano. Tragically, John's mother died when he was seven years old, and his father died when John was eleven. As a teenager, Gano attended a school that was operated by Barton W. Stone, pioneer gospel preacher. In his classes Stone not only taught secular subjects, but he also taught his students the Bible. In commentary on Stone's effectiveness, J.M. Powell said, "With his invincible logic of flowing from a heart of love, he influenced a number of outstanding men to become a part of 'the good cause.' Among those stalwarts that he enlisted was John Allen Gano ... (70, p. 223).

At age twenty-one John Allen obtained his license to practice law. He was on his way by steamboat to Texas to set up his practice when he became very ill with lung hemorrhage. The captain, not wishing to have a death on his boat, put John off on the lower Ohio River. Fortunately, a compassionate family took him in and nursed him to health. It was during this period that he determined to be a gospel preacher. (70, p. 223)

All of Gano's family were associated with the Baptists, but John Allen had never become a member. He heard both Barton W. Stone and T. M. Allen preach the primitive gospel. It was T. M. Allen who baptized him July 10, 1827 at Georgetown, Kentucky. It was at a gospel meeting that Gano was so moved by the message that T. M. Allen preached that he responded, confessed Christ, and was baptized. (70, p. 223)

John Allen's sisters were devout Baptists and were very much concerned about his religious convictions. They sent for a well known Baptist preacher by the name of Jacob Creath, Sr. in order to "straighten him out." Creath traveled the distance of seventy miles in order to bring Gano back into the Baptist foal. Richard Gano described that meeting:

> Entering his room and finding him seated at a little table with his Testament, Mr. Creath said, "Brother John, I am glad you have determined to devote your

life to the service of Christ, but I think you had better have taken your stand with the church of your fathers; your family have been identified with the Baptist Church for probably a hundred years, and your grandfather, John Gano, was an eminent Baptist minister and chaplain in the Revolutionary War under George Washington, and immersed General Washington during that war." John A. Gano replied, "If you will show me in this Book," laying his hand upon the Testament, "where it says, 'Deny yourself, take up your cross and follow your grandfather,' I will follow mine while I live; but I read it, 'Deny yourself, take up our cross and follow Christ,' and I intend to follow this teaching if it separates me from all the kindred on earth." (70, p. 223)

Creath was an honest man and this discussion had such an impact on his life that he would never be the same again. Richard Gano wrote, "They spent twelve hours in conversation and the old minister was so impressed that he returned the next day and they renewed the conversation, and Jacob Creath, Sr., became convinced and soon after came out publicly and took his stand with the church that has no book or creed but God's Word and will wear no name but the name of Christ, the only position on which the friends of Christ can ever be united, and John Allen Gano went with all his might to preaching the Gospel of Christ and had success in winning souls to Christ unequaled in that state." (70, p. 224)

The year that Gano was instrumental in converting Jacob Creath, Sr. was 1827. In the same year Gano married Mary Catherine Conn. The ceremony was performed by Barton W. Stone. As a wedding gift the parents of Mary Catherine gave the young couple a very valuable farm. (70, p. 225)

From 1827 to 1836 Gano traveled and preached with T. M.

Allen. When Allen returned to Missouri in 1836, Gano and John T. Johnson began traveling together and preaching the gospel. This association continued until Johnson died in 1856. Many churches were established during these two periods.

John Allen Gano became critically ill in the fall of 1887. His last words were spoken to J. S. Sweeney. They were, "I am almost home." He passed away at 6:00 A.M. on Friday, October 18, 1887 at the age of eighty-two. John W. McGarvey conducted the funeral service at the Gano home which was called "Bellview." The home was located about half way between Georgetown and Paris, Kentucky. He was buried in the Georgetown cemetery.

CHAPTER 23
TOLBERT FANNING
1810 - 1874

Tolbert Fanning was described by Earl West as, "Unquestionably, the most influential preacher in the South before the War between the States. There were other great men, of course... but when one considers the lasting influence, Tolbert Fanning has to be ranked above them all." (1, p. 108)

When Fanning was eight years of age, his parents moved to Alabama and settled in Lauderdale County where he remained until  he was nineteen years old. Since his father raised cotton, young Fanning spent much of his time in the cotton fields. While it does not seem such to us today, Fanning was very fortunate to be able to attend school from three to six months each year. He acquired a fondness for study early in his life and excelled in his studies. His father was not a religious man, although he was highly respected in his community. His mother was a member of the Baptist Church, and was recognized as an intelligent woman.

CONTACT WITH THE RESTORATION

Young Fanning received his early religious training from his mother, as well as an occasional preacher that he heard speak. Since his teaching came from those with the Baptist persuasion, Fanning

305

at first accepted the doctrine that man could not do anything toward his own salvation. In fact, he was taught that he could not even understand the Bible without a special illumination from the Holy Spirit. Fanning was spiritually burdened under this gloomy and hopeless impression of false Calvinistic teaching for several years of his young life. When he was sixteen years old, he began to give attention to two preachers who claimed to be "Christians only," E. D. Moore and E. J. Matthews. These men encouraged him to read the New Testament and find for himself what the will of the Lord was. As he did so, his understanding of the plan of salvation took the place of the gloomy doubts that he previously possessed. (1, p. 111)

BAPTIZED AT AGE SEVENTEEN

According to H. Leo Boles, Tolbert Fanning attended a gospel meeting in 1827 near Florence, Alabama conducted by James E. Matthews. One sermon that especially impressed Fanning was "The Gospel and Its Conditions." At the conclusion of the sermon, young Fanning made the good confession of his faith in Jesus, and was baptized immediately into Christ. (36, p. 151) Earl West writes the account of Fanning's conversion a little differently. He states that B. F. Hall had come from Kentucky into Lauderdale County to preach. On Sunday evening he preached at Cyprus Creek. Tolbert Fanning, age seventeen, was present and heard the lesson. When the invitation was given, Fanning came forward and made the confession, but was not baptized until the next morning. According to West, the one who did the baptizing was James E. Matthews from Mississippi. (1, p. 108)

Even though the accounts vary, the end result was the same and that event would completely alter the life of Tolbert Fanning. His next two years were spent primarily in studying the Scriptures and attending school. On October 1, 1829, he left home for the purpose of preaching the gospel to all who would listen to him. He was only nineteen and inexperienced, but he was determined to preach Jesus Christ. His earnestness and zeal and his clear, logical manner of presenting the truths of the gospel attracted thousands of people to attend his meetings, and large numbers were delivered from the kingdom of darkness into the kingdom of light. (36, p. 151)

MARRIED CHARLOTTE FALL

In 1831 Fanning entered Nashville University and graduated in 1835. While a student at the university, Fanning was able to preach in several locations. During one vacation he made a preaching tour with Alexander Campbell into the states of Ohio and Kentucky. At Perryville, Kentucky, he debated a Methodist preacher by the name of Rice. The debate was successful for Fanning and meant a great deal to the cause of truth in that area. In 1836 he again spent the spring and summer with Alexander Campbell in a preaching tour that took them through Ohio, New York, Canada, New England, and many cities in the East. (36, p. 152)

Fanning married Charlotte Fall in 1837. Charlotte Fall was the sister of Philip S. Fall who was an early preacher of Restoration principles in Nashville, Tennessee. It was also in 1837 that he opened a female academy in Franklin, Tennessee. He taught in the academy, and during the same period preached in the Nashville area through 1839. On January 1, 1840, Fanning moved to a location about five miles from Nashville where he directed a female academy until 1842. In 1843 Fanning spent most of his time preaching on tours through Alabama and Mississippi.

ESTABLISHED FRANKLIN COLLEGE

In 1844 Tolbert Fanning established Franklin College. Fanning was elected the first president of the school. He also taught in the school for the next seventeen years, at which time he resigned for the purpose of raising money to enlarge the school. That same year, 1861, the Civil War began which canceled any plans for expansion. In 1865 the college building was destroyed by a devastating fire. After Franklin College burned, Fanning purchased the Minerva College property, which was a short distance from Franklin College.

In conjunction with his wife, they began to teach in the new school and called it "Hope Institute." (36, p. 152)

Much good was done by Franklin College under the direction of Tolbert Fanning. Among the alumni were A. J. Fanning, E. W. Carmack, William Lipscomb, David Lipscomb, F. M. Carmack, J. E. Scobey, and E. G. Sewell. (36, p. 152) Tolbert Fanning's efforts in three areas can be appreciated by Restoration students. He was a powerful preacher of the gospel, an educator of the young, and an effective and influential writer.

PUBLISHED THE CHRISTIAN REVIEW

While he was president of Franklin College, Fanning began publication of the Christian Review in 1844. His first article published in the Christian Review was title "Our Position in Reference to the Different Religious Denominations." In this article he stated, "While we have the Bible, we can see no authority or plausible reason for the existence of any church not designated and portrayed in the New Testament, and consequently we consider ourselves called of heaven to state our reasons in a friendly and courteous manner for such a conclusion." (36, p. 153) The name of the paper was later changed to Christian Magazine. After this paper ceased, Fanning became the senior editor of the Gospel Advocate. In 1866, Volume VIII of the Advocate listed the following: "T. Fanning and D. Lipscomb, Editors." (36, p. 153) His name still appears as one of the editors of Volume IX in 1867. After finishing as an editor for the Advocate, he began publishing monthly journals in 1872 known as The Religious Historian. In this paper he discussed the vital subject of church government. As a preacher, teacher, writer, Fanning was always clear and sound. (36, p. 153)

"Fanning was a physical giant--six feet six inches tall. David Lipscomb, his student, said, 'He was as tall, well-muscled, and active a specimen of lithe, vigorous manhood as is often seen. He gradually grew more portly, and at forty to sixty was one of the finest specimens of majestic and graceful manhood to be seen anywhere.'" (59, p. 48) He was a man of great energy and activity. It was not unusual for him to spend his day in the classroom, then conduct his business interests on his farm for several hours, and then sit up and write until midnight or later, and then get up in the morning to start the routine all over again. (36, p. 154) When Fanning made up his mind about a matter, he was hard to move in a different direction. What was a matter of strong conviction for Fanning was unfairly considered by some as unyielding.

A MAN OF STRONG CONVICTIONS

Fanning was a man of the Book. He was opposed to everything religiously that he could not find authorized in the Bible. He was, therefore, opposed to the missionary societies and other such organizations. He was also opposed to instrumental music in worship. He opposed denominationalism with all of his might. He was bold and courageous in speaking out against error. Without question, Tolbert Fanning was one of the greatest and most useful men of God of his generation.

DEATH COMES TO A GREAT MAN OF GOD

"One day in the early spring of 1873, Fanning went to the lot to see his livestock. He asked Frank Manier, a farm hand, to lead out a fine bull for him to examine. Manier was afraid of the animal and so Fanning, showing signs of impatience with his farm hand, stepped into the yard to do the work himself. The bull made a lunge for Fanning and almost killed him on the spot. He was carried to the house and for a week or two remained in bed. But he was not accustomed to inactivity and hardly knew what it meant to be sick. By April 30, which fell on Thursday, he felt strong enough to be up again and so he went back to the lot. But when he returned to the house, he felt something tear inside his body as he started up the stairway. For several days he suffered great agony in his side. On Saturday the day was gloomy and rainy. Then on Sunday morning he told the physician that this would be his last day. He summoned a group of his friends to his room and asked that they worship with him. Together they broke the loaf in memory of the death of Christ. But when Fanning asked them to sing, everyone was at first too filled with emotion. Fanning continued to beg, 'sing, sing.' When they finally started the hymn, he was too weak to join them. Soon he went away into death." (59, pp. 256-257)

If Fanning had lived seven more days, he would have been sixty-four years old. It was 10:30 Sunday morning, May 3, 1874 when he observed the Lord's Supper. It was 12:30 P.M. that same day when he passed away. His mind was clear to the end, but his pain was so great that he could hardly talk. During his life he served the Lord and His church with all of his being. The church suffered a tremendous loss the day that Tolbert Fanning passed from this life.

CHAPTER 24
BENJAMIN FRANKLIN
1811 - 1878

"Benjamin Franklin was of the sturdy, pioneer brand of preachers who had characterized the Movement in the early days, and were still numerous in Indiana. He was essentially a man of the people, forthright, able but withal plodding." (66, p. 141) Earl West gives Benjamin Franklin a very high standing in importance to the Restoration Movement. "It is not exaggerating in the least to say that after the death of Alexander Campbell in 1866 the most prominent man in the brotherhood was Benjamin Franklin." (1, p. 99)

Benjamin Franklin was born February 12, 1811 to Joseph and Isabella Franklin in Belmont County, Eastern Ohio. He was a direct descendent of Josiah Franklin, an English non-conformist, who numbered among his seventeen children Benjamin Franklin, the inventor, diplomat, and signer of the Declaration of Independence. Benjamin Franklin, preacher of the Restoration, may have been named for his great uncle, but he was directly a descendent of the inventor's brother, John. When Benjamin was an infant his parents moved to Noble County, Ohio where they lived until 1833.

In May, 1833, Joseph Franklin moved his family and worldly effects into Henry County,

311

Indiana, where he entered a tract of land, near where Middleton now stands. The country was new and unpromising, and the population as very sparse. Here Joseph Franklin and his sons erected saw-mills and flour-mills, and this business they conducted for a considerable length of time, according to varying circumstances. A turning-lathe was set up on the farm, a vat for tanning sole-leather was built, and the father made his own shoes and drove his own pegs.

Benjamin had preceded his father one year, having accompanied his uncle, Calvin Franklin, into Henry County in 1832. During the summer and autumn, Benjamin employed himself at whatever he could find to do. When winter came he worked a few months on the National Road, which was in course of construction across the State. ... When twenty-one years of age, he bought eighty acres of land, which he immediately began to improve. On this farm, with his own hands, he built his own log-house, which after a lapse of forty-five years, still stands, good and sound, as a memorial of the brave man who designed it, and of the honest hands that constructed his own forest home. (71, pp. 13-14)

During the time that Franklin was working on his farm he met Mary Personett. They were married December 15, 1833. "She went with him through all his long career, bore him eleven children, and cared for them with a mother's patient and tender care through many long years of privation and sorrow, keeping up courage and hope when many a woman would have sunk under the heavy burden." (71, p. 14) Franklin traded his land for an interest in a gristmill on Deer Creek in 1837. His uncle Calvin Franklin was a partner in this venture. This did not prove to be successful financially and was sold in 1840. With no farm and no business to produce income, the family struggled greatly during this period. Benjamin worked occasionally whenever he could find employment, and received small donations as a preacher. (71, p. 22)

EXPOSED TO THE PRIMITIVE GOSPEL

When Joseph Franklin moved into Henry County, Indiana in 1833 the Franklins had not showed the slightest interest in religion. All of this changed when Samuel Rogers moved his family to Henry County in the same year. Samuel Rogers and Joseph Franklin agreed to meet in each other's cabins on Saturday afternoon and study the Bible through. They studied honestly, agreeing to mark each passage on which they could not agree with the intention of later returning to that passage for further discussion. They avoided every sign of disagreement or prejudice. When they finished, they found that not a passage had been marked. 1, p. 100 These studies resulted in the conversion of Joseph Franklin. As a result of the teaching of Rogers a number of other Franklin family members were also converted. "Early in December of the same year the preaching of Rogers began to produce visible results. Benjamin and his brother Daniel ... submitted to the authority of Jesus the Christ, and were baptized for the remission of sins on a confession of faith. A week later, Benjamin's wife, along with his brother Josiah, were baptized into the one body. In a few days some thirty or forty persons became obedient to the faith. Among these were Joseph Franklin, another brother of Benjamin, and John I. Rogers, a son of Samuel Rogers." (71, p. 18)

FRANKLIN THE PREACHER

Ben Franklin went to work zealously studying his Bible and preparing himself to preach. Although he developed into a very polished and effective speaker, his early efforts showed his backwoods upbringing, lack of education, and poor grammar. John Longley, one of Indiana's early pioneer preachers, often went to hear Franklin, and was one of his severe critics. Franklin had unconsciously formed the habit of saying, "My dear friends and brethering." At one meeting Longley took a piece of paper and a pin and made a hole every time

Franklin repeated the phrase with the word "brethering." At the conclusion of the sermon he counted one hundred and fifty holes. (1, p. 102)

Despite this early handicap, Franklin developed into one of the most powerful proclaimers of the ancient gospel ever known on American soil. While Franklin gained wide fame as an editor and debater, in the pulpit he came as near to representing perfection as any gospel preacher that could be found. He preached without notes and quoted scriptures voluminously. He did not pretend to be a philosopher, a politician, a teller of stories, or anything of the kind. He was a gospel preacher in everything the term implies. (1, p. 103)

The pioneer preacher, Alfred Ellmore said of Ben Franklin in an article for the Christian Leader in 1890: "...even now, after listening to many men of varied abilities, I am firm in the conviction that Benjamin Franklin was the greatest gospel preacher I ever heard." (1, p. 103) Franklin was praised highly by men such as J. W. McGarvey and David Lipscomb for his effective style and substance as a gospel preacher, as well as being an excellent debater. Earl West paid Franklin a great compliment when he said, "It is not likely that a greater, nobler, truer, purer preacher of the gospel lived since apostolic times than Ben Franklin." (1, p. 104)

TRAGEDY STRIKES FRANKLIN

"1845 marked one of the saddest years in Benjamin Franklin's personal life. He had recovered from a serious illness when he received word of his father's death, and on November 18, 1845, his brother Joseph died while visiting in Benjamin's home. Joseph Franklin, Jr. was a medical doctor and had been a minister in the Church of Christ for some four or five years, although he was only twenty-six years of age at the time of his death. Three years earlier Benjamin Franklin's infant daughter, Sophia, had died suddenly while he was away preaching, and several years later his infant son, Walter Scott, succumbed to smallpox. Although Franklin became saddened and subdued by these losses, he expressed no bitterness and looked forward with increased hope to a Resurrection." (72, p. 12)

FRANKLIN THE EDITOR

In 1835, shortly after his conversion, Franklin wrote his first article for the press. It set forth the plan of salvation, and was published in the Heretic Detector, a paper published in Middleburg, Ohio. Meanwhile, Franklin earned a living by farming as well as by working in his own mill. In 1842 he moved to New Lisbon, Indiana where he remained for two years. A part of this time he preached for the church at Bethel. In 1844 he moved his family to Centerville, county seat of Wayne County, Indiana. In 1845 Franklin started a journal that he called The Reformer. In 1847 he moved to Milton, Indiana and changed the name of the paper to The Western Reformer.

During this time Franklin found himself getting into several religious discussions. In 1843 he debated George W. McCune, a Universalist preacher. In 1847 he held a four day discussion with another Universalist preacher, Erasmus Munford. A month later he debated with a Methodist preacher by the name of Henry R. Pritchard.

In 1850 Franklin merged his paper with Alexander Hall's The Gospel Proclamation and the result was The Proclamation and Reformer. The next of Franklin's editorial attempts came as co-editor with D. S. Burnet on The Christian Age. The years between 1850 and 1855 were disappointing for Franklin. His publishing interests proved to be a financial loss. During this time, he divided his time preaching for the Clinton Street Church in Cincinnati and the church at Covington, Kentucky. On January 1, 1856, the first issue of the American Christian Review came off the press. Moses E. Lard, C. L. Loos, John Rogers, Isaac Errett, and Elijah Goodwin were then listed as contributing editors. For many years the Review was to be the most influential paper in the brotherhood. (1, p. 106)

THE MISSIONARY SOCIETY AND INSTRUMENTAL MUSIC

After the establishment of the American Christian Missionary Society in 1849, the influence of Ben Franklin went wholly behind that organization. For a short time in 1856 and 1857, he was the Corresponding Secretary. However, as time went on, his ardor for the Society cooled and by 1866 he turned solidly against it. Why such a drastic change? David Lipscomb wrote an article evaluating Franklin's life shortly after he died. Lipscomb writes that Franklin was ordinarily a man of great firmness, but at times was influenced by others against his own judgment. It would seem, then, that the great heart of Ben Franklin was torn between two great desires. On the one hand he had a passion for unity among the brethren, and on the other, he had a passion for an independent stand for the truth. It grieved Franklin deeply when his own passion for the truth conflicted with his desire for unity, but in the end, he was always faithful to his conviction. Lipscomb points out that Franklin was persuaded, even at times against his better judgment, that the adoption of societies would bring about better unity and activity. When he saw that they failed, he returned to the more conservative position. (1, p. 106)

"Back in the earlier days, while Franklin was advocating the societies, he paid a visit to Franklin College, and spent a night with Tolbert Fanning. They talked of the societies 'that were then engulfing the brotherhood.' Both of them agreed they were wrong. At the end of their conversation each gave the other his right hand as a pledge to 'resist them and to walk in the good old ways.'" About that same time Franklin paid a visit to Jacob Creath, Jr., and Creath remembered Franklin's promise that he was going to get out of the societies and 'wash his hands of them as soon as possible.' ... At heart Franklin was convicted that the societies were unscriptural, but he patiently waited to see if there was any way he could harmonize his convictions with the existence of the societies before he spoke out." (1, p. 107) Franklin was bitterly opposed to the use of instrumental music in the worship. He regarded the instrument as an innovation and refused to preach where the instrument was used.

THE END COMES

Benjamin Franklin died October 22, 1878 in Anderson, Indiana where his family had lived for the past eighteen years. His son, Joseph, described his father's last hours on earth:

> So encouraging were the symptoms that his family thought he was really improving. He ate regularly and slept well, and his writing was done with great ease. In the morning of the 22nd of October, 1878, he took a long walk upon his farm. Returning about nine o'clock, he said to his wife: "Mother, I feel very much better today, and I hope I shall get well." He then seated himself at the table and wrote some two or three hours. When called to dinner he ate heartily, and still talked of how well he felt. After dinner he lay down for his customary sleep. He slept somewhat longer than usual and attracted attention by his labored breathing. At two o'clock he awakened and sat up in his chair, but seemed very dull, as if he were hardly awake. After a time he began to show symptoms of distress, and complained of heaviness, "as if a fifty-pound weight lay on his heart." His wife was the only person in the room at the time. She soon saw that something very unusual was the matter, and called their daughter from another part of the house. When she came to him he was gasping for breath. She made an attempt to rub his side with a view to restore the circulation, but he said, "Don't trouble me; my time has come." She now became seriously alarmed ... a messenger was dispatched to call a physician, and to notify the other members of the family residents in Anderson. The physician came within one hour, but Mr. Franklin was too far gone to swallow, and nothing could be done. His last words were spoken to his wife: "Mother, I am sorry to have to leave you." Leaning back in the arm chair ... and with his eyes fixed on the companion who had shared all his joys and his sorrows for forty-nine years, his breathing grew shorter, until it could not be

observed that he breathed at all. About five o'clock in the afternoon of October 22, 1878, it became evident to the loving eyes fixed upon him, but nearly blinded by their tears, that Benjamin Franklin was dead. (71, p. 49-50)

Benjamin Franklin was only sixty-seven years old. He passed from this world at a time when the church surely needed his steady hand and keen mind. He was buried near Anderson, Indiana. Franklin's death was a severe blow to the aging Jacob Creath, Jr. who looked upon Franklin as the savior of the Restoration. Creath wrote: "If our brethren believed in canonizing men, he could soon be placed in the front ranks on the roll of canonization among our great men, and if their mantles ever fell upon any man, that man was Benjamin Franklin.... His death is universally regarded by the readers of the Review as a great loss to our restoration. He has none who can fill his place, and we shall not see his like soon again." (1, p. 106)

On October 24, 1878 a memorial service was held for Franklin at the home of his son-in-law. M. T. Hough and W. W. Witmer conducted the funeral. "Asleep in Jesus" was sung. The fifteenth chapter of I Corinthians and a part of the fourth chapter of II Timothy were read, and W. W. Witmer spoke at length on those two texts. Following the service, the body was taken to a cemetery near Anderson, Indiana where it was laid to rest. The head stone is in the shape of a marble pulpit with the open Bible on it and these words: "He was determined to know nothing save Jesus Christ, and Him crucified." I Cor. 2:2.

TRIBUTES OF PRAISE

Franklin was ranked by some as the second generation leader of the Restoration Movement. In reporting his death, David Lipscomb grieved over the death of Franklin with these words, "The cause loses its most able and indefatigable defender since the days of Alexander Campbell, and his loss is simply irreparable." (37, p. 4) Samuel Rogers, who baptized Franklin, felt that his part in converting this dedicated man of God was adequate payment for a lifetime of preaching. Rogers said, "If I had done no more for my Master than to have been instrumental in giving to the world Benjamin Franklin, I would have no reason to be ashamed; but would feel that I had by no means lived and died in vain." (37, p. 4)

Franklin was a debater and a strong defender of truth. W. T. Moore said of him, "He was a strong force to deal with when he was in opposition." (37, p.5) Franklin's oral debates numbered more than thirty in addition to a number of written discussions. Six of his debates were published and distributed widely. It has been reported that Franklin baptized as many as 10,000 individuals.

CHAPTER 25
WILLIAM KIMBROUGH PENDLETON
1818 - 1899

William Kimbrough Pendleton was born in the year of 1818 to Virginia aristocrats, Edmund and Unity Yancey Kimbrough Pendleton. His mother was an Episcopalian, but his father claimed no religious affiliation until about 1833 when he became intensely interested in the writings of Alexander Campbell. Edmund Pendleton was baptized into Christ along with his wife and brother, Mathison. They formed a small congregation in Gilboa in order to worship after the New Testament pattern.

William was sent to the finest schools and received a good education. He entered the University of Virginia in 1836 to study law. While he was in school he read the Millennial Harbinger as well as some of the older copies of the Christian Baptist. These, along with the Bible gave him his religious training. It was the custom of Alexander Campbell to travel extensively and preach as well as edit the Millennial Harbinger. His tours took him over a wide range of territory, and often took him to Virginia. Quite often Campbell would take one of his daughters on these trips. Campbell's daughter, Lavina, accompanied her father to Charlottesville, Virginia, where Pendleton was a student at the University. Lavina and William met on that trip.

BAPTIZED BY CAMPBELL

Pendleton left the University in the spring of 1840 and returned to Louisa County. In June of that year he heard Campbell preach the gospel and was moved by the message to be baptized. Alexander Campbell baptized him near the Mount Gilboa church building. On October 14, 1840, William and Lavina were married in the Campbell mansion at Bethany. It had been Pendleton's intention to go into politics, but he changed his plans and joined with his father-in-law in the establishment of Bethany College. Pendleton taught in the school and became vice-president in 1845. William and Lavina had a daughter September 1, 1841 and named her Campbellina. Lavina died of tuberculosis, called "consumption," in 1846 at the young age of twenty-nine. In 1848 he married another daughter of Alexander Campbell, Clarinda Campbell, who also died of tuberculosis in 1850. Pendleton married a third time in 1855 to Catherine King.

CO-EDITOR OF MILLENNIAL HARBINGER

It was about 1846 that Pendleton became co-editor with Alexander Campbell on the Millennial Harbinger. In 1849 he attended the first meeting of the American Christian Missionary Society and supported it. In 1864 Alexander Campbell turned the Millennial Harbinger completely over to Pendleton. It continued until 1870. Campbell died in 1866 and Pendleton was named President of Bethany College. He was also associate editor of the Christian Quarterly.

In 1855 he renewed his interest in politics and ran for Congress, but was defeated. However, in 1873 he was a delegate to the State Constitutional Convention. In 1873 he was appointed as State Superintendent of Public Schools, a post he held for several years. In 1884 Pendleton resigned as President of Bethany College. He spent the last years of his life in Florida, but died in 1899 while making his last visit to Bethany. Through his close association with Alexander Campbell, his editorship of the Millennial Harbinger, and his presidency of Bethany College, W. K. Pendleton was one of the most influential leaders of the Restoration Movement prior to the Civil War and the years that followed shortly thereafter. (1, p. 94)

CHAPTER 26
MOSES EASTERLY LARD
1818 - 1880

The life of Moses Easterly Lard began at Shelbyville, Bedford County, Tennessee, October 29, 1818. His parents were extremely poor. His Scottish parents, Leaven and Mary, joined in the migration westward in 1829 toward Missouri. His father went to Missouri because of the plentiful game. Tragedy struck in 1835 when Moses' father died of smallpox. Mary Lard found the financial burden of providing for six children impossible. She lost the land on which they were living and had no support for her family. Moses, who was eleven years old, and his brother had to leave home and go out on their own to make their own way. Mary gave to each of the boys her blessing and a small New Testament. Of this scene Lard in later years wrote:

> As my brother and myself stood beneath the little cabin eaves, just ready to take leave of the only objects on earth dear to us, and thus close the saddest scene of our lives, my mother said: "My dear boys, I have nothing to give you but my blessing and these two little books." Her soul was breaking, and she could say no more. She then drew from her bosom two small testaments; and as her tears were streaming,

and lips quivering, she screamed as if it were her last, and placed them in our hands. We all said good-bye, and that family was forever broken on earth… To that little book and the memory of that scene my future life owes its shaping. I never neglected the one, thank Heaven, nor forgot the other. (1, p. 291)

The family would never be united again on earth. Mary Lard lived long enough to see Moses preach. By 1835, when Lard was seventeen years of age, he could read but he could not write. Van Deusen in his book Moses Lard, the Prince of Preachers states that the story that he was illiterate at seventeen was not correct. In fact, he had learned to read before his father died, but he did not learn to write until he was seventeen. While living in Clinton County, Moses taught himself to read by cutting the letters out of old advertising posters and tracing them.

Lard, at seventeen, worked as a tailor. However, in 1835 an opportunity came to Moses and his brother. Arthur King ran the King Academy. King invited the boys to attend the Academy. In exchange for room, board, and schooling, the boys would work for him, doing chores. King stated that Moses Lard was the best student he ever had.

EXPOSED TO THE PRIMITIVE GOSPEL

During the next few years Lard listened to denominationalism and heard the pleas of Calvinistic preachers urging sinners to get an experience. From these Lard turned away in disgust. Feeling there was nothing to religion, he finally turned toward infidelity. Finally, however, he began to hear of preachers who were advocating a return to the first century gospel. Lard then came into possession of Walter Scott's "Gospel Restored." Lard devoured it. A number of years after this, Walter Scott made a trip to Missouri and for the first time met Lard. Immediately Lard threw his arms around Scott and said, "Brother Scott, you are the man who first taught me the gospel." (2, p. 142)

Lard was twenty-three years old in 1841 when he first heard a man preach the true gospel in its primitive purity. This man was Jerry P. Lancaster, who at one time had been a Methodist preacher. Lancaster migrated to Missouri from Kentucky, and began to preach the true gospel. Most of his preaching was done in the upper counties of the state. Lard went to hear Lancaster, and accepted the gospel, later being immersed by this same man.

In 1849 Lancaster moved west to California during the gold rush. In California he became unfaithful. Several years later, when the war was over, Lancaster came back to Missouri, friendless, penniless, and in need of assistance. He went to a meeting being conducted by T. M. Allen, one of Missouri's oldest pioneer gospel preachers. Allen had talked to him privately before the meeting, and at the invitation Lancaster came forward and back to the Lord. He was always faithful afterwards. Lard always had a tender feeling toward him, and spoke kindly of this man who had immersed him. (1, p. 292)

BEGAN PREACHING

It was in Clay County that Lard was immersed. It was in this county also that he preached his first sermon. Soon he was preaching in Richmond and Lexington, also practicing his trade as a tailor at the same time. He married Mary Riffe of Lexington about 1842. By 1845 he had two children. To think seriously of going to school at this time was almost out of the question. He had little education, was married, and was the father of two children. Education was costly. To go to school and support a family at the same time was something Lard could only dream about. Nevertheless, circumstances were paving the way in his favor.

ENROLLED AT BETHANY COLLEGE

At Richmond, Lard had become the good friend of General Alexander W. Donaphan, one of Missouri's leading citizens, and an ardent and faithful Christian. Donaphan encouraged him to make the sacrifice and to go to Bethany College. He enrolled on March 4, 1845, at the age of twenty-seven. Lard worked hard and completed a four years' course in three years. Even though he worked at physical labor while going to school, he graduated as valedictorian in his class on July 4, 1848. After school, Lard and his family returned to Missouri where he preached in various places for the next ten years. His first local work was in Independence, Missouri.

REVIEW ON CAMPBELLISM EXAMINED

In 1857 J. B. Jeter, a Virginia Baptist preacher, wrote a booklet called A Review on Campbellism in which he gave an extremely critical picture of Alexander Campbell and the Restoration Movement associated with him. Campbell gave some attention to the Jeter book in the Millennial Harbinger, but decided that a more thorough examination should be given to it. Since Campbell's schedule was too heavy to write a detailed response, he selected Moses Lard for the work. The title of Lard's book was Review on Campbellism Examined. That Campbell would select Moses Lard for this work indicates the high opinion that Campbell had of Lard by this time. (2, p. 144)

There is no record of Moses Lard participating in a great number of debates. Perhaps they were not significant enough to attract the attention of historians. One public discussion that he did have was conducted at Brunswick, Missouri in October of 1860 with W. G. Caples, presiding elder of the Methodist Church. It was a lengthy discussion, lasting some eight days. The audiences ranged from fifteen hundred to three thousand at each meeting. Many outstanding preachers were present to hear the discussion, including Raccoon John Smith, W. H. Hopson, T. M. Allen, J. W. McGarvey, and John R. Howard. After hearing Lard defend the truth, John R. Howard paid Lard a high compliment: "He came closer to possessing the character of the real orator, the true Christian orator than almost any man I ever heard. His words generally fell from his lips, like coins from the mint, correctly struck and properly impressed by the organs of speech, and seemed to be ready for the press without any correcting or revision." (1, p. 295)

LARD'S QUARTERLY

Moses Lard was determined to publish a quarterly periodical. With inadequate support he began in 1863 during the Civil War to publish Lard's Quarterly. In the summer of 1868 it ceased to be published due to financial problems. It is the judgment of many Restoration students that this quarterly contains possibly the richest of all Restoration literature. Lard wrote three-fourths of the articles. (2, p. 144)

After the closing of the, Quarterly, Lard, with four other brethren, edited a weekly called the Apostolic Times. This paper took a strong stand against the use of instrumental music during the 1870's. Lard could never do anything he conscientiously thought was wrong. He found it impossible to cooperate with brethren who were using the instrument of music. The following indicates Lard's strong convictions regarding instrumental music in worship:

> Let every preacher resolve at once that he will never enter a meeting house in which an organ stands. Let no brother ever unite with another using an organ... Let brethren remonstrate in gentle, kind, but decided terms and, if unheeded, let them abandon the church. Thus, these organ-grinding churches will be broken down, and the sooner they are in fragments the better for the cause of Christ. (2, p. 145)

Also, Lard was critical of the American Christian Missionary Society, but he did so on the basis of expediency, stating that it was an unnecessary expediency. He wrote: "The right of Christian men to have them is a right we by no means call in question; but a claim to have them based on any really necessary ground is a claim the force of which we must in candor say we have not felt." (1, p. 299) Many liberals who favored the Society and the instrument would not support the Quarterly as a result of Lard's opposition. More than anything else, this probably contributed to the financial failure of the Quarterly.

Lard was given to moods. He was despondent at times over the issues in the church and because of illness in his family. Lard was a man of great loyalty. He took it personally when anyone attacked his friends. Lard loved a good debate. He loved to get into discussion and the hotter the better. Lard described his feeling in this way:

> I am so sorry Brother Shepherd is adverse to controversy. Were he not, what a nice time he and I could now have. I like controversy. I like it all the better the hotter it grows. I like to see it leap up even to a white heat. Give me a foreman over on the other side deeply entrenched in great banks of error. Only let the truth be with me; and then let the battle rage. I like sharp practice at close range. What if error shoots up high, and hisses and blazes like rockets? There is no cause for alarm. The rainbow with its soft, blending colors, lifts its arch high over the storm that rages below. So with truth. (1, p. 289)

COMMENTARY ON ROMANS

In 1875 Lard presented to the brotherhood what he considered to be "the work of his life," his commentary on the book of Romans. After one hundred years it is still used. While Lard will always be recognized as an effective writer and journalist, it is as a preacher of the gospel that Lard will be especially remembered. Without question, he was one of the most eloquent speakers to come out of the whole Restoration. Yet, sometimes, like Walter Scott, he did not measure up to his true capabilities.

On one occasion Lard was preaching on the subject of baptism when a man arose and said, "Mr. Lard, if you were on the plains, a thousand miles from water, and a man sent for you, and you should convince him of his sins, and he should believe on Jesus as the Christ, and be willing to confess Him, and you knew that in all probability he would die before you could find water to baptize him, what would you do?" Instantly he replied, "Sir, I would start for water, and if he should die, he would die on his way to obedience." (2, p. 145)

This straight forwardness made Lard a favorite preacher of many audiences. It is doubtful that many preachers, modern or pioneer, could have had the emotional impact on his audiences as did Moses Lard. It is said that when he preached on the Prodigal Son, he painted so vivid a picture that the audience would look back to the door to see if the Prodigal was coming home. When Lard was up and the emotions were aroused, he would pour forth a stream of eloquence that would sweep his audience away. "Once when he finished an eloquent discourse, he called suddenly on the audience to stand and sing. Not a word was uttered. It took several minutes for that great sea of emotion to calm down enough that the people could sing." (1, p. 289)

One of the last acts of his life was to serve as president of the College of the Bible at Lexington, Kentucky. Lard's one year of leadership at the school saved it from liberalism at that time, although it later digressed from the truths of the New Testament.

DEATH COMES TOO SOON

Lard was a large man, being 6'3" tall, and was physically strong. However, at the age of sixty-two his body gave way to stomach cancer and he died in June of 1880. Prior to his death, Lard remarked, "There is not a cloud between me and my heavenly Father." His body was taken from Lexington back to St. Joseph, Missouri where he was buried at Mount Mora cemetery.

CHAPTER 27
JOHN WILLIAM McGARVEY
1829 - 1911

John William McGarvey was a second-generation Restoration leader who is said to rank next to Alexander Campbell in greatness as a preacher, teacher, and writer. J. W. McGarvey was born in Hopkinsville, Kentucky on March 1, 1829. His father, who had emigrated from Ireland, died when he was four, leaving his mother with four small children. Mrs. McGarvey then married Dr. G. F. Saltonsall, a widower with nine children. This made a family of thirteen children. In time, six more children were born, for a total of nineteen children. Fortunately, Dr. Saltonsall was able financially to support this large family.

Physically, McGarvey was a man of small stature, being only 5'7" tall and of medium weight. Some affectionately called him "Little Mac." All of his adult life he wore a beard. He used a long ear trumpet during his last years because of a hearing problem. In character he was very kind. A daughter said, "I never did see father display irritation toward any family member." (2, p. 76) He enjoyed being with people but he also loved the truth and sometimes even his friends felt his sharp pen. However, he had the unique ability of being able to mete out discipline tempered with kindness. Because he stood for the truth, he was called a "legalist" by some. In spite of being called a legalist, he was able to keep control of himself. McGarvey was a man of courage. Once he stated, "If I were floating on a plank in mid-ocean, and a man should try to take it from me, I would fight for my life." Spiritually, he fought for the plank many times. (2, p. 76)

BAPTIZED AT BETHANY COLLEGE

Dr. Saltonsall was a successful businessman and a board member of Bethany College to which he made financial donations. In his will, Saltonsall made Bethany his twentieth child. When it came time to select a college, McGarvey chose Bethany College and entered in March of 1847. Dr. Saltonsall went to Cincinnati and bought his stepson all the books needed for the whole college curriculum. As a young person, McGarvey heard very little preaching that was instructive. He heard the doctrine that faith only was all that was necessary in becoming a Christian. He commented frequently, "I believe in Christ as much as that preacher does, but I am not saved." (2, p. 176)

While a student at Bethany College, McGarvey heard Campbell and others present the simple New Testament plan for becoming a Christian. In the spring of 1848, McGarvey made the good confession and was baptized into Christ. One of his instructors, W.K. Pendleton, baptized him in Buffalo Creek near the college.

McGarvey was an outstanding student. Alexander Campbell presented young McGarvey with a copy of the New Testament with an inscription that it was for proficiency in knowledge of the Scriptures. This was treasured by McGarvey for many years as one of his most highly prized books. Unfortunately, this volume was destroyed many years later in a fire that consumed his house and all of the contents. (62, p. 14)

IN THE CAMPBELL HOME

McGarvey was deeply impressed with the family prayer-life of Alexander Campbell, as were all the students who happened to be in the Campbell home at 8:00 in the evening:

> At 8 o'clock every evening a bell was rung, and all inmates of the house, including servants and visitors, promptly assembled in the large family room. When all were seated, Mr. C. himself could recite a verse of Scripture, and then all present in the order in which they were seated would do the same. Young men who were visiting the girls in the parlor, of whom there were always from two or three to half dozen daughters, nieces and cousins, must come in with the rest and recite their verses. ... After the recitation of verses, a chapter was read by Mr. C. and all kneeled in prayer. (62, p. 16)

Another thing that McGarvey always remembered about being in the Campbell home was the presence of "grandfather" Thomas Campbell. This was after Thomas had lost his eyesight. He customarily was seated in one corner of the large family room, where he loved to recite psalms and hymns and chapters of Scripture long ago committed to memory, and which he never wanted to forget. In order to be sure that he correctly remembered every word, he would ask some young person who might be present to hold the book and correct him if he missed a word. (62, p. 16)

THE TRIP HOME

McGarvey graduated valedictorian of his class of twelve students on July 4, 1850. While he was a student at Bethany, his family had moved to Fayette, Missouri. The trip home was rather complicated. McGarvey describes the journey home in his autobiography:

> The trip home was a steamboat from Wellsburgh, Virginia to Beaver, Pennsylvania, thence by canal boat to Erie on the southern shore of Lake Erie, thence by steamer to Chicago, thence by canal boat again to Lasalle on the Illinois River, thence by steamer

down that river to Peoria, and thence by stagecoach to Tremont where a visit made to old friends and some remaining members of the family. Thence by stagecoach to Springfield, Illinois, thence by railway, the only one in Illinois and the first he had ever seen, to Naples on the Illinois river; thence by stagecoach to Quincy, thence by rowboat down the Mississippi ten miles to Hannibal, Missouri, and thence by stage coach to Fayette. (62, p. 18)

BEGAN PREACHING

In Fayette, Missouri McGarvey taught in a secular school system for several months and then determined that he wanted to preach the gospel. He studied his Bible diligently, not only in English, but in the Greek language as well. In 1852 the church at Fayette invited him to be their preacher. As was the custom then, he was ordained by the laying on of hands by T. M. Allen and Alexander Proctor. Allen came to be a helpful counselor and helper for young J. W. McGarvey in those early days. Allen was very strong in exhorting sinners to respond. Where Allen was very moving, McGarvey was somewhat lacking. One time when Allen and McGarvey were in a protracted meeting together, Allen preached in the morning and McGarvey in the afternoon. Just before McGarvey got up to deliver his lesson, Allen bent over and whispered this advise to him: "Now, John, come out under the whip and spur, head and tail up." (1, p. 303)

In January of 1853 McGarvey began his work with the church at Dover, Missouri. He remained with them for nine years. It was here in Dover on March 23, 1853 that he married Frances Hix, a marriage that would last for fifty-five years. McGarvey was preaching in Dover when the Civil War broke out. He maintained that it was wrong for Christians to go to war, a position he held all of his life. The church at Dover became divided over this issue. Many criticisms were directed at McGarvey because of his position.

In addition, there was controversy regarding the black

members of the church. The congregation had a large black membership, and a large gallery was assigned to them during the services. However, since the number was large and McGarvey wanted a better teaching arrangement for them, he arranged for them to have the full use of the auditorium one Sunday afternoon each month. This was not acceptable to some of the members, but they were not successful in stopping the meetings. Nevertheless opposition against McGarvey came because of this. McGarvey was prepared when the right invitation came to make a change of congregations. (62. p. 22)

MOVED TO LEXINGTON

That invitation came from Lexington, Kentucky in the spring of 1862. The preacher in Lexington, W. H. Hopson, had come under fire for his sympathizing with the South and therefore needed to move. He recommended McGarvey, who sided politically neither with the North or the South. McGarvey taught that both sides should lay down their arms and settle their troubles without bloodshed. The Main Street congregation had been organized in 1831 with nine members. A dozen preachers had worked with the congregation by the time McGarvey arrived in 1862. At that time the church ranked fourth in size of all churches in the city, but in a short period it became the largest. His work was relatively uninterrupted by the war, except during the battle at Richmond. At that time the Main Street church building was used for a hospital. On January 1, 1871 McGarvey became the preacher for the Broadway congregation in Lexington that had been established in 1870. He preached at Broadway until his resignation in 1881. He continued to serve as an elder until 1902 at which time his deafness caused him to resign. He withdrew his membership from Broadway that same year because the organ was introduced into its worship. He and his wife went to the Chestnut Street Church where I. B. Grubbs told him, "Brother McGarvey, we would rather have you than 10,000 aids to worship." (2, p. 182)

When the Broadway congregation moved into the Presbyterian building, McGarvey remarked humorously that he would be the first to preach the gospel in that building. Numerous citizens of Lexington took his remark at face value and were offended at the comment. Accordingly, McGarvey announced his subject in advance and then preached on the subject, "What Makes up a Gospel Sermon?" In his lesson he contrasted the gospel with Calvinism, and then spelled out how to become a Christian. At the end of the sermon, the Presbyterians were silent, and the church was pleased that the truth had been preached.

AN EFFECTIVE PREACHER

Unlike the humor and personal illustrations used by other preachers, McGarvey was effectively unique as he would select a text from the New Testament and derive from it a single basic principle, and then take up an Old Testament story bearing on his theme. McGarvey was a strong preacher, not afraid to preach sound doctrinal lessons. He delighted on preaching on the conversions found in the book of Acts. Those who listened could learn clearly how to become a Christian.

As a teacher in the classroom McGarvey excelled. "The classroom was the throne of J.W. McGarvey, as he knew what he taught, and then taught what he knew. The London Times stated, 'In all probability, John W. McGarvey is the ripest Bible scholar on earth.'" (2, p. 184) He never weakened the faith of any young man entrusted to him nor poisoned a single soul with doubt. Although he had additional educational ties, McGarvey's name is associated principally with the College of the Bible in Lexington, Kentucky.

COLLEGE OF THE BIBLE

McGarvey began his teaching career with the College of the Bible in 1865 where he remained for forty years. Sixteen of those years he was president. The highest enrollment at the school was one hundred and eighty-seven in 1877, and the lowest was seventy-eight in 1902. McGarvey was eighty when he resigned as president. One of the last courses he taught was Biblical criticism, and his hearing was so poor toward the end that his students would come to his desk and recite into his hearing trumpet.

In 1895 a $20,000 building was erected for the College of the Bible. It was torn down in 1960, and a new building was erected at an approximate cost of $400,000. When the old building was torn down a tin box was found in the cornerstone that contained some pictures, song books, Bibles, and religious journals, including an 1895 copy of the Gospel Advocate. Many people in Lexington believe that McGarvey had put the tin box in the cornerstone. (2, pp. 185-186)

A WRITER

As a writer, J. W. McGarvey, after Alexander Campbell, was the most prolific among the Restoration leaders. For over forty years articles flowed from his pen to various publications, including the Millennial Harbinger, American Christian Review, Apostolic Times, The Christian Standard, and Lard's Quarterly. In addition, he wrote a number of books that helped to spread his influence in a wider circle. At the age of forty-three McGarvey wrote a commentary on the Book of Acts that appeared in 1863. Thirty years later in 1893 he wrote a second commentary on Acts. In 1875 he completed one on Matthew and Mark.

In 1879 McGarvey made a six month trip to the Bible Lands and the following year his book, Lands of the Bible, made its appearance. While on the trip, he almost drowned in the sea near Sidon. He was caught in an undercurrent and became exhausted, sinking twice and losing consciousness. Through the effort of a companion, H. S. Ear, he was rescued. McGarvey wrote the popular Fourfold Gospel in 1905 in cooperation with P. Y. Pendleton. This gospel harmony has been used as a textbook in a number of Christian Colleges. In 1897 he produced the Bible Study Guide, and in 1886 he wrote the first half of the book entitled Text and Canon of the New Testament. Five years later he completed the second half which he titled, Credibility and Inspiration. In 1902 he wrote Jesus and Jonah and the Authorship of Deuteronomy. In 1894 The Guide

Publishing Company printed a book of his sermons. McGarvey died before completing a commentary on the New Testament Epistles. He was able to complete the books of I and II Thessalonians, I and II Corinthians, Galatians, and Romans before his death.

POSITION ON THE ISSUES

To understand the man, we need to look at his position on issues. "McGarvey took an unpopular course during the Civil War when he opposed the Christian engaging in carnal warfare. He gave five reasons for his position: (1) Christians could not participate in a fraternal strife; (2) The unity of the church must be maintained; (3) War destroys the Christian character of those who participate in it; (4) A united course of action would give the brotherhood great power when the war closed; (5) Non-participation would harmonize with the policy of early Christians." (2, p. 189)

Admirers of McGarvey are usually surprised to learn that he favored support for the Missionary Society. Although he lacked full sympathy with this human machinery to preach the gospel, his influence was used to encourage the organization.

He strongly opposed instrumental music in worship and felt it was a source of corruption in worship. He refused to be a member of a congregation where the instrument was used. He wrote many articles in the brotherhood journals in opposition to the instrument. The Broadway church in Lexington where McGarvey was a member voted to accept the instrument on November 2, 1902, and on that date McGarvey turned in a letter of resignation. He also wrote a short article in the Lexington Leader, stating his reasons for leaving.

On October 5, 1911, the eighty-year old Mrs. McGarvey left for Martinsville, Indiana to seek help for her rheumatism. The next evening McGarvey became critically ill, and when the end approached at 10:15 p.m. he said serenely, "Lord, I come, I come." And with that the life of J. W. McGarvey came to an end. The funeral was conducted at the Central Christian Church building in Lexington, Kentucky, on October 9, 1911. The Chestnut Street building where the McGarvey's were members was too small and the

Broadway building was under renovation. Ironically, at his funeral, an organ was used with the three songs that were sung. An aged woman remarked, "This is a great wrong for he opposed it all his life." (2, p. 190) The body of "Little Mac" was placed by loving hands in the Lexington cemetery near the final resting places of "Raccoon" John Smith and Henry Clay.

CHAPTER 28
DAVID LIPSCOMB
1831 - 1917

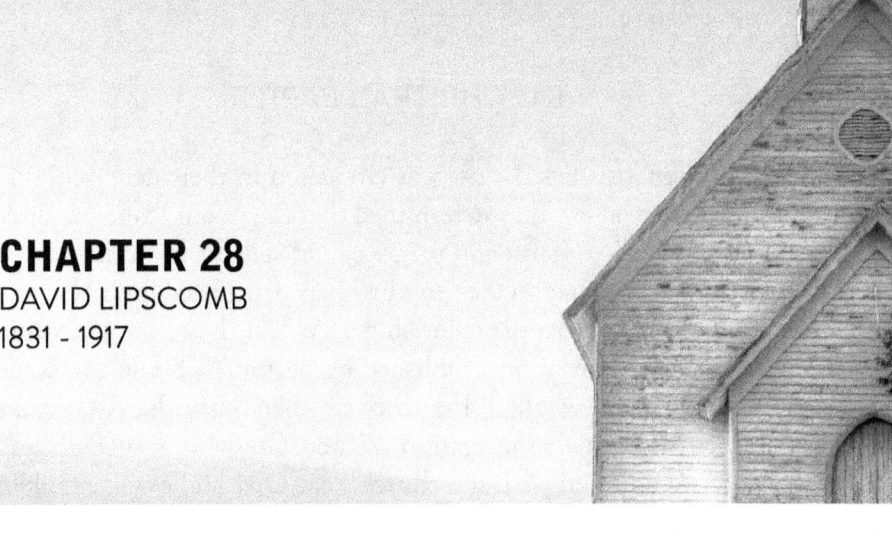

David Lipscomb was born in Franklin County, Tennessee in 1831. "At that time Franklin County was hardly more than a wilderness. Mail service was unknown. Newspapers never reached back into the farm homes. A stagecoach line from New York to New Orleans ran through the county near the farm of Granville Lipscomb.

A tavern was located not far away where the stages changed horses on the journey. News came in from the outside world in this manner. Roads were but winding snake paths of mud. Life was rugged, simple, primitive and difficult. Clothes were of the home-spun variety, and meals consisted not of the dainties of modern-day living, but primarily of that which was grown on the farm. Schooling was hard to secure, and the man who could read and write was looked upon as an educated individual." (38, p. 6)

David's father, Granville Lipscomb moved to Franklin County from Virginia in 1826. He was the oldest of ten children born to William and Ann Day Lipscomb. Granville, Dabney, and John were brothers and members of the Primitive Baptist Church that met on Bean's Creek in Franklin County. Granville was a deacon in that congregation.

THE CHRISTIAN BAPTIST

The Christian Baptist was circulated in their neighborhood and all three read it. They determined that they would take the Bible as their only rule of faith and practice, and stated this to the Baptist Church. This resulted in the three brothers being tried for heresy and excluded from the Baptist fellowship. "At Winchester, not far from them, was a congregation established by Barton W. Stone that some referred to as "Newlight." The three brothers immediately became identified with this congregation. Later, Granville Lipscomb and his wife were united with the church near Owl Hollow in Franklin County." (38, p. 7)

The three brothers, after accepting the New Testament as their only rule of faith and practice, began a diligent study of the Scriptures. Soon they concluded that slavery was against the will of God and determined to do something about it. All three were now married and had families. They each owned a farm and a few slaves, although the exact number is not known. To carry out their convictions, they moved in 1835 to Illinois and freed their slaves. (38, p. 7)

Among the first recollections of David was the year that the family spent in Illinois. It was there that two sisters and a brother died. In a short while his mother also died. Disheartened by these tragedies, all of which took place in a very short time, Granville decided to take what was left of his family back to Franklin County, Tennessee. All three of the remaining children were close to death from malaria fever.

Once they got back home the children recovered from their illness. David's father, Granville, remarried. David attended Sunday school where his father was the teacher. Each night at bedtime the children listened to their father read from the Scripture and comment on them.

At the age of thirteen, David and his brother William went to Virginia to spend a year with David's grandfather. His grandfather was a deacon in the Baptist Church at Lower Good Mine in Louisa County. There was an active Sunday school in which the pupils memorized Scripture. During this time David memorized the four gospels in addition to the book of Acts. He argued with his grandfather that baptism was for the remission of sins and refused to join the parade of young people to the mourner's bench. 38, p. 8

David's father, Granville, became a successful and moderately wealthy farmer. He bought a few slaves to assist with the work. "According to David Lipscomb's recollections in later life, his father did so because of necessity, although he always regarded slavery as an evil to the country and to the people.'" Granville Lipscomb provided instruction to his slaves in reading and writing, and they also were assembled regularly for worship.

BAPTIZED

It was in 1845 when fourteen-year-old David was baptized by Tolbert Fanning. Fanning had recently opened Franklin College near Nashville. He made a trip through Franklin County, preaching on the way. Young David was just recovering from typhoid fever. He sent for Fanning, requesting baptism. He did this without telling anyone else. Fanning tested David by asking him why he wanted to be baptized. David answered, "to obey God." With this statement, Fanning baptized David Lipscomb in a box that had been filled with water. (38, p. 9)

In January of 1846 Lipscomb entered Franklin College and three years later graduated, delivering the valedictory address. During the school period David was constantly under the influence of Tolbert Fanning. He was truly Fanning's protégé. Lipscomb adopted the fearless independence of mind that was so characteristic of Fanning. In years to come Lipscomb would show no fear in standing alone on an issue. He held the same position as Fanning did on such issues as missionary societies, Christian participation in war, and the use of instrumental music in worship. Tolbert Fanning influenced David Lipscomb in his life more than any other living man.

SUCCESSFUL FARMER

After graduation, Lipscomb moved to Georgia and became the manager of a large farm. He only stayed about two years and returned in 1852 to Franklin County. Here he worked on a farm as well as taking a contract, in partnership with his father, to help construct a railroad from Nashville to Chattanooga. Unfortunately, Granville Lipscomb, David's father passed away about a year later at the age of fifty-one. This left the burden of the care of the family, including five small children, the care of the farms that his father had owned and run, and the supervision of Granville's slaves. (61, pp. 45-46) The following will give us information about David Lipscomb's farming career as well as his use of slavery:

> He moved in 1857 to Davidson County where he and William had purchased a farm of six hundred and forty-three acres in White's Bend or Bell's Bend, as it was most usually called, from Tolbert Fanning. A purchase price of $16,275 was paid for the acreage in the northwest section of the county. ... It was not the finest piece of land in Davidson County. It was rather rocky, covered with snakes, and overgrown. But it offered possibilities for farming, milling, and the cutting of cordwood to supply the fireplaces of Nashville. David established bachelor's quarters on the farm. Probably he had inherited a few slaves from his father's estate. The census records of 1860 show that Lipscomb owned five slaves ranging in age from nine to thirty-five. Likely he freed the Negroes prior to the Civil War. Family history from the Zellner side--David Lipscomb married Margaret Zellner--relates that slaves were never a part of the Lipscomb household after their marriage in 1862. (61, p. 61)

Slavery and its abolition became a constant topic of controversy following the Civil War. Isaac Errett and

Lipscomb had a lengthy discussion concerning the subject in their respective papers in 1868. Lipscomb took exception to much that Errett wrote, especially his attitude toward the Southern people. Lipscomb recalled in 1892 that he told Mr. Errett on one occasion: '... the difference between myself and him was, I and my parents were willing to free our own slaves; his conscience made him anxious to free other peoples." With the exception of this one statement, Lipscomb does not indicate how his slaves were freed. However, he asserted that he was not an advocate of slavery and that, '... if the war did nothing worse than free the slaves, I would not complain of it." Again he remarked: "... slavery was an incubus and hindrance to the Southern people and I was at all times willing to surrender all my interests in it to see it abolished." (12, p. 57)

Like his father, Lipscomb was a very religious man and studied the Scriptures diligently. He did not think of himself as a preacher, but as a Christian doing what a Christian ought to do. In 1875 Benjamin Franklin went to Franklin, Tennessee and conducted a gospel meeting, and became better acquainted with Lipscomb. Benjamin later wrote his impression of Lipscomb. "Brother Lipscomb is a plain and unassuming man, with the simplicity of a child. He has good native sense, much power and influence, and is greatly devoted to the cause. There is not the least danger of his ever turning 'clergyman.' He has not an inkling in that way. He lives in utter disregard of the notions of the world, puts on no airs, wears just such coat, hat and pants as suit him. We were much pleased with him as far as our short acquaintance went." (38, pp. 11,12)

Lipscomb greatly admired a preacher by the name of Jesse Ferguson who preached in Nashville, Tennessee. He was extremely popular and drew large crowds. Unfortunately, Ferguson went off into false teaching and became a spiritualist. This discouraged young Lipscomb and many other Christians of Middle Tennessee. He even considered going back to the Baptists. With this in mind, he purchased the standard book of the Baptist Church, and made a close study of Baptist doctrine and church government. His investigation was very thorough. At the conclusion of his study he was convinced that he was on solid ground just being a Christian. He determined to strengthen the brethren in the faith of the Bible. (36, p. 245)

FIRST SERMON

David Lipscomb began preaching about 1858. George Stroud of Warren County, Tennessee, was apparently the first to suggest to Lipscomb that he should preach the gospel publicly. Lipscomb accompanied Stroud to a preaching appointment one Sunday. Stroud had previously asked David to preach that day. Lipscomb had carefully studied about ten verses of Scripture and felt that he was fully prepared to discuss them. When he stood up to speak he read the verses, but completely forgot what he had planned to say. He finished reading the chapter, hoping the thoughts would come to him, but they did not. He was embarrassed and sat down, asking Stroud to preach in his place. Stroud, not expecting this, also got flustered, and couldn't get his thoughts organized to preach either. The meeting closed with two embarrassed speakers. After services both men had dinner at the home of a brother, neither mentioning the embarrassing meeting. After dinner, they got on their horses and rode together. Finally Stroud spoke to Lipscomb, not wanting the embarrassing experience to discourage him and said, "Brother David, I hope you will not let this discourage you." Lipscomb, probably about twenty-six years old, replied, "Well, brother Stroud, I will not be discouraged if I can help it; but, I confess that it is enough to discourage a young man to see a man who has been preaching fifty years make such a failure as you made today." (8, p. 13)

POSITION ON WAR

The Civil War came in 1861. Prior to its becoming a reality, Lipscomb had made up his mind what he would do. His conviction was that Christians could not take part in war. At this time Lipscomb lived on a farm at the edge of Nashville and preached regularly. He established several congregations of the Lord's church. (36, p. 245) He publicly spoke out against the war, and took no part in the politics of the North or the South. However, Lipscomb was denounced by men on both sides of the War, but this did not deter him from preaching his convictions.

F.D. Srygley relates this interesting insight into David Lipscomb and his preaching:

> During the Civil War, Lipscomb took strong ground against Christians going to war, and preached his conviction with boldness that attracted much attention and excited bitter prejudice against him. Zeal for the Southern Confederacy ran high, and impetuous spirits denounced him as an abolitionist, a Yankee spy, and enemy to the South, etc., but none of these things moved him. When Forrest occupied Columbia, complaint was made to him that David Lipscomb was preaching doctrine that was disloyal, and he ought to be arrested and stopped. Forrest sent a member of his staff to one of Lipscomb's appointments where, by special announcement, he was to preach the disloyal doctrine that Christians cannot scripturally go to war. The staff officer took a seat immediately in front of the speaker, and gave close and respectful attention to the sermon. During the sermon, the military officer was moved to tears several times and, after the audience was dismissed, he remarked to a gentleman in the congregation, "I have not yet reached a conclusion as to whether or not the doctrine of the sermon is loyal to the Southern Confederacy, but I am favorably convinced that it is loyal to the Christian religion." (55. p. 161)

Lipscomb tried to live apart from the war as much as possible. He took care of his farming and preached the gospel.

THE GOSPEL ADVOCATE

David Lipscomb will forever be identified with the Gospel Advocate. The Gospel Advocate was begun in July of 1855. The first editor was Tolbert Fanning. William Lipscomb, the older brother of David, was the assistant editor. During the Civil War the paper ceased publication for a period of four years. When it reopened on January 1, 1866, its editors were listed as Tolbert Fanning and David Lipscomb. Due to Fanning's various activities, the editorship responsibilities were handled mostly by Lipscomb. (2, p. 234)

Lipscomb eventually became the chief editor of the Gospel Advocate. His approach was always conservative. Through the Gospel Advocate, both Fanning and Lipscomb opposed the Missionary Society, instrumental music in worship and Christians engaging in warfare. Lipscomb's writings were simple and frank. He was aided through the years by such writers as E. G. Sewell and F. D. Srygley.

Dabney Phillips said of Lipscomb and the Gospel Advocate:

> During Lipscomb's fifty years as editor of the Gospel Advocate, he was frequently involved in a controversy on a vast range of topics. He wrote numerous articles opposing the Missionary Society, stating his belief that the work of the church should be done through the local congregation. He insisted that the society was a substitute for the church. Lipscomb felt that if the society could do the missionary work of the church, then societies could do the other works of the church, causing the church to become an empty and meaningless form. (2, p. 234)

Lipscomb was ever vigilant to make the Bible the basis for his conclusions. He wrote, "The cardinal thought in my religion has ever been to follow the will of God, as expressed in precept, or approved example; to stand on safe ground; to be sure of the approval and blessing of God. (2, p. 235)

STAND AGAINST INNOVATIONS

Through the pages of the Gospel Advocate David Lipscomb and Tolbert Fanning performed a great service to the brotherhood. The good that they did in keeping the churches of the South from falling headlong into digression cannot be overstated. The division that was caused by the liberal element in the church was devastating. However, without the Gospel Advocate the damage to the Lord's church by those advocating unscriptural innovations would have been far greater. Lipscomb and the Advocate bitterly opposed the use of instrumental music in worship as well as the Missionary Society. Consequently, churches in the South, for the most part stayed loyal to earlier Restoration principles. In the North, where the Advocate was little read, and where the Christian Standard was far more influential, the majority of the churches went with the general movement, accepting the innovations that the Advocate resisted. (38, p. 17)

Bringing the Gospel Advocate back into existence was directly related to the strained relationship between the brethren of the North and the South. Lipscomb, in speaking of the need for the Gospel Advocate, said that there was not a single paper known to him that that Southern people could read without having their feelings wounded by political insinuations and slurs. He said that this had more to do with calling the Advocate back into existence than all other circumstances combined. It is no wonder that almost immediately the Advocate was accused of harboring a sectional spirit and a Southern bias. It was never the intention of Fanning and Lipscomb to make the Gospel Advocate a paper exclusively for the South. The bulk of the brethren in the North felt that the Advocate was championing the rights of Southern people, so they looked upon Lipscomb's view of civil government as "sour grapes" since the South had been beaten in the War. This background considerably aided the Advocate's growth in the South, but hindered its growth in the North where it had little or no influence. In the years to follow, this fact was to have even more significance. (38, p. 15)

The efforts of Fanning and Lipscomb were courageous and effective, but this is not to say that they fought the battle alone. There were other stalwart, courageous men who were true to the Word who should also be given recognition in this regard. Included are Jacob Creath, Jr., Moses Lard, and Benjamin Franklin. J. W. McGarvey fought against the instrument, but he accepted the missionary society.

H. Leo Boles said of Lipscomb:

> Perhaps he did more to keep the churches in the South loyal and faithful to the New Testament order of work and worship than any other man. He had deep convictions and profound faith in God. He studied the Word of God daily and was loyal to it throughout his life. Near the close of his life he said, "I am conscious of mistakes and improprieties in dealing with the Word of God and with my fellow men, but I have a conscience void of offense toward God and man that I have always done what I thought at the time was best. I have always studied the Word of God to learn what is God's will, never to prove preconceived opinions. I have always tried to be true to his teachings, believing that they alone will benefit the human family." (36, p. 246-247)

ADMINISTRATOR, TEACHER, AUTHOR

David Lipscomb was a great admirer of Tolbert Fanning. After the death of Fanning in 1874, Lipscomb created an endowment fund to equal the value of Tolbert Fanning's property and, with the help of Mrs. Fanning, established the Fanning Orphan School near Nashville. Lipscomb was president of the Board of Trustees of that institution from its beginning until his death in 1917. (38, p. 246)

In 1891, in association with James A. Harding, Lipscomb founded the Nashville Bible School, later to be known as David

Lipscomb University. He taught the Bible daily in the school.

In addition to his editorial writings, Lipscomb was the author of several books, Civil Government -- Its Origin, Mission, and Destiny, Commentary on Acts of the Apostles, The Life and Sermons of Jesse L. Sewell, Commentary on the New Testament, Salvation from Sin, Queries and Answers, and Questions Answered.

Lipscomb was married to Margaret Zelner on July 23, 1862. To this union only one child was born, but the baby died in infancy. However, the Lipscombs raised several children that were not born to them. David Lipscomb died on November 11, 1917 at the age of eighty-six. Funeral services were held in the College Street Church building where David had been an elder for many years.

CHAPTER 29
ALFRED ELLMORE
1838 - 1925

Alfred Ellmore was born August 11, 1838, the eighth child of a family of ten children. The family lived near Owl Prairie in the southern part of Indiana. At the time of Alfred's birth his father, Eleazor, was a Christian. His father read all the information he could get on religious matters and had read his own New Testament. He passed through the Missionary Baptist denomination and then through the old Christian Church, sometimes called the "New Light" group, and then finally settled down to being nothing but a Christian. He became a member of the New Testament church and nothing else, and stood against all denominations.

Young Ellmore's mother was a pious woman, and she carefully taught her children from the cradle up the importance of living a pure and holy life. In this way the all-sufficiency of the New Testament as the rule of life for Christians was impressed on the children. They were taught that the New Testament was the standard of authority on all religious questions and practices. Srygley said that Ellmore's whole life had been in keeping with his early home training. "He has always and everywhere been steadfast, persistent, and determined to maintain just what is written in the New Testament--nothing more or less, in all matters of religious work and worship." (54, p. 130)

Ellmore was raised in poverty and hard work. In the rural region of Indiana where he was raised he spent his boyhood at hard labor, dividing his time in clearing land, digging ditches, plowing rough ground, gathering corn, killing hogs, hauling wood, and riding eighteen miles on horseback to the mill. His educational opportunities consisted of from twenty to thirty days per year, between jobs and at odd times, attending school in an old log schoolhouse in which he never so much as saw a textbook on English grammar. He had ambitions and aspirations, which seemed beyond his opportunities to achieve.

BECAME A CHRISTIAN

At the age of nineteen, Alfred Ellmore went six miles to a place of meeting, confessed his faith in Christ, and was baptized into Christ by Samuel Otterman. Soon after he was baptized he began to take part in the public worship in the church. He was an excellent singer and led the congregational singing. He also led in prayer and began to make talks. He had a desire to be a preacher, but could not see how he could overcome his poverty enough to realize this desire. At the age of twenty-one he married and the cares and responsibilities of a home pushed his hope of preaching even further away. He was despondent that he could not be a preacher. When he was twenty-seven years old, and in this state of mind, he opened his New Testament and read the parable of the talents. When he had finished the reading, he was so affected that he could not rest.

BEGAN PREACHING

He started to school under the teaching of Professor John C. Ridpath. For three years he went to school and taught school alternately. During that time he took advantage of every opportunity to talk to people on the subject of religion. This was the beginning of his life and his work as a preacher. His first effort to preach a formal sermon was in his home church, among the people who had known him all his life. This was in March of 1865. The rest of his life was spent in preaching and teaching the gospel. He preached in meeting houses, schoolhouses, dwelling houses, opera houses, storehouses, courthouses, halls, depots, sawmills, on board ship in the Atlantic Ocean, in groves in the woods, on boxes in the streets, and under tents and brush arbors. His preaching carried him from Illinois, Ohio, Pennsylvania, West Virginia, Kentucky, Missouri, Iowa, Michigan, Kansas, Arkansas, Texas, Colorado, California, and Canada.

Ellmore's first protracted meeting was in Wabash County, Indiana. There was no church at the place, but the meeting resulted in the establishment of a congregation of fifty-eight members. The night before he was to travel to the place of the gospel meeting which was more than a hundred miles away, he sat in his log cabin by a big log fire nearly all night, studying his Bible in preparation for the meeting. He was poorly provided with clothes, and even more scantily supplied with money. He borrowed a coat and took his wife's plaid shawl for an overcoat. He depended upon collecting a few dollars that a neighbor owed him in order to pay for his railroad ticket, but on the morning of the day he was to leave he was told that the money could not be paid. Fortunately, a neighbor learned of the situation and loaned him the money.

SUCCESS AS A PREACHER

For twenty-five years Ellmore preached every year or so for the church at Elnora, Indiana, and under his preaching over five hundred members were added to that one congregation. In 1875 he was invited to preach at Lawrenceburg, Indiana, where there was no church. In six weeks a congregation was established with one hundred and twenty-four, seventy-five of whom were baptized during the meeting. On his first visit to Meaford, Canada, he found five denominations in that place. After his meeting had been going on about ten days, an interdenominational union revival was started in opposition to him, with twelve preachers, a big choir, and several musical instruments to attract the people away from Ellmore's meeting. Both meetings continued for six weeks. Ellmore closed with eighty-three persons added to the Lord's church, but the inter-denominational union revival closed without a single convert or addition.

About 1886 Alfred Ellmore began to take a position regarding the order of worship that caused some difficulty in the brotherhood. In 1888 Ellmore wrote in the Christian Leader, explaining his position that Acts 2:42 furnished a divine pattern and order of worship that had to be observed:

> Within the last seventy-five years, Acts 2:42 has been quoted perhaps ten thousand times as describing the order of the worship of the first church, and yet, in about nine thousand nine hundred and ninety and nine and a half times, the advocates have failed to adopt this order. I have often heard of men carrying dark lanterns, but I am inclined to think that nothing is so dark as the man who is religiously blind. Fifty years hence, children in the gospel will wonder at our stupidity in not being able to see the harmony of the order of the worship in the Jewish temple and that of the Church of Christ.
>
> And upon this divine order I comment again. Let the bishops go up into the stand: one read and another offer the opening prayer. (1) Then, under the supervision of the bishops, let a half-dozen occupy five minutes each in the lesson, which was announced the Lord's Day before teaching. (2) Take up the fellowship. And I would be understood here as teaching that they should take up the fellowship, and not do something else in the place of it. (3) Break the loaf. (4) The prayers. Let from two to five offer prayers of two to three minutes each time. Now, if Acts 2:42 is the divine model, then nothing else is. And I insist that we wheel into line at once. Professing to be apostolic, let us be apostolic... (38, p. 456)

Ellmore was vociferous in insisting that all the churches adopt this "divine model." "Why continue in that hireling-pastor-every Sunday system? If it be inquired, if Acts 2:42 is intended to be the 'divine model,' why does it exclude singing?" Ellmore's reply was that it was implied in the "teaching." (38, p. 456)

Alfred Ellmore loved the Lord and was among the most tireless preachers in the church. Under the preaching of Ellmore, approximately 7,500 persons were baptized as of 1898. He lived for another sixteen years after that time, so it is quite safe to conclude that the total number of baptisms would be even higher. For twenty-three years Ellmore wrote regularly for the American Christian Review edited by Benjamin Franklin. For seven years he was on the editorial staff of the Christian Leader, edited by John F. Rowe. In later years he bought one-half interest in the Gospel Echo which he edited for many years. In 1901 he turned his paper over to the Gospel Advocate and began a column called "Silver Chimes."

Of all the gospel preachers, Ellmore's favorite was Ben Franklin. Franklin once told Ellmore something that he remembered all of his life. He said, "Brother Ellmore, do all the good you can and no harm." (56, p. 194) As age approached, Ellmore sought to extend his labors into the warmer climate of Texas, and he began to shuttle back and forth between Texas and his home in Covington, Indiana.

Ellmore often visited Gunter College to lecture and conduct meetings. It was in May of 1912 that he stopped by the college and discovered that N. L. Clark had resigned the presidency. While there, the faculty met, voted and unanimously asked Ellmore to assume the office, which he did, bringing with him his son, Will, and his family. He served as president of the college from 1912 to 1922.

HIS LOVE OF PREACHING

A quotation from Ellmore as he wrote in the Firm Foundation in 1908 gives us insight into the importance that he placed on preaching:

> I have no desire to live again in this world, only that I might do more good than I have done. Instead of being immersed at 19, I would go into the church at 15, and instead of waiting until 27, I would enter the ministry at 20, and I would preach, yes sir. If I were the son of a rich man, I would preach. If I were the son of a poor man, I would preach. If too poor to make a living, and the brethren did not support me, I would work on the bench, in the field, in the garden, in the schoolroom, and then preach as I had opportunity. I might keep some cows and some chickens, but I would preach the gospel. (56, p. 193)

Alfred Ellmore passed from this life December 11, 1925 at the age of eighty-seven.

CHAPTER 30
T. B. LARIMORE
1843 - 1929

T. B. Larimore was born July 10, 1843 near Sequatchie Valley in Jefferson County, East Tennessee. He was a poor boy and had little schooling in his early years. As a youth he worked on the McDonough farm for $4.00 per month, and went to school only ten or twelve weeks per year. He stayed with the farmer through the week, sleeping in his loft with two of the farmer's sons. On Monday morning Larimore would get up early and walk the distance to the McDonough farm, work all week, collect his small pay and then walk back home on Saturday night.

Larimore fondly remembered his mother meeting him on his return home each Saturday night. "... There was a small stream not far from the house where his mother had waited all week so at that place he had to walk a log across the creek. Invariably his dear old mother was on the other side shining her old oil lantern for young Larimore to see how to walk the log. She never failed him, rain or shine, which left a lasting impression upon him concerning a mother's love. Someone asked if he thought his mother would be across the valley to help him to his eternal home. In his unbounded faith he said he did not know, but he did know JESUS WOULD." (54, p. 51)

CONFEDERATE SOLDIER

When young Larimore was sixteen years old he entered Mossy Creek Baptist College in East Tennessee. The year was 1859. To enter the school he had to walk more than forty miles. Larimore remained in the school until 1861, receiving a diploma. When the Civil War began, he entered the service of the Confederate Army. His unit, under the command of General Zollicoffer, went to Kentucky where the commander was killed in battle, his body remaining in the hands of the Union Army. Larimore was one of several who volunteered to bring back the body. In the next few weeks Larimore was placed in Captain Spiller's unit as a scout under General Albert Sydney Johnston. General Johnston was killed at Shiloh. Fortunately for Larimore, he was never personally involved in combat and never took the life of an enemy. (56, p. 82)

In the fall of 1863 Larimore was captured by two Union soldiers while he was on scout duty. He was able to take an oath that he would not fight against the Union and was allowed to go home. He was twenty years old and not yet a Christian.

BAPTIZED

After returning from his service in the War, Larimore moved his mother and sisters to Hopkinsville, Kentucky, where his mother identified her family with the church. His mother had become a Christian while he was a away at Mossy Creek Baptist College. Larimore attended services of the church with his mother. It was on his twenty-first birthday, July 10, 1864 that he made a public confession of his faith in Christ and was baptized for the remission of his sins.

While teaching at the Hopkinsville Female Institute in 1866, he preached his first sermon in the same meeting house where he made his good confession. The subject was "Christian Union," drawn from John 17:20, 21. At the close of the sermon, Editha Retter, the daughter of a congressman was baptized. In the same year, 1866, he entered Franklin College near Nashville. While attending school, Larimore, in June of 1867, again preached on John 17 and at the close of the lesson C.G. Payton was baptized. Larimore spent about two years in Franklin College and in 1867 was graduated with honors. (56, p. 83) After leaving Franklin College Larimore traveled and preached with R. B. Trimble in middle Tennessee and northern Alabama.

In 1868 Larimore married Esther Gresham near Mars Hill, Alabama. They had seven children. Esther passed away in 1907. In 1911 Larimore married Emma Page.

MARS HILL COLLEGE

After Larimore and Esther Gresham were married, they both taught at Mountain Home School near Florence, Alabama. When that institution failed, the young couple determined to start a school of their own. They used twenty-eight acres of land that Esther had inherited, and borrowed money to build the school in Florence, Alabama. With the two working together they built a three story house with twelve rooms and three halls at a cost of $10,000, including the furnishings. It was originally called "Mars Hill Academy," but was later changed to "Mars Hill College." The school opened January 1, 1871, and operated successfully for sixteen years. Many young people passed through the doors of Mars Hills, forever benefiting from the association with T. B. Larimore. The school closed in 1887, not because it was a financial failure, but because T. B. Larimore was in such demand for evangelistic meetings that he could no longer ignore the many calls. There was not enough time to devote both to the school and preach continually in gospel meetings. He chose to give up the school.

EVANGELIST

After 1887 Larimore was engaged in preaching in evangelistic meetings almost constantly. He was in great demand as a speaker. In 1889 he had 500 requests to hold gospel meetings. He is well remembered for the length of some of his meetings, the longest being at Sherman, Texas in 1894. It began on January 3 and closed on June 7, a duration of five months and four days. During this meeting he preached 333 sermons, speaking twice every day and three times on Sunday. There were more than 200 baptisms during the meeting. His second longest meeting was in Los Angeles, California in 1895. It began on January 3 and closed on April 17, a period of three months and fourteen days. There were 120 persons baptized during the meeting. In 1890 he preached a gospel meeting at the Pearl and Bryan Street congregation in Dallas, Texas that lasted for two months with seventy-three baptisms.

Even from his earliest efforts Larimore was an effective speaker. As he gained more experience he became an outstanding orator. "In his preaching there was no bombast, no pomposity. He stood before his audience dignified, self-possessed, almost motionless, as there flowed from his lips the wisdom of God couched in the purest of English. Like Paul, he determined to know nothing in the pulpit save Jesus Christ and him crucified. Without putting forth an effort to be eloquent, he was eloquent; without resorting to the tactics of a rhetorician, he was rhetorical. The magnetism of his poise and voice and eye had its origin in his intellect, his heart and his emotions. He did not resort to humor, sentimentality or vituperation. His style of address was unique. Alliteration and a free use of descriptive adjectives coupled with a mellifluous voice combined to hold his audience spell-bound." (73, p. 5)

Larimore did not write any books, but there were three books written about him, Larimore and His Boys, Letters and Sermons, and From Maine to Mexico, and Canada to Cuba.

AVOIDED CONTROVERSY

By nature, Larimore was kind and gentle in his preaching. He chose his subject and presented it in a simple, straightforward way with no notice taken of religious error that might be relevant to his subject. Larimore seemed intent on avoiding controversy. One day after finishing his sermon he asked if anyone had anything they wanted to say. It was a denominational preacher who stepped forward and expressed disagreement with some of the things that Larimore had preached. When he had apparently finished, Larimore asked "Is that all?" The denominational preacher answered in the affirmative. The audience no doubt expected Larimore to then refute what the denominational preacher had said, but he made no reply, except to kindly say, "Let us stand and be dismissed." (73, p. 6)

Unfortunately, Larimore's spirit of non-controversy caused him to be very slow in taking a position about the Missionary Society and the use of instrumental music in worship. There can be little doubt that the cause of truth could have been aided by Larimore at this painful period had he taken a firm stand on the issues much earlier. He was held in very high esteem in the church and could have been a good influence at the time when many congregations were making up their minds about joining with the innovators or standing for the "old paths." Eventually he did make his decision to align himself with the smaller and less popular group that was still pleading for a strict adherence to the New Testament pattern.

On his death bed Larimore stated, "When it is God's will for me to go, I shall tenderly kiss the hand divine that severs the silver cord of life, and joyfully lay down my burden at the foot of the cross. (2, p. 270) T. B. Larimore died on March 18, 1929 in Santa Ana, California. He is buried in the very peaceful Fairhaven Memorial Park in that city. He was eighty-six years old. H. Leo Boles said of him, "Brother Larimore still lives in the hearts of thousands whom he taught the Word of God and encouraged to live faithful to God. He left his imprint on his students and all who listened earnestly to his preaching. ... The world is better and happier because T. B. Larimore lived in it." (36, p. 336)

CHAPTER 31
JAMES A. HARDING
1848 - 1922

James A. Harding was born in 1848 in Winchester, Kentucky to J. W. and Mary Harding. Both of James' parents were members of the Lord's church before James was born. J. W. Harding had obeyed the gospel in 1839. After his conversion, the elder Harding preached on Sundays and worked either as a tailor or a merchant through the week. He married Mary E. McDonald in 1844, and to them fourteen children were born. (38, p. 333)

J. W. Harding was an elder in the Court Street Church in Winchester, Kentucky until the instrument of music was forced into the worship in 1887. He and fifteen others left and became the nucleus for the Fairfax congregation. It was nothing for young James to see his father lead fifty to one hundred people to Christ in the course of one gospel meeting. This impressed young Harding. J. W. Harding was a successful gospel preacher, actively preaching up to one month before he died at the age of ninety-seven in 1919. He only preceded his son James in death by three years. (38, p. 333)

BAPTIZED

James A. Harding, even as a young person had a deeply pious nature and early in life turned his thoughts to the subject of religion.

He was baptized into Christ during a gospel meeting conducted by his father and Moses E. Lard at Winchester, Kentucky, in October of 1861. James was only thirteen years old when he became a Christian. At age sixteen he began his studies in a preparatory school which was taught by J.O. Fox. The purpose of the school was to prepare young men for college. His studies lasted two years, and he then entered Bethany College in West Virginia in 1866. He remained there for three years and graduated at age twenty-one in the class of 1869. (36, p. 365) After he graduated from college young Harding moved to Hopkinsville, Kentucky where he began teaching a school for young men and boys. He remained in Hopkinsville for five years. He was an active member of the Lord's church in Hopkinsville and began to preach the gospel.

MARRIED

While teaching school, Harding made the acquaintance of V. M. Metcalfe, a popular Kentucky preacher in 1870. Metcalfe strongly encouraged Harding to preach. Often when Metcalfe was on his way to a preaching appointment, he would stop by and pick up Harding. Before long he had Harding preaching. During the time that he was teaching in this school he married Carrie Knight, the oldest daughter of Judge John B. Knight, a prominent member of the church at Hopkinsville. Unfortunately, his wife only lived about five years after they were married, passing away in 1876. Two years after she died, Harding married Pattie Cobb of Estill County, Kentucky. Pattie was unselfishly devoted to her husband's work. A women's dormitory at Harding College was later named "Pattie Cobb" in honor of Harding's second wife.

BEGAN TO PREACH FULL TIME

It was because of ill health that Harding gave up his school teaching at Hopkinsville in the fall of 1874. This allowed him to devote his full time and energies to the work of an evangelist. (36, pp. 365-366) There is an interesting story that led to this work. While at the school, Harding had contracted malaria fever and was taken to Winchester to recover. "Just as he was recuperating, an old brother, Jon Adams, came to get him to go back into the country and hold a protracted meeting. Harding protested that he had never held a meeting and had no meeting sermons. Adams talked roughly to him, and reminded Harding that he had been brought up in church and Sunday school and besides had been to Bethany College, and that he ought to be killed if he could not preach, and for him to 'shut his mouth,' get his horse and go hold that meeting. Harding went and held his first protracted meeting." (38, p. 334)

Harding possessed a great faith in God. He was fully convinced that if he discontinued teaching school, which was the source of his income, in order to preach full time, God would take care of his needs. His whole life was built on that premise.

DESCRIPTION

In 1899 Harding made a visit to Dallas, Texas. On this trip he met T.R. Burnett. Burnett wrote an excellent description of Harding:

> Physically, he is a fine specimen of the genus Homo, weighing perhaps over 200 pounds, and has a large blue eye and a big red head. His fat, flush cheeks and thick, red neck indicate that he is of thoroughbred stock or has been fed well at the pie counter. He has doubtless made "full proof of his ministry" among the yellow legged chickens of the blue grass regions of Tennessee. I take it that he wears a no. 17 collar, sleeps well at night, has a conscience void of offense toward God and man, and is full of a laudable ambition to do a great work for the Master's cause. In personal appearance and manner of address, he is very much like C. M. Wilmeth, only he is larger in size. Like Brother Wilmeth he fills his sermons with illustrations. It is no uncommon thing for his eyes

to fill with tears while he is speaking, but it is rather a help, and not a hindrance to his speech. ... He is in all respects the soundest gospel preacher that I have heard preach in Texas. He believes the Bible from "lid to lid." 38, pp. (335-336)

UNTIRING EVANGELIST

Harding was constantly busy in his work as an evangelist. For seventeen years he labored wholly in evangelistic work. He conducted over three hundred gospel meetings that lasted from three to ten weeks each. Often, for months, he would preach two sermons a day. Harding conducted seventeen meetings in Nashville, Tennessee alone. For this work he received an average of five dollars per meeting. An eight-week meeting at Foster Street in Nashville resulted in one hundred and twenty-three baptisms. In 1883, Harding preached five hundred times in three hundred days. He insisted that the baptisms take place immediately following the service, and usually brought clothing for all ages. He traveled in twenty-two states and in two provinces of Canada. His travels extended from Canada to Florida, and from New York to Texas. He preached in all the large cities of these states and in many small towns and rural sections.

In many places he conducted meetings for ten years in succession. One year he spent six and one-half months in meetings in Nashville. He preached more in Nashville than in any other city. He held seventeen gospel meetings in Nashville and thirteen in Detroit, Michigan. Harding spoke in a conversational tone but with an intense earnestness, and with occasional flashes of humor. He was enthusiastic and impressive. He had the power to stir men and move them to action. He was a great teacher and a good writer, but his greatest power was as a preacher in the pulpit. (36, p. 366) Harding was a man of conviction, standing against the use of instrumental music in worship and the Missionary Society.

THE DEBATER

Debating was a great joy to Harding. He conducted more than fifty debates in his career. Four of his debates were published in book form. In 1884 he debated for six days with a Methodist preacher named T. L. Wilkerson in Ontario, Canada on the theme of baptism. This debate was published in book form under the name Debate on Baptism. The second published debate was the Harding-Nichols Debate. This debate was held in Lynville, Tennessee in 1888, and was published by the Gospel Advocate. His most widely acclaimed debate was with a Baptist named J. N. Moody in 1889. The debate lasted for sixteen nights, and was published under the title, The Nashville Debate. The next published debate was the second debate with Nichols and was also titled Harding-Nichols Debate. It was conducted in Murray, Kentucky, in 1890. (36, pp. 367-368)

NASHVILLE BIBLE SCHOOL

While Harding was preaching meetings in Nashville, and debating with J. N. Moody, he stayed much of the time with David Lipscomb. Lipscomb talked to Harding about his concerns for the church in Nashville, and the need of more faithful gospel preachers. Lipscomb placed before Harding the plan for starting a school. Lipscomb had been thinking about such a work for nearly twenty years. When he mentioned the idea of a school to his friend, Harding enthusiastically endorsed the plan and encouraged Lipscomb to proceed. Lipscomb asked Harding to join with him in establishing the school. (36, pp. 366-368)

Harding became a "school man." He gave up the work of a full-time evangelist in 1891 to help Lipscomb start the Nashville Bible School. He felt that his most effective work was yet to be done with the students in the classroom. On October 5, 1891, on Fillmore Street in Nashville, in a rented house, the Nashville Bible School started. Only nine young men were in attendance the first day, but during the session thirty-two students were enrolled. Harding was selected as the first principal of the school, and later the more prestigious title of "Superintendent" was given to him. Nashville Bible School was later to be known as David Lipscomb College, and still later as David Lipscomb University. Harding remained with the school for ten years and saw it increase in number and influence each year.

POTTER BIBLE COLLEGE

After leaving the Nashville Bible School, he went to Bowling Green, Kentucky and founded the Potter Bible College in 1901. C. C. Potter and his wife proposed to Harding to devote one of their farms to a Bible school and to erect the proper buildings if he would secure the necessary faculty. The Potters had a one hundred and forty-acre farm two miles from Bowling Green, Kentucky. It was their intention to use the proceeds of this farm to support the school. Harding believed that each college should be self-supporting. Unfortunately, the time came when Potter Bible College no long could support itself. When this time came, Harding paid the outstanding bills and locked the doors. (38, p. 337)

HONORED

David Lipscomb University honors James A. Harding as one of its founders. The old chapel hall bears his name, as well as the present high school administration building on the Lipscomb campus. In addition, Harding University in Searcy, Arkansas was named after James A. Harding. There is no indication that Harding left the Nashville Bible School because of any differences with David Lipscomb. He left because he felt that more good could be done with an additional school. David Lipscomb wrote in the Gospel Advocate June 6, 1901, that Harding's leaving was not the result of any disagreement. He said he wished there were a college in every county. 38, p. 338 It is interesting to note that Harding accepted no salaries from the two schools, only room and board. While teaching daily in the school during each session, he preached four or five times a week in and around Nashville. During the vacation periods, he again became the powerful evangelist, proclaiming the Word from the various pulpits across the land.

THE WRITER

Harding was a clear and powerful writer. While teaching at the Nashville Bible School and preaching as he found opportunity, he wrote weekly for the Gospel Advocate and other religious papers. In April of 1899 he began publishing The Way, a religious weekly. This was published in Nashville until Harding moved to Bowling Green, and then it was published in that city. The Way was finally combined with the Christian Leader of Cincinnati, Ohio, and the new paper bore the name The Leader and Way. (36, p. 367)

LIVED SACRIFICALLY

The character of James A. Harding is seen in the sacrificial way that he lived. He never preached for a "stipulated" income. He increased his giving to the point that, toward the end of his life, he was giving sixty percent of his income to the Lord. While traveling, Harding never took a Pullman sleeping car, but traveled the more economical class in order to "save the Lord's money." W. L. Karnes, who taught with Harding at Potter School stated, "Harding has inspired more people to read the Bible than any man in the past one hundred years." (2, p. 266)

THE END COMES

The last years of his life, Harding was plagued with the loss of memory and blackouts. He and his wife Patti lived those years in Atlanta, Georgia with their son-in-law, Dr. Paine. Following a three day coma, James A. Harding passed away on a Sunday afternoon, May 28, 1922 at the age of seventy-four. He was buried in Bowling Green, Kentucky. His wife, Patti, passed away in 1945 at the Paine home at the age of ninety-two. She was buried beside her husband. (2, p. 266)

Jesse P. Sewell spoke of Harding in these glowing terms:

> I wish I could fix the name of James A. Harding in the hearts of disciples of Christ throughout the generations to come as "James A. Harding, the Magnificent." He was magnificent culturally, he was magnificent spiritually, he was a genuinely magnificent personality.

The faith of James A. Harding was noble, lofty, sublime. With him God was as real as James W. Harding, his father in the flesh. To him Jesus was as real as his fleshly brother, Walter. To him the Holy Spirit was as real as the spirit in his own body. To him the Bible was as literally a personal message from God as were letters from his earthly father. To him heaven was as real as Nashville, and as far superior in goodness and beauty as are the mind and soul of man superior to his aging and decaying body.

In faith he was like Abraham. He was constantly going forth in obedience to the command of God, without knowledge of whither, except that given in God's word -- and that without the slightest fear as to the present or the future...

In his presentation he was logical, clear, and easy to understand. As a teacher, he was earnest, eloquent, and persuasive. To him preaching the gospel was man's highest and noblest activity. He went about it with profound reverence, and proceeded always with becoming dignity. The pulpit was never desecrated by anything common or coarse when James A Harding occupied it. By him the process of salvation was never presented as a mere mechanical form. It was always a life-saving, spiritual experience -- a new birth, giving entrance into a new life. (60, pp. 264-265)

John T. Glenn wrote of Harding's last days with these touching words:

Brother Harding was a happy man. It shone in his face; it was magnificent in his life -- and that he never lost! I had the great pleasure of having him and Sister Harding (Sister Patti, as I always called her) in our home for a day's visit just a short time before he went to be with his Lord, whom he loved with all his heart. Over and over, through the day he would say, "I am so happy! I am so happy! In my Father's house are many mansions -- not huts, mansions. And I want to go home!" And maybe a tear would be rolling down his dear face. That was my last sight of him, but it is a blessed memory. (60, p. 267)

CHAPTER 32
CONCLUSION

In the eleventh chapter of Hebrews, after the writer had mentioned those in the past who possessed great faith, he then stated in verse 32, "And what more shall I say? For the time would fail me to tell of..." The writer then continues to list a few more of the faithful. When we attempt to recount those great men of faith in the Restoration Movement we are presented with a similar problem. If we intend to list all of them, we are doomed to failure from the beginning. There are so many that deserve to be recognized but are not. Many fine brethren who worked sacrificially for the Cause are not remembered by history at all. They quietly went about their work as faithful servants of the Lord, without recognition or applause. While we do not mention them in our books of history, nevertheless, we deeply appreciate them and their labor in the Lord.

In this book we trust that we have presented enough information about principal figures and issues of the Movement to remind us of where we have been, and hopefully, to give us some insight in charting the course for the future. Unfortunately, many in our present time are not of the same mind as those faithful and courageous brethren of the past. Those men were content to abide by the principle, "Where the Bible speaks, we speak. Where the Bible is silent, we are silent." Those great men of the past labored to draw good and honest people out of the denominations and into the church that we read about in the New Testament.

Tragically, in our time a new generation has arisen who care nothing for "the old paths," but appear all too eager to turn the Lord's church into a denomination. They are willing to give up the ground that was gained by our pioneer preachers of the past. As we looked back into the 1800's we saw two major departures from the course that had devastating results. With the introduction of the American Christian Missionary Society in 1849 and instrumental music in worship in 1860, the way for division was paved. Add to these innovations a major change in attitude toward the authority of the Scriptures. That lack of respect for the authority of the Scriptures reached such an extreme in some circles that even the plenary inspiration of the Bible was denied. Combining all three of these factors together it became obvious that there was no way to avoid a major division. The census of 1906 merely recorded a division between the Churches of Christ and the Christian Church that had already existed for at least two decades.

Indeed, history does seem to be repeating itself today. The same errors that divided the Lord's church in the late 1800's are being advocated all over again by some brethren. Such a selling out of truth would bewilder and disgust those grand brethren of the past who gave their very lives to preach the primitive gospel. Will we learn from our history or are we doomed to repeat the mistakes of the past?

Jeremiah 6:16: "Thus sayeth the Lord, stand in the ways and see, and ask for the old paths, where is the good way, and walk therein."

RETURN TO THE OLD PATHS
A History of the Restoration Movement

BIBLIOGRAPHY

1. Earl West
   The Search for the Ancient Order, Vol. I,
   Religious Book Service, Carmel, IN. (1990).
2. Dabney Phillips
   Restoration Principles and Personalities, Youth in Action, University, AL, (1975).
3. Garrison and DeGroot
   The Disciples of Christ, A History, Bethany Press, St. Louis, MO (1948).
4. James R. Rogers
   The Cane Ridge Meeting House,
   Standard Publishing Co., Cincinnati, OH (1910).
5. F. W. Mattox
   The Eternal Kingdom, A History of the Church of Christ, Gospel Light Publishing Co., Delight, AR (1955).
6. J. M. Powell
   The Cause We Plead,
   A Story of the Restoration Movement,
   20th Century Christian, Nashville, TN (1987).
7. George A. Klingman
   Church History For Busy People,
   Gospel Advocate, Nashville, TN (n/a).
8. John D. Cox
   Church History,
   DeHoff Publications, Murfreesboro, TN (1951).
9. Alvin Jennings
   T. M. Allen, Pioneer Preacher of Kentucky and Missouri, Star Bible & Tract Corp., Ft. Worth, TX (1977).

10. Everett Ferguson
    Church History, Reformation and Modern,
    Biblical Research Press, Abilene, TX (1967).
11. P. Donan
    Life of Jacob Creath, Jr.,
    Religious Book Service, Indianapolis, IN (1862)
12. Robert E. Hooper
    A Call to Remember, Chapters in Nashville History,
    Gospel Advocate Co., Nashville, TN (1977).
13. Monroe Hawley
    The Focus of Our Faith,
    A New Look at the Restoration Principle,
    20th Century Christian, Nashville, TN (1985).
14. W. J. Seaton
    Five Points of Calvinism,
    Banner of Truth Trust, Inverness Reformed Baptist
15. William Herbert Hanna
    Thomas Campbell, Seceder, Christian Union Advocate,
    Standard Publishing Co., Cincinnati, Ohio (1935).
16. Louis Cochran
    Raccoon John Smith,
    College Press Publishing Co., Joplin, MO (1985).
17. C. Leonard Allen and Richard T. Hughes
    Discovering our Roots: Ancestry, The Churches of
    Christ, ACU Press, Abilene, TX (1988).
18. Alan Highers, editor
    Spiritual Sword, October,
    Getwell Church of Christ, Memphis, TN. (1991)
19. Edward Deming Andrews
    "Shakers," Colliers Encyclopedia,
    Crowell-Collier Educational Corp., (1970).
20. Johnny Ramsey
    Unpublished Notes on Church History (n/a)
21. C. A. Young
    Historical Documents Advocating Christian Union,
    College Press Publishing Co., Joplin, MO (1985).

22. Perry E. Grisham
    The Sage of Bethany, a Pioneer in Broadcloth,
    College Press Pub. Co., Joplin, MO   (1988).
23. M. Tucker, Editor
    Restoration Then and Now, E. Tennessee School of
    Preaching, Knoxville, TN (1983).
24. Robert E. Hooper
    A Distinct People,
    Howard Publishing Co., West Monroe, LA (1993).
25. B. W. Stone and John Rogers
    The Biography of Barton W. Stone,
    College Press, Joplin, MO (1847).
26. L. G. Tomlinson
    Churches of Today,
    Gospel Advocate Co., Nashville, TN (1964)
27. Louis Cochran
    Fool of God,
    Duell, Sloan & Pierce, N.Y., N.Y. (1962)
28. Barton W. Stone
    Biography of Elder Barton W. Stone, Written by Himself,
    Cane Ridge Meeting House Pub.
    Cane Ridge, KY. (1847)
29. Lynn McMillian
    Restoration Roots,
    Gospel Teachers Publishing Co., Dallas, TX (1983).
30. Robert Richardson
    Memoirs of Alexander Campbell,
    Religious Book Service, Indianapolis, IN (1897).
31. B. W. Stone
    The Christian Messenger,
    Star Bible & Tract Corp., Ft.   Worth, TX (1978).
32. William Baxter
    Life of Elder Walter Scott, William Baxter,
    Gospel Advocate Pub. Co., Nashville, TN (1874).

33. William A. Gerrard
    Walter Scott, American Frontier Evangelist,
    College Press Pub., Joplin, MO (1992).
34. Daniel Schantz
    Walter Scott, God's Pied Piper,
    Standard Publishing Co, Cincinnati, OH (1984).
35. Louis Talbet
    What's Wrong With Mormonism?
36. H. Leo Boles
    Biographical Sketches of Gospel Preachers,
    Gospel Advocate Pub., Co., Nashville, TN (1932).
37. Otis Castleberry
    They Heard Him Gladly,
    Old Paths Pub. Co., Rosemead, CA (1963).
38. Earl West
    The Search for the Ancient Order, Vol. II,
    Religious Book Service, Indianapolis, IN (1950).
39. Thomas Campbell
    What Is Wrong? Campbell Pub., L. A., CA (1950).
40. Marvin W. Hastings
    Saga of a Movement,
    Christian Schoolmaster Pub., Manchester, TN (1981).
41. Bill Humble
    The Story of the Restoration,
    Faith Facts Press, Indianapolis, IN (1994).
42. Keith Moser
    "Roman Catholicism," Bible Light, December Issue,
    Sunny Slope Church of Christ, Paducah, KY (1995).
43. James M. Powell and Mary Nelle Hardeman Powers
    N. B. H., A Biography of Nicholas Brodie Hardeman,
    Gospel Advocate Co. Nashville, TN, (1964).
44. Cane Ridge Bicentennial Planning Committees
    Cane Ridge Bicentennial Sampler, Paris, KY, (1991).
45. Hoke S. Dickinson, Editor
    The Cane Ridge Reader,
    Cane Ridge, KY, (1972).

46. Williston Walker
    A History of the Christian Church,
    Charles Scribner's Sons, N. Y. (1970).
47. John Waddey, Editor
    Life and Lessons of J.W. McGarvey,
    Gospel Light Pub. Co., Delight, AR, (1988).
48. John Laws, Lectureship Director
    The Restoration: The Winds of Change, Lectureship Director, Sain Publications, Pulaski, TN.
49. Dabney Phillips
    A Medley of the Restoration,
    Bible and School Supply, Montgomery, AL (1978).
50. Everett Donaldson
    Raccoon John Smith, Frontiersman and Reformer,
    North Ridge Pub. Co, Mt. Sterling, KY, (1991).
51. Jerry C. Brewer
    Firm Foundation, "What is Calvinism?," October
    Firm Foundation Pub., Houston, TX, (1996).
52. Dabney Phillips
    "Restoration Tragedies,"
    Bible Light, September/October Issue, (1996).
53. James DeForest Murch
    Christians Only, A History of the Restoration Movement,
    Standard Pub. Co, Cincinnati, OH, (1957).
54. J. Porter Wilhite
    The Trail Blazers,
    Lambert Book House, Shreveport, LA (1965).
55. F. D. Srygley
    Biographies and Sermons,
    Gospel Advocate Pub., Nashville, TN, (1961).
56. Earl West
    The Search For the Ancient Order III,
    Religious Book Service, Indianapolis, IN (1979).
57. John Rogers
    The Biography of Elder John T. Johnson,
    Gospel Advocate Pub. Co, Nashville, TN (1956).

58. J. W. Shepherd
    The Church, the Falling Away and the Restoration,
    Faith and Facts, Inc., Indianapolis, IN (1929).
59. James R. Wilburn
    The Hazard of the Die: Tolbert Fanning and the
    Restoration Movement,
    Sweet Pub. Co., Austin, TX (1969).
60. Lloyd Cline Sears
    The Eyes of Jehovah: The Life and Faith of James
    Alexander Harding,
    Gospel Advocate Co., Nashville, TN (1970).
61. Robert E. Hooper
    Crying In The Wildernss: A Biography of David
    Lipscomb, David Lipscomb College,
    Nashville, TN (1979).
62. J. W. McGarvey
    The Autobiography of J.W. McGarvey (1829-1911),
    College of the Bible, Lexington, KY, (1960).
63. W. C. Rogers
    Recollections of Men of Faith,
    Old Paths Book Club, Rosemead, CA, (1960).
64. Paul Vaughn, editor
    Triumph and Tragedy, Cane Ridge to the College of the
    Bible and More, Pub. by author, Corinth, MS.
65. Williston Walker
    A History of the Christian Church, Charles Scribner's
    Sons, N.Y., N.Y., (1970).
66. Louis and Bess White Cochran
    Captives of the Word,
    College Press Publishing Co., Joplin MO (1987).
67. Adron Doran
    "Cane Ridge," Firm Foundation, February,
    Damon, Texas (1998).
68. Dean Mills
    Union on the King's Highway,
    College Press Pub. Co, Joplin, MO, (1987).

69. B. A. Abbott
    The Disciples, An Interpretation,
    Christian Board of Pub., St. Louis, MO, (1924).
70. Jack L. Ray
    "John Allen Gano," Triumph and Tragedy,
    Paul Vaughn, editor, Corinth, MS.
71. John F. Rowe and G. W. Rice
    Biographical Sketches and Writings of Elder Benjamin Franklin, Lambert's Book House,
    Shreveport, LA (1880).
72. Otis L. Castleberry
    They Heard Him Gladly,
    Old Paths Pub. Co, Rosemead, CA, (1963).
73. S. P. Pittman
    "T. B. Larimore," 20th Century Christian, January, Nashville, TN (1959).

www.ingramcontent.com/pod-product-compliance
Lightning Source LLC
Chambersburg PA
CBHW070418010526
44118CB00014B/1803